"A Class-V ride through both big waters and a fast-changing culture."

—**Jon Bowermaster**, *National Geographic Adventure* author and adventurer

"This is a book in which the author is on fire with his subject. Eugene Buchanan studies, chases, and pours down one of the world's wildest rivers in a journey sometimes terrifying, often chilling, but always mesmeric and drenched with resonance. The story is swiftly moving, yet it superbly delineates the cultural and political context out of which this expedition arose. Buchanan is a gifted narrator with seeming total recall and a lucid candor and self-awareness, as well as a talent for painting topographical views of gorges and rapids that have an almost surreal power. *Brothers on the Bashkaus* is, in a fashion, an elegy for a lost moment of cultural and environmental first contact. It is a torrent of a book … Take the plunge!"

—**Richard Bangs**, founding partner of Mountain Travel/ Sobek, author of eleven books, including *Mystery of the Nile*, *Adventures without End*, *The Lost River*, *River Gods*, and *Riding the Dragon's Back*

"Adventure paddling is fun enough, but it becomes epic, zany, and outrageous when it's set in the manic madness of modern Russia. Imagine Hunter S. Thompson—without the drugs— running Class VI. Can't conjure up the image? Sit down on a comfortable chair, get some raw pork fat for munchies, and read Eugene Buchanan's *Brothers on the Bashkaus* for a wild, hungry ride in improbable boats with a bunch of crazies. The book exposes the unadulterated spirit of whitewater adventure—stripped clean of all the fancy stuff, like paddles and lifejackets."

—**Jon Turk**, author of *In the Wake of the Jomon* and *Cold Oceans*

"Buchanan's blood is two parts river. This is a memorable tale of adventure, friendship, and a confluence, or collision, of cultures. Buchanan and his cohorts get tossed almost by happenstance onto the wildest of rivers in a land where the gear is homemade, local horsemen go crazy on strong tea, memorials to dead paddlers perch on the banks, and, as at an execution, nothing can happen until a last cigarette is smoked."

—**Peter Heller**, author of *Hell or High Water* and *Outside* magazine contributor

"Your fate is tied to strangers in a strange land in—strangest of all—a craft hewn from the forest primeval ... a monster Siberian whitewater river before you. A reader could want for no better guide than Eugene Buchanan, an expert storyteller who knows firsthand that if you are good, lucky, and don't mind daily fat cubes, the best expeditions sometimes emerge out of the worst predicaments. Superb."

—**Todd Balf**, author of *Last River* and the forthcoming *Comet: The Untold Story of Major Taylor and How He Beat the Color Line* (Crown Publishing, 2007)

"Eugene Buchanan's paddling expertise and sharp reportorial eye will sweep you breathlessly down one of the world's wildest, toughest, and most remote rivers, in company with the knights-errant of Siberian whitewater. A fascinating cultural and adventure read."

—**Peter Stark**, author of *The Last Breath* and *At the Mercy of the River*

Brothers on the

BASHKAUS

Terri —

Happy paddling

Best,

Eugene Buchanan

Eugene Buchanan

Brothers on the
BASHKAUS

A Siberian Paddling Adventure

Fulcrum Publishing
Golden, Colorado

Library of Congress Cataloging-in-Publication Data

Buchanan, Eugene.
 A Siberian paddling adventure / Eugene Buchanan.
    p. cm.
 Includes bibliographical references.
 ISBN-13: 978-1-55591-608-4 (pbk. : alk. paper)
 ISBN-10: 1-55591-608-2 (alk. paper)
 1. Siberia (Russia)--Description and travel. 2. Buchanan,
Eugene--Travel--Russia (Federation)--Siberia. 3. Canoes and
canoeing--Russia (Federation)--Siberia. I. Title.
 DK756.2.B825 2007
 915.7'3--dc22

                                  2006033718

Printed in the United States of America by Color House Graphics, Inc.
0 9 8 7 6 5 4 3 2 1

Cover and interior design: Jack Lenzo
Cover photographs by Van Wombwell

Fulcrum Publishing
4690 Table Mountain Parkway, Suite 100
Golden, Colorado 80403
800-992-2908 • 303-277-1623
www.fulcrumbooks.com

To my wife, Denise, whom I fell in love with on the Colorado River in the Grand Canyon and who supported this project behind the scenes while I holed myself away in my office. I love you more than words can describe.

Also to my daughters, Brooke, eight, and Casey, four, each of whom took to the river while still in diapers, and will hopefully continue learning from it as I have for years to come.

"Each of us puts his person and all his power in common under the supreme direction of the general will, and, in our corporate capacity, we receive each member as an indivisible part of the whole."

"The undertakings which bind us to the social body are obligatory only because they are mutual; and their nature is such that in fulfilling them we cannot work for others without working for ourselves."

—Jean-Jacques Rousseau

Contents

Boris (left) and Ramitch taking their positions at the stern of their four-man cataraft on Siberia's Bashkaus River.

Acknowledgments .... *xi*
Regional Map .... *xii–xiii*
Bashkaus Map... *xiv*

CHAPTER ONE
A Paddle Sign in Moscow............................... 1

CHAPTER TWO
The Siberian Brainstorm 7

CHAPTER THREE
Team Konkas.. 19

CHAPTER FOUR
Across Siberia: The Train.............................. 29

CHAPTER FIVE
Decision Time.. 41

CHAPTER SIX
The Rest of the Way 47

CHAPTER SEVEN
Yuri and the Bus 55

CHAPTER EIGHT
The Bashkaus Put-In 71

CHAPTER NINE
Final Preparations 81

CHAPTER TEN
Rafting's Roots 93

CHAPTER ELEVEN
On the Bashkaus 105

CHAPTER TWELVE
Penetrating Deeper 123

CHAPTER THIRTEEN
The Lower Canyon 141

CHAPTER FOURTEEN
The Bashkaus Memorials 155

CHAPTER FIFTEEN
The Dreams 173

CHAPTER SIXTEEN
The Rapids Continue 189

CHAPTER SEVENTEEN
Perestroika 199

CHAPTER EIGHTEEN
Heading Home 205

Epilogue.. 223
Selected Bibliography.................................... 237

Acknowledgments

Sergei the Small (left) and Andrew backpaddling away from an undercut wall in the lower canyon.

In writing this book, I tried to be as factual as possible with the events of the expedition. But even with copious notes and research, thirteen years is a long time for any such reconstruction.

Several people were instrumental in helping me put this work together. First and foremost, I'd like to thank my expedition partners, Van Wombwell, Ben Hammond, and Bruce Edgerly, as well as W. L. Gore and Associates, Inc., for believing in us enough to award us the first-ever Shipton/Tilman Grant applied to a river expedition. I'd also like to thank Team Konkas—in particular, Boris, Ramitch, and Olga—for taking us under their wing. I'd like to thank fellow editor Frederick Reimers, adventurer and author Jon Turk, and my mother, Mary Estill Buchanan, for their editing suggestions; Yury Voronov, for aiding my understanding of Russia's rafting history; and Jib Ellison, for piecing together the early history of Project RAFT. Finally, I'd like to thank my wife, Denise, for waiting for me at the airport upon my return.

Regional Map

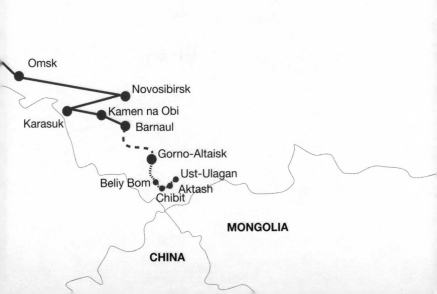

Omsk

Novosibirsk

Karasuk

Kamen na Obi

Barnaul

Gorno-Altaisk

Ust-Ulagan

Beliy Bom

Aktash

Chibit

RUSSIA

MONGOLIA

CHINA

Bashkaus Map

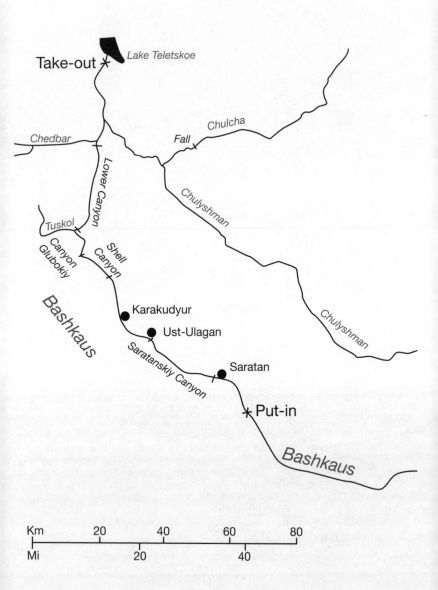

CHAPTER ONE

A Paddle Sign in Moscow

St. Basil's Cathedral in Moscow, one of the last signs of civilization.

The sign catches us by surprise. Duct-taped to a paddle blade waving above a sea of heads in the windowless Moscow airport is a piece of paper that reads, "We look for four American kayaker to go Kalar River."

I look at Edge, Van, and Ben, counting with my finger. "That's us," I say. "That has to be us."

It's 3:00 P.M. Moscow time on July 23, 1993. If we were at home, we might have been tossing a Frisbee at a summer barbecue. Here, our future matches our bleak surroundings. Hordes of dark-clothed travelers scurry around the gray confines of the concrete terminal. Jet-lagged and tired, we aren't sure who, if anyone, is going to meet us. Wondering who is holding the paddle, we shuffle over for introductions.

At the end of the shaft is Boris Jahnis, his full brown beard and ponytail giving him the air of a Berkeley professor, only scruffier. If he's a professor, he's obviously off duty, as indicated by his black T-shirt with a gold-and-red coat-of-arms

insignia across the breast. Light-blue surfer shorts with red and
blue palm trees and yellow pineapples end just below his knees,
exposing hairy, muscular calves. A black plastic-mesh baseball
cap barely covers his forehead, which is as prominent as the
paddle waving above him. On his feet is a pair of sagging socks
tucked inside a worn-out pair of white canvas sneakers.

Joining him is a taller dark-haired man and a wavy-brown-
haired accomplice. Their eyes dart quickly to our pile of gear.

"Do you speak English?" I ask tentatively. "We're the
Americans looking to go to the Kalar River."

"I'm Boris," comes a hearty-voiced reply. "This is Igor and
Sergei. We take your things."

He pauses before stooping down to pick up an army-
green amoeba-shaped canvas bag housing our frame and oars.
Igor bends over to help him.

"What is this?" asks Boris in a thick Latvian accent.

"That's our frame," admits a sheepish Ben.

"And our oars and raft," adds Van, justifying its weight
and cumbersome appearance.

Boris grunts and turns away. In a few seconds, we see
why: Sergei's white two-door car has to carry seven people
plus all of our gear. After loading our gear atop a makeshift
car rack and squishing everything else inside the hatchback,
the car's lone mud flap touches the pavement before we even
pile in. With the four of us on each other's laps in back, topped
by even more gear on the top rider's thighs, we drag out of
the passenger-pickup area and emerge into an even drearier
outside.

The sky is overcast, a dull gray that matches our travel-
weary brains. Like bleached dominos, row after row of identical
concrete apartment buildings blurr by on the two-hour drive to
Igor Petrovich and Sergei Milov's apartment. Laundry dries in
the wind, hanging over almost every balcony rail. Despite their
scale, none of the apartment buildings have parking lots; most
of their inhabitants don't own cars. Power lines casually criss-
cross the highway, as if put there as afterthoughts. If one of the

dominos were to tip over, they'd likely all fall, those not in line caught in the tumble through these archaic wires.

Two boys playing soccer with a half-flat ball wave as we park on a broken slab of concrete marking Igor and Sergei's place. We leave our gear atop the car and head to an elevator, which reeks of urine. Sergei delicately presses *12*, his finger conditioned to dodge wires sticking out of the control panel. When the door opens, we emerge into a long dark hallway. At its end, we pile into a two-room apartment shared by Sergei, his wife, Irina, and their three children.

Despite the impoverished existence, Irina wastes no time in serving us herring, bread, and vodka in their crowded dining room. Before we know it, our glasses are full and Boris, Igor, and Sergei break into simultaneous toasts of *"Nastrovia!"* Exchanging glances, we tentatively sip our oversized glasses. Then our hosts drain their cups and we realize we have to do the same. Four shots later—as well as a cup of golden root tea, a mild narcotic that grows in Siberia's Altai Mountains—Boris explains why we should abandon our plans for the Kalar and join his group on a river called the Bashkaus.

"It is strong river," he says gruffly. "You meet my team and come with us."

Boris is a member of Team Konkas, a Latvian whitewater team from Riga that has been running rivers together for twelve years. This year, while we're planning to run the Kalar, they're tackling the Class V to VI Bashkaus, one of the hardest and most committing multiday river trips in the former Soviet Union. Sergei ran it four years earlier with three other members of Team Konkas. Igor ran it a year later, in 1990, and most likely won't be going back.

It's a fluke that Boris met us at the airport; we were expecting someone else. During our search for Russian partners to join us on the Kalar, Ben stumbled upon another Latvian, named George Aukon, from Flagstaff, Arizona, while rafting the Dolores River in Colorado. When Ben mentioned that we had secured a grant to run a river in Siberia, George told his friend Boris about us and sent him our flight schedule. Boris then took the liberty of intercepting us at the airport. For the time being, it seems a good thing.

Still, we can't shake the feeling that we have been kidnapped. We are in the apartment of a friend of a stranger who seems to know everything about us and our plans, while we know nothing about them or theirs. Shutting out the effects of the vodka, we decide to have a say in our fate.

"Boris, can you ask Sergei if we can use his phone?" asks Ben. "We want to try calling Andre, our contact here."

Boris turns to Sergei and Sergei nods, pointing to the corner. It's a rotary, but it works, its ancient crackling traversing the web of wires holding the apartment dominos together. A few minutes later, after Boris gets on the phone and interprets, Ben returns to the herring- and vodka-filled dining table.

"He's not there," he says. "He's stuck in Turkey, delayed by a storm on the Black Sea."

"When's he getting back?" asks Van.

"His wife doesn't know," Ben answers. "Could be a week. Could be a month. But there's more—she says she's never even heard of us."

"What do you mean?" I ask.

"She has no idea who we are," confesses Ben. "Her husband never mentioned us or our expedition."

It's a big blow. According to faxes received by Ben, Andre was to build us three breakdown whitewater kayaks, which we were going to use to run the Kalar. Van was going to row a cataraft, housed with our breakdown oars and frame in the canvas body bag now atop Sergei's car.

"Well, that sucks," sums up Edge. "What about the other guys who were supposed to come along?"

"They were all friends of Andre's," answers Ben. "I don't even know their names."

What we do know is that, well vodka'd and still groggy from the flight, we have some serious decisions to make. Quickly. Boris is meeting the rest of his team at the Moscow train station the next day for a three-day ride east to Barnaul. Do we wait around here indefinitely hoping that Andre will return, or cut our losses and join the Latvians?

The decision becomes tougher when we walk across the hallway to Igor's apartment and watch him turn on a scratchy video of a Bashkaus trip he took three years earlier. The rapids look horrendous, and the homemade equipment—including bulky life jackets that make the paddlers resemble cosmonauts—looks even worse. Catarafts surf uncontrollably in holes above sure-death swims. Eddyless Class V rapids continue for what looks like miles. If they're not running a death-defying rapid, they're struggling their gear over a slippery, steep portage. Igor then drops the bomb, describing how he had to wait ten days in the heart of the canyon for the water to drop, witnessing three deaths during that time. After first leading another group out on a four-day hike to safety, he returned to lead his own group out—all in all, a ten-day hike for him to escape the canyon.

With a job and family now, Igor is not going this time. Neither is Sergei, who also has kids to take care of. Given what we saw on the video, we wonder if this is an omen.

When Ben asks a question about their rafts, Igor's answer causes even more chagrin.

"We make it," he says through Boris. "We make everything—rafts, paddles, life jackets, even tents."

Shaken, inebriated, and tired, we drag ourselves back across the hall to Sergei's apartment. There, Boris hands me a short description of the river written in broken English. He borrowed it from their trip leader, Ramitch, who picked it up at a river runner's library in Moscow. Sitting at the table, I flip the page.

"Among all the rest Altai routes," it reads, "this one is to be pointed out because of its unity and the combination of impressions of fairy landscapes and difficult and worth-overcoming rapids, leave alone the extremely high psychological tenseness connected with the danger and long staying alone in the isolated deep canyon."

Fairy landscapes, difficult rapids, mental tension, remote, steep canyon, and isolation. It sums up what we saw on Igor's video, and more.

We share a tiny room vacated by Sergei's kids, who join their parents in their bedroom, while Boris sleeps in the dining room. I part the drapes and take in the rows and rows of identical buildings, which match the gray clouds. Lightning flashes in the distance. "Well, what do you guys think?" I ask. "What do you want to do?"

The choices are clear. Either we stick to our plans and try to run the Kalar, which means waiting indefinitely for our boats and phantom point person, or embark with a group of complete strangers on a nightmarish-looking river on homemade equipment, all three of which we know absolutely nothing about.

It's as clear as our vodka that we've stumbled upon a Land of the Lost when it comes to river running. The sport here has evolved much like Australian wildlife: completely free of outside influences. If we join the Latvians, we'd get an up close and personal look at Russian-style rafting on one of the most difficult whitewater rivers in the former Soviet Union. The "extremely high psychological tenseness" from "long staying alone in the isolated deep canyon" would likely be magnified with complete strangers who don't speak English. So would the difficulty of running Class V-VI water on homemade equipment.

Sergei knocks on the door and pokes his head in.

"*Spokoynoy nochee*," he says. "Good night."

"*Spokoynoy nochee*," we reply in unison.

When the door shuts again, Ben echoes what's on all of our minds.

"I don't know," he says. "We don't even know these guys."

CHAPTER TWO

The Siberian Brainstorm

Buried in a wave, Andrew (left) and Sergei the Small struggle to pull their cataraft forward in Kamikaze rapid.

Our predicament came about like many others I'd found myself in—via a fax that curled its way onto my office desk. This one announced the second year of W. L. Gore and Associates' Shipton/Tilman Grant. Created in 1990, it was a new grant named for British explorers Eric Shipton and H. W. Tilman, two twentieth-century mountaineers known for mounting fast and efficient expeditions. Shipton was the first to climb the 7,756-meter peak Kamet in the Himalayas in 1931. He hooked up with Tilman, and they became the first people to traverse Mount Kenya's West Ridge, explore Nepal's Nanda Devi region, and survey the flanks of K2. The pair also bicycled across Africa and traversed the polar ice cap.

Repeating a mantra adopted by Tilman, the grant maintains that "any worthwhile expedition can be planned on the back of an envelope." It's intended for small groups that can travel lightly and not be burdened by sponsor and media obligations and is awarded to "small unencumbered teams of friends with daring and imaginative goals" who tackle expeditions "in a self-propelled, environmentally sound, cost-effective way."

It sounded too good to be true and the rest of the work-day was shot. I was a die-hard river runner, eager for another ticket to adventure. My mind started racing.

The next day I called my friend Ben Hammond. The application had to have credibility, I reasoned, and Ben, as the assistant director of the Rocky Mountain branch of the National Outdoor Leadership School (NOLS), could provide just that. A seasoned trip organizer and skilled outdoorsman, he had led numerous expeditions to the boondocks, from Alaska to New Zealand. He was also a skilled and strong river man, with a keen eye for detail and scouting water. Most important, he was easygoing, diplomatic, and capable of mak-ing light of the most miserable situations—the perfect expedi-tion partner. His balding head, Paul Newman blue eyes, and crow's-feet seemed to belong in the outdoors.

I had first met him about six years earlier while raft guid-ing outside of Anchorage, Alaska. He was working at the NOLS branch in Palmer. My older sister, Helen, was friends with his older brother, Kris, and one day after guiding, I took the com-pany Suburban to the NOLS commune in Palmer to introduce myself. We did a Cataract Canyon trip together on the Colorado River a year later. After another summer guiding in Alaska, I heard from him again. He had landed a November permit for the Grand Canyon and asked if I could help line up equipment and guides. I moved down from Alaska, met my wife, Denise, on the trip, moved to Telluride, and eventually landed at *Paddler* magazine in Steamboat Springs, Colorado. That's where I was when the grant announcement rolled onto my desk.

I told Ben of two other people I thought would round out the team. Bruce "Edge" Edgerly was a kayak instructor for the Boulder Outdoor Center; his whitewater experience would be invaluable. Jackson, Wyoming, local Van Wombwell, an ex–Alaskan river guide who had joined Ben and me on the Grand, was also a strong candidate. Single and adventurous like Ben, he was working as a real estate appraiser in Teton County but could probably be easily persuaded to join in. Ben agreed wholeheartedly.

The next day, I called Van, who jumped at the chance. He was an experienced world traveler with a healthy reverence for characters such as Shipton, Tilman, and Ernest Shackleton, whose exploits had inspired him to go climbing in Nepal, hitch-hike to Antarctica on a Chilean air force cargo plane, and spend a summer working in Africa. A friend since our college days at Colorado College in Colorado Springs, he was also responsible for getting me started guiding by returning from a summer in Alaska with tales that lured me north. Together we had survived a mapless sea kayak foray into the depths of Prince William Sound and organized a spring-break trip down Utah's San Juan with twenty-five coeds. Back of an envelope was just his style.

My next call was to Edge.

"I'm thinking of trying to land a new grant to run a river somewhere," I said. "You interested?"

A pause filled the line. I could almost hear his cheeks suck in as he thought about it—an Edge trademark.

"Who all's going?" he asked.

He didn't know Van and Ben, but that didn't matter. He, too, was in. So in, in fact, that he'd end up quitting his job with an environmental remediation company to come along.

Our elder at thirty-three, Edge was also our strongest kayaker. I had paddled several whitewater runs with him, and he was always the first to run a problem rapid. I first met him five years earlier on Colorado's Clear Creek while he was getting his master's at the University of Colorado and teach-ing kayaking on the side. Waiting my turn in an eddy at a local playhole—a place where water circulates back on itself, allowing a kayaker to surf—he appeared out of nowhere from upstream, intentionally tipping upside down and flushing into the hole. Then he rolled up and surfed it, his plan all along. It was a yahoo showboating move, but it showed his confidence in a kayak. If there was a horizon line on whatever river we chose, we'd send him to the brink of it to probe.

A few weeks later, we met at Ben's house in Lander, Wyoming—Van driving over from Jackson and Edge and I driving up from Colorado. I introduced Edge, and we settled in on Ben's screened back porch. Apparel from a recent NOLS trip hung on a clothesline outside.

"What do you think?" I asked, showing everyone the fax. "What would be a good trip to pitch?"

Ben took a long draw from his beer before answering. "I don't know," he said. "Probably nothing in the United States. Everything here's been done."

We all agreed that we wanted to do a long trip, spending a minimum of three weeks on a river that was unknown to us.

"Maybe something in Africa or South America?" I suggested.

I had done a couple of river trips in South America already, one to the Quijos in Ecuador and another to the Tambopata in Peru. I spoke Spanish well enough and had connections that might ease logistics.

"I think we need someplace more exotic, more different," Ben said.

Edge mentioned Africa's Zambezi, but we all agreed there wasn't much left to explore there. Van then shared some advice from a college professor who had helped him secure field research funding for a lake-mapping trip to Africa.

"He said that to win a grant, the idea has to be both timely and significant," he said. "I think the blank spot on the map these days is Russia."

It was 1992, only a few months after the breakup of the Soviet empire. Glasnost and the fall of Communism were opening up the region to unprecedented Western exploration. A few beers later, we decided on Siberia, vast and wild, its rivers long and largely unknown to Westerners. And Edge would lend credence to the application as our inside man; he had run a Soviet river before, the Chatkal, on an expedition with Mountain Travel/Sobek.

"Think about it," said Ben. "It has an entire continent's watershed, and probably a ton of rivers that have never been run. And it's 'out there' enough that they just might buy it."

I contacted the W. L. Gore office as soon as I returned home. A few days later, I received a form outlining the grant's specifications. It required a detailed itinerary, a budget, a list of expedition members, and a time frame. With Siberia's sixty-three rivers longer than 1,000 kilometers, a harder task was narrowing down our choice of an actual river to run. Before the application's deadline, Ben stumbled upon a kayak instructor from North Carolina's Nantahala Outdoor Center who happened to mention something about the mighty Manuska, a tributary to Siberia's Ob River. The Ob is one of four massive arteries—including the Yenisey, Lena, and Irtysh—draining Siberia and flowing north into the Arctic Ocean. A tributary to one of them seemed to fit the bill. With the grant's deadline fast approaching, Ben took the lead and started scribbling.

Landing a grant, we found, is a lot like landing a fish. You have to cast, but you also have to set the hook. We tried to do both with our pitch:

> What was once the Soviet Union has recently undergone irreparable transformations. Areas previously undiscoverable have opened up for outside exploration. Available to us for perhaps the first, and possibly last, time is an environment similar to our North Slope in Alaska: an ecosystem rich in wildlife and unexplored natural resources. We feel our proposal to be worthy of consideration for the unique opportunities it offers not only to us as participants, but those lives we influence as outdoor educators. Taking part in an exploratory expedition is consistent with our ethical orientation of self-reliance and simplicity. Consistent with this is an unquenchable desire to follow our dreams.

He was purposefully vague in the first few paragraphs, filling it with such buzz phrases as "ethical orientation of self-reliance" and "lives we influence as outdoor educators," but then he hit his stride:

> There are very few places left on this Earth that have not been quantified, measured, dissected, and sieved through some intellectual filter. … Expeditions take on a character and life all their own once the wheels have been set in motion. Our wheels have begun turning; we share a strong conviction that the expedition is both feasible and an opportunity not to be squandered. Particularly intriguing is the sense of adventure in traveling to an area no one can point to on a map—because it does not exist on any map. As yet, no information exists on the Manuska River, outside of a description given over the telephone from someone who swears it exists. Fair enough …

The proposal went on to say that we planned to reconnoiter several rivers, including the Manuska, and pick one to navigate a first-known descent. We included a budget (down to the last potato and crate of vodka), as well as an expedition itinerary outlining the steps to achieving our goal. But something, we felt, was missing. A few weeks later, Ben mailed us a letter, catching us up on what he thought we should add to the proposal:

> Comrades, I got pretty tired by the time I got to the appendices, so I just cranked them out. I did lay it on a bit thick, but am confident we can punt. The glaring omission in my mind is a stinking map pointing to where we think this friggin' river is … can you come up with anything? From the sound of things, the committee is meeting in about a week, winding down to the final decision by mid-April. Seems they are intrigued and curious, which does

not surprise me given the vague, uncommitted, and flowery proposal we sent them. My thought at this point is to convince them we are not a pack of poets out to experience nature, but are truly committed to this thing (for a price, of course). So, I've been trying to pass along as much objective, logistical info as I can muster in this subsequent letter I'm sending them. Best of luck. Tread firmly but directly, there is nothing to fear but fear itself. Yours, etc., Ben.

After we all added our thoughts, we mailed a secondary letter to the judges, explaining expedition objectives, a more detailed budget, new revelations in logistics, and other information we thought would work to our advantage. Whether it was our back-of-a-redneck-bar-napkin organizational prowess or down-to-the-potato budget, two months later we received our response:

Congratulations on being awarded a 1992 Shipton/ Tilman Grant. Your endeavor is one of four that the judges felt most exemplified the philosophies of Eric Shipton and Bill Tilman. Evaluation of all 103 applications was a difficult and lengthy process, as they were all worthy in their own right. I personally want to congratulate you … you will be setting a precedent for all future applicants to follow …

We'd nailed it—the first paddling-oriented grant ever awarded by W. L. Gore.

Writing the proposal was one thing, but following through was quite another. The grant's whole premise was that we travel lightly and quickly, unburdened by minute details, but one slight detail still caused us problems. Though we tried to confirm the location of the river—Van tracked down aeronautical maps, and we contacted countless Russian river runners—no one had ever really heard of the Manuska, save for our "reliable" source over the phone.

At least Shipton and Tilman knew Kilimanjaro was there before traipsing halfway across the globe to climb it. We won a grant to run a river that, it turns out, didn't exist. So we dug in the heels of our Tevas and, as Ben so eloquently put it in our letter, punted. Originally hoping to get underway that summer, we put the trip off until the following year, trying to determine once and for all the existence of the Manuska. If it turned out to be a Grey Goose chase, we had to find a suitable alternative. So, grant in hand, we scrambled to form a plan B and find another river.

A letter from Ben the following fall summed up both our frustrations and our commitment to following through with some sort of expedition:

> Gentlemen … I figure a letter to all updating our status on Siberia is in order. I think we're well placed to begin kicking into high gear, and by our March meeting, we'll know, to our satisfaction anyway, the WHERE, WHEN, and HOW of this expedition into oblivion. I'm particularly curious, Bruce, to see what you came up with in your "Vanya Briefing." By the sounds of it, you've hit upon a great little river in the Baikal region. I'll see if we can score a deal on a case of Bear Mace-off and some track shoes.

By June—after rounding up such sponsors as Finnair, REI, and NOLS and poring over Van's maps—we had settled on an alternative river: the Kalar, a long, twisting waterway near Lake Baikal, the largest freshwater lake in the world.

It was nowhere near the supposed Manuska, but at least it was still in Siberia. We envisioned an idyllic, crystalline river teeming with fish and flanked by flowery meadows, berry bushes, and craggy mountains. In our research, Ben had stumbled on a Russian in Moscow who made breakdown whitewater kayaks suitable for rapids up to Class III to IV. (This was the phantom Andre.) He could have three of them ready for us by July. Our plan was to fly to Novosibirsk in Siberia then travel by train for three days to a small village where we would backpack for two days to reach the put-in. From there, we'd float the Kalar back to where it intersected with the train tracks. We'd bring the three breakdown whitewater kayaks and two specially made lightweight cataraft pontoons, as well as a breakdown frame and oars, to carry the gear. We'd take turns rowing, alternating between time in the kayaks and time behind the oars. Andre would bring two of his friends in their own boats. We estimated the 300-mile float would take us about two and a half weeks.

We felt confident of our itinerary, and the plans progressed rapidly. As they did, word got out about our expedition. On a trip to Telluride, I bumped into my former Outward Bound instructor, who had applied for the same grant for a climbing expedition to China.

"How do you like that?" he said after learning we had nudged him out of contention. "I teach you everything I know and what do you do? You stab me in the back." He was joking, of course, at least until I grabbed the last bratwurst from the barbecue.

Then we had to deal with the inevitable cling-ons. "You guys need a photographer?" came inquiries at the office. "Pencil holder? Someone to cook potatoes?" People I hadn't heard from in years suddenly acted like best friends, touting skills they thought would come in handy. Even my mom tried to get in on the action as a pencil-pushing cultural documenter. We turned them all down, sticking to our core four, as Shipton and Tilman would have done.

Months of preparation later, we learned the hard way not to host a Siberia send-off celebration the night before you leave.

"You got the first-aid kit?" asked Ben, carrying an assortment of unrelated items to our packs in the garage while dodging our friends at the nearby keg. "Where should we pack the granola?"

"Put it in the bag with the pump," yelled Edge over the

din of the party. "There's still a little room in it."

"How about the water filter and stove?" asked Van.

"I'll take it over here," I replied. "There's still some room in this duffel."

"Jesus, this thing weighs a ton," added Ben, dragging a giant canvas bag housing our frame, oars, and pontoons to the car.

The previous night, I survived a similar send-off party in Steamboat. This one had a vodka-and-potato theme, with mashed potatoes, boiled potatoes, au gratin potatoes, French fries, and baked potatoes. It didn't take long for the two substances to come together. Gouging a shot glass–sized divot in a baked potato with his thumb, my cousin Homer then filled it with vodka for a toast.

"Shot glass, Siberia-style," he said.

Homer is Steve Holmes, a second cousin whom I didn't even know before I moved to Steamboat. We had boating in common as well as blood. He was a world-class C-2 paddler vying for a spot in the Olympics. I'd paddled with him on local runs and considered him a mentor.

"*Nastrovia!*" he said, raising the potato, draining it, and then eating half of the vessel as a chaser.

Things weren't as rowdy in Boulder, largely because we were too busy. By 3:00 A.M., we had our personal gear loaded into backpacks, river gear stuffed inside dry bags, and food packed in duffels. We'd raided the bulk-food bin at the NOLS headquarters in Lander for everything from PowerBars to jelly beans, anticipating buying such staples as rice, sugar, and flour in Moscow. Our mound of equipment required two cars, racks and trunks completely loaded, to get us to the Denver airport an hour later. For a group trying to travel as lightly and unencumbered as possible, we weren't doing a great job.

"Final destination Moscow?" asked the ticket agent.

"Yep," said Ben.

"You'll be changing planes in New York and again in Helsinki. Any bags to check?"

We directed her attention to the pile behind us. A

chagrined look crossed her face. We were allowed two each, plus one carry-on. Because it was heavier than the limit, we designated the bag housing our raft, frame, and oars as "extra." We gladly paid the extra fifty dollars not to have to deal with it.

We had to deal with something else as soon as we reclaimed our bags at JFK. Behind us, from deep in our pile of gear, came an ear-piercing siren that caused two armed security guards to rush over. Our motion-sensor alarm, a gimmick I had received at the office to review and had brought along to protect our gear, went off accidentally, and none of us knew how to turn it off.

"Don't worry," I exclaimed to the guards. "That's just our bag. I'll take care of it."

I dug deep into a duffel to find the culprit and pulled it out, siren wailing. A few more guards came over as I fumbled with various button combinations before finally taking out a pocketknife and unscrewing the battery cap. The screeching finally stopped, and our gear was once again all over the floor, just like the night before.

"Way to go, Euge," Van said. "That thing's come in handy already."

"Everything's going so smoothly so far that I think we're in for a great trip," added our diplomat, Ben.

After rechecking our bags, we made our way to the gate. A duty-free bottle of scotch and tequila later, as well as four cartons of Marlboros for bartering, we boarded our flight.

On board, our morale rose with the aircraft. Our assigned seats were first-class.

"I just don't know if I'm cut out for all this adventure stuff," said Van sarcastically as we all clinked champagne glasses.

As if we'd been doing it all our lives, we then began riffling through the complimentary ditty bags for items that might come in handy in Siberia—perfume, a comb, socks, shaving kit, lotion, even a travel toothbrush with plastic carrier. "We could probably use this," said Ben, twirling a napkin ring in his fingers. "Might make a good fishing lure."

"And we can always use another signal mirror," said Edge, pocketing a compact.

Knowing we'd soon be subject to spoils from the bulk-food bin, we devoured the five-course meal. All in all, we blended in admirably, save for our river sandals sticking out in the aisles. It was a good way to start an expedition into the unknown.

The only foreboding omen came in Helsinki, when Ben accidentally left his fly rod on the wrong plane. It was expensive, and we were counting on using it to supplement our rations.

"Oh well," I said. "At least you still have your napkin-ring lure from the ditty bag."

When night came, I plugged my earphones into the armrest's radio and settled on "Sympathy for the Devil" by the Rolling Stones. It somehow seemed appropriate, heading to Russia while Mick Jagger bellowed on about St. Petersburg and Czar Nicholas II's daughter Anastasia. As it was for the subject of his song, it was a time for a change for us as well.

CHAPTER THREE

Team Konkas

Sergei the Tall (left) and Edge brandishing the Latvians' homemade paddles at the put-in.

Guttural dog barks echo off the rows of apartment buildings outside our window in the morning. Our heads hurt. I part Sergei's drapes again and the gray overcast seeps in like water flooding a basement. Before going to sleep, we agreed to join the Latvians for the train ride east to Barnaul. This will allow Andre four days to return, at which point we can try calling him again. Besides, it's the direction we need to go anyway to get to the Kalar, and it's a way to delay our decision and get to know these guys. It's also better than staying here.

After toast, soft-boiled eggs, and another cup of golden root tea, we haul our overnight bags back downstairs, where Igor's brother, Nicolai, is waiting to drive us to the train station. Like last night's drive to Sergei's apartment, it's another escort far off the beaten tourist track.

"That still running?" asks Ben when we pass an aging nuclear power plant.

"Yes," Boris replies. "It was broken for a while but now is

strong again."

"Strong like Bashkaus," I add from the backseat.

"Hah, not that strong," Boris says, laughing.

My mind flashes back to the video we saw of the Bash-kaus. I am not sure if he is joking or not.

Nicolai tunes the radio and settles on a news station. On it, we learn through Boris that the Russian government is issu-ing a new currency on July 26, while we'll be on the train.

"Not smart to exchange money yet," says Boris. "Better to wait until Barnaul."

Broken down cars litter the highway like crumpled leafs on a riverbank. There are no rules of the road here. Do what works to get where you're going and act for the common good. Right now, that good is getting to the train station on time. Nicolai swerves to miss a car that cuts him off.

Thanks to Nicolai's NASCAR moves, we make it with time to spare. While waiting, we take rides on the massive Stalin-built subway system where people scurry about as part of their daily lives. In one passageway, what appears to be a dead man lies prone on the stairs, arm in a cast extended upwards. His body is as rigid as his plaster-covered arm. No one gives him a second look. Over the heads of commuters, we see the huge telltale homemade backpacks of other Rus-sian river runners and backpackers setting out for their annual reprieves. The packs extend far above their bearers' heads and are as crammed with provisions as the subways are with people.

We ride a couple of stations away, switch subways, and return to where we started. Had we known what kind of train ride we are in for, we might not have pursued any extra time on the tracks.

We return to meet the rest of Boris's Team Konkas, whose members have already traveled thirteen hours from Riga, Lat-via, and now face a seventy-three-hour ride to Barnaul. They are all what is referred to as *splavniki*, Russian for "whitewater tour-ist." Besides Boris, they include four Sergeis (whom we nick-named Sergei the Tall, Sergei the Medium, Sergei the Small, and just Plain Sergei); two Valeris; Andrew; Yevgheny (whose name in Russian matches my own); and Ramitch and Olga.

Short, solid, and with wavy brown hair, Olga reminds me of a schoolteacher who always busted kids for passing notes. Despite enduring a thirteen-hour train ride, her clothes match, with a light-green T-shirt highlighting a pair of dark-green nylon pants. Below her unkempt hair rests a pair of large round glasses. We'd soon learn that these help her see everything, especially inequitable portions of food. She is the team's only woman and Ramitch's wife of thirteen years. Ramitch, the trip leader, was on the Bashkaus with Apartment Sergei four years earlier. This will be his second trip on the river and everyone else's first. Together, with the unflappable Boris, they make a team of ten, with Olga and Boris—and to a much lesser degree, Yevgheny—the only ones capable of carrying on any sort of conversation in English.

Ramitch is Valerij Ramkovitch, born November 17, 1957, in the small Latvian village of Gorniki. The son of farmers, he is one of five children and the youngest of four brothers. Perhaps it was those early, youngest-sibling years that give him the resolve and respect he needs for his leadership role in Team Konkas today. He met Olga, who is originally from Lithuania, while studying chemistry and living in the student hostel at Riga's Latvian University. They married in 1980. After graduating and having a daughter, Julia, in 1981, Ramitch went to work for the Inorganic Chemistry Institute of the Latvian Academy of Science before branching out on his own. With Latvia now separated from the Soviet Union as well as Russia, and scientific work hard to find, Ramitch and a few friends, all with a passion for whitewater, founded their own business, called Konkas, in 1991. The company makes pavilions and umbrellas for commercial use, and catarafts for their own.

Though some members of their whitewater team have come and gone—Boris is still a relative newcomer—the core has remained much the same during the team's twelve years. Its main cogs are now all here at the train station for the most difficult expedition they have ever attempted.

As well as satiating their adrenaline needs, this trip also has bragging rights at stake. Every year, Team Konkas enters a contest with Latvia's other outdoor clubs for best expedition of the year. Konkas has won the annual celebration for the past three years straight. This year, it will be easier: due to hard times, Konkas is the only team taking part in a river expedition— a shame for the expedition of the year competition, as the team is undertaking one of the greatest river challenges possible. They have the title locked up before even stepping on the train, as long as they beat out one other Latvian group heading on a mountaineering expedition to the Pamir Mountains, 1,500 miles southeast of Moscow.

"There will be no contest or party this year," Olga says after introductions. "People can't make trips when their money has to go to food."

This year, Team Konkas is lucky. Yevgheny Sokolov, an amicable—and employed—industrial wire salesman and long-time member of Team Konkas, is subsidizing the trip. He looks far too friendly and personable to be a wire salesman, characteristics emphasized when he looks us in the eye, smiles, and shakes our hands vigorously during introductions. With a circle of short dark hair making a lunar eclipse of his shiny, balding head, he's tall and jovial, laughing easily with all three Sergeis. Apart from Olga and Boris, who speak the best English, we'll get to know him, as well as Ramitch, better than the others solely because of his attempts to communicate.

It's a good thing he's subsidizing the trip. Though the Russians and Soviets have fought off the biggest empire builders in the world—including the Mongols, Napoleon, and Hitler— embracing a free market is proving a much harder battle, especially for countries such as Latvia. Long used to a Soviet umbrella guaranteeing employment, housing, and health insurance, Latvia, which seceded from the Soviet Union in 1991, is in hard times. Newly independent, its people no longer have Mother Russia looking after them. There are no more state supports for such things as food, clothing, shelter, or even employment.

Barely a year and a half after the country's independence, many factories are only operating three days a week. Boris, a computer programmer who taught himself English from a book, makes forty dollars a month. Ramitch is an unemployed chemist launching a fledgling manufacturing business. He spent eight years living with Olga and Julia in a hostel while waiting for a better place to move. It wasn't until last year that they were able to join a group of fifty families in a communal apartment building. Plain Sergei works as an auto mechanic eighteen hours a day just to make ends meet.

The new government doesn't make things any easier, either. Shortly after the country's independence, it decreed that Latvian citizenship requires parents born in Latvia before 1941, the year Russia took over to beef up its troops against Hitler. This means that people such as Boris, a Ukrainian Jew whose grandfather was killed in a Nazi raid, have no real nationality. They are no longer Russians and no longer Latvians. And they don't have the benefits of either country's citizenship.

On the bright side, the Latvians are accustomed to such changes in nationality. It started with the Germans, who took over while spreading Christianity in the thirteenth century. Then the region became part of Livonia until it fell to Poland in 1562. Next, it was Sweden's turn, which took over in 1629. In 1721, it passed to Russia, which ruled it until the Communist Revolution in 1918. Twenty years later, Russia reoccupied the country and incorporated it into the Socialist Soviet Union. Then it came full circle back to Hitler's Germans, who ruled it for three years before it returned once more to Stalin.

Boris's grandfather was far from the only casualty during that time. Of the 70,000 Jews living in Latvia under Germany's rule, 95 percent were massacred.

When Russia regained control again in 1944, Latvia was turned into one of the most industrialized regions of the Soviet Union. When the coup against Mikhail Gorbachev failed, the Latvians seized their chance for freedom and, following Lithuania and Estonia, declared their independence on August 21, 1991.

For people such as Boris, however, this has been a mixed blessing. Because the country's ethnic identity has been so diluted by foreign rulers—in much the same way that we would later see the Bashkaus muddied by the many creeks tumbling into it—the new government set up strict laws, limiting citizenship to ethnic Latvians and to those who lived, or whose parents lived, in the region before the Soviet's rule in 1941. Several classes of people now live in the country, from Latvians to exmilitary, ex-KGB, and ex-Communist party members, all of whom have a different status. While things are settling down, more than half of the country's 740,000 ethnic Russians have been denied citizenship and declared aliens, with a respective mark in their passports.

"We have both living in Latvia," says Boris as we wait for Ramitch to strike a deal for our train tickets. "Latvian citizens and aliens. And then we have those like me."

If their nationality is convoluted, their role on Team Konkas is straightforward. "We have people from both sides on our team," continues Boris. "And we get along great. Which is good, because we have to run strong river."

Indeed, a river doesn't care what nationality you are. It will flip a mixed raft of Latvians and Russians as readily as a boat of purebreds. Perhaps in Team Konkas's case, that helps. Like water converging from different streams, not everyone is from the same background. Together, when working as a team, they grow stronger, just like the Bashkaus as it picks up tributaries. The team's peformance in its expedition competitions is proof of that.

That Team Konkas has fared so well in their country's river competitions owes largely to their leader, Ramitch. His hard features—sharp nose and matching chin and straight black hair cropped to the side—underscore his shrewd, steadfast rule. He got his start river running in 1980, organizing a trip just north of Riga on the Amata River. The spring-fed waterway didn't so much test his recruits' early whitewater skills as their ability to function as a team. Though it was an easy Class II, Ramitch made it known from the beginning that he was in charge.

"He went through everyone's packs and took things out he thought they didn't need," Olga says. "They didn't like it much, but they obeyed."

Traveling light has been the team's trademark ever since, in ways that would do Shipton and Tilman proud. Ramitch's squad put the concept to its first serious test a few years later when tackling their first Class V, a rapid called Kiviristi on Latvia's Ohta River. The success of this trip cemented their status as perhaps the strongest and closest-knit whitewater team in Latvia. The year before we arrived, they embarked on their toughest expedition to date, running a river called the Kitoy near Lake Baikal. It marked the first time they didn't have to hike to a put-in. Instead, like we were about to do, they took a train.

Now, however, they have extra baggage along—us. Through the doors leading inside, I hear Ramitch arguing with the ticket clerk. Boris tells me he's trying to secure them at the Russian rate so as not to incur any unnecessary "travel" fees. Though I can't understand a single word, it sounds like the conversation is going in his favor. Trip leader, travel negotiator, head guide, comrade—Ramitch wears all these balaclavas and more for Team Konkas. And he seems perfectly suited for each role.

Throughout the 1970s and '80s, many Soviet paddling clubs gave out an annual Sports Master of Whitewater award, for which Ramitch would easily qualify. To earn the title, one had to have successfully led at least two Class V to VI multiday whitewater trips. The accolades weren't bestowed just for surviving the run's rapids, but a panel rated the whole trip, from the portages to travel logistics. Though lean of frame, Ramitch is heavy with experience, having already led three expeditions that would qualify.

The awards were worth more than simple bragging rights. They were based on a Soviet Masters of Sport system whereby bureaucrats who depended on government funding allocated for sports could demonstrate that their program was working by producing a certain quota of Sports Masters. The more masters they had, the more funding they'd receive. For white-water paddlers, the honor also helped expeditions gain access to logistical help, making it easier to procure transportation in remote villages, food supplies, and even equipment.

As well as doling out awards to one another, Russian paddlers also share information freely. After each trip, Ramitch sends his journal notes to an expedition library in Moscow, which chronicles data on all of the country's private expeditions. So far, the library has amassed more than 5,300 expedition reports, including mountain climbing, river running, and bicycling trips, dating back to 1935. It's a good system, born of necessity; without any commercial outfitters to provide information, private groups such as Team Konkas have to rely on each other for information about different runs. The library's river-running department catalogs trip reports and maps, and even has its own sort of vice squad, or river police, that issues travel papers to qualified groups. Like the Sports Master accolade, these papers help expeditions secure assistance from local villages.

Ramitch, Boris tells us, has secured such papers for this expedition.

"They send them to him in Riga," he says. "Ramitch, strong leader."

If he's done nothing else for Team Konkas over the years, he's instilled an indelible sense of camaraderie in his squad, a microcosm of all the paddlers in the region and the solidarity that seemingly permeates the sport here. This shows itself the moment the train arrives. Accustomed to the ins and outs of confined travel, the team intrinsically forms a fire-bucket brigade to schlep all the gear inside one of the cars. We join in, eager to prove our worth. As if they've done it a hundred times, Sergei the Tall and Valeri methodically place everyone's paddles across the top bunks to create an additional platform to store the backpacks and other gear. It's simple and ingenious.

It also affords us our first close look at what propels their homemade rafts. The paddles are obviously homemade, with fiberglass blades fastened to aluminum shafts. One is beet red, with a large yellow hammer and sickle inlayed into the fiberglass. Another, belonging to Ramitch, has an intricate design that reads "Team Konkas" on one side and "Riga, Latvia" on the other. Sergei the Tall's shows a centaur rearing up on his hind legs and shooting an arrow.

The backpacks we load onto the makeshift paddle platform are equally improvised. While ours carry labels of such brand names as The North Face and REI, the Latvians' are made from old parachutes and army cots, with hand-sewn leather straps riveted to sawed-off bed frames. Stuffed to the gills until they're listing like the Leaning Tower of Pisa, each one is a different color—yellow, green, blue, or red. Laying them across the paddles spanning the bunks yields a giant rainbow of gear.

We're happy to add ours to the mix.

"We might not know where we're going," Van says nonchalantly, throwing his pack onto the heap and filling in gaps with assorted other gear, "but at least we won't have to worry anymore about lugging our gear around for the next three days."

"That in itself is worth joining these guys," adds Edge.

CHAPTER FOUR

Across Siberia: The Train

Strumming the oft-requested "Rocky Raccoon" halfway down the upper canyon.

We barely load all of our gear on board before the train starts rolling toward Siberia. Since Ramitch bought us tickets at the Russian rate—10,000 rubles, or about $10 apiece, instead of the exorbitant $1,000 per person charged newly approved foreigners—he cautions us to keep quiet as soon as the conductress, wearing a gray uniform and cap, passes by. We need to pass as locals instead of Americans. If she wasn't monitoring the rail lines, the conductress would be a shoo-in for Nurse Ratchet in *One Flew over the Cuckoo's Nest*: all scowl and jowl. Though our unlobotomized brains aren't at risk, our comfort is. We want to keep on her good side.

Although we look as if we could pass for Russians, or at least Latvians, with our four-day stubble and wrinkled clothes, Olga quickly sets us straight. The giveaway is our mouths.

"You smile too much and your teeth are too good," she says. "You no look Russian."

Andrew smiles behind her, exposing three empty slots.

Olga is right. Compared with Andrew's stumps and the conductress's scowls, we stick out more than we did in the first-class section of Finnair. But the technique works. With mouths clamped shut, we hand Ratchet of the Railways our Russian tickets when she passes by. She eyes them suspiciously before moving on as we glumly stare down at the floor.

"*Nyet*," Edge says after she is out of earshot.

"*Nyet, nyet*," I reply.

Van and Ben also chime in, until we sound like the Knights who say Ni in *Monty Python and the Holy Grail*. It's the only Russian we know so far, apart from a token toast and *good day*.

"*Dobre utra*," Van adds, trumping our linguistic ineptitude.

Van represents our best chance of communicating, tutoring with a Russian woman in Jackson for six months before the trip. It helps tremendously. I tried to take a cram course in Russian before we left, listening to a *Russian Made Easy* book on tape every time I drove. But the title is a misnomer. My studies proved as effective as our attempts to blend in on the train.

Not counting us and our *nyet*s, Russian is spoken by nearly 240 million people—including those in the new Russian Federation, the fourteen other countries in the former Soviet Union, and Eastern Europeans in Warsaw Pact countries. It's also a key language across the Caucasus and Central Asia. Though more consequential, learning to read whitewater is far easier. You get caught up in a hole rather than in pronunciations. The modern Cyrillic alphabet has thirty-three letters, seven more than English. Of the thirty-three, seven look like ours (*H*, *P*, and *Y*, for instance) but are pronounced entirely different ways. What's more, accent can be placed on any syllable, meaning every word's pronunciation has to be learned separately.

"*Nyet*," I say again, this time focusing on the *ny*.

When we manage the courage to look up from the floor, the conductress is gone, glaring at other passengers at the far end of the car. We survive close call number one.

Across the aisle, Sergei the Tall pulls out a plastic baggie filled with reams of paper. He pulls out a page, reads it, and passes it to Andrew. While we brought four books each for the trip, the Latvians brought one for all ten of them to share. As it isn't bound together, they take turns reading the pages one by one. Read a page, then pass it along. Read a page, pass it along. They can carry everything they need for a twenty-eight-day river expedition on their backs, from rafts to reading material. We feel even more misgivings about our own excessiveness. Less than a quarter of our total gear on our backs would likely grind us to a crawl. Of course, we also imagined that we'd likely have transport all the way to our put-in in the Siberian wilderness.

"Wow," says Edge. "I never thought I'd feel guilty about bringing a book."

"*Nyet*," replies Ben.

We're able to bridge the cultural and language gap by speaking the universal language of whitewater. In a summit of sorts, Ramitch calls us over to his bunk and asks about our plans for the Kalar. He then spreads a map out on a small table between the two sets of bunks, closing a pair of white drapes to block the glare. Boris and Sergei the Small lean their heads over from prone positions on the bunks above, trying to be part of the conversation. With Boris translating from his suspended position, Ramitch says there is a reason no one has run the Kalar: it is a mosquito-infested bog.

"Many bugs. Slow water," he says through Olga.

He also says the train we had hoped to take to its put-in isn't running, a victim of frost heaves that have buckled the tracks. He then pulls out Mylar maps of all 212 named rapids on the Bashkaus and points, with Boris interpreting. "We go here," he says. "Difficult, strong river."

Still hesitant to join their group, we ask him about another river we had researched, called the Kitoy. "Perhaps it would be a better alternative?" Ben asks Boris.

Boris translates while Ramitch listens intently.

"Not with your equipment and not without someone who

has been there," says Boris, adding that Team Konkas did the river the year before.

"Tell us about it," I reply.

"A few years ago," Boris continues, waiting for Ramitch to finish before translating, "a group missed a portage and four people drowned."

Ramitch draws a skull and crossbones on a makeshift map on a napkin, pinpointing the tragedy's location. It didn't happen on their trip, but they clearly respect the river.

"Very many people have died there," adds Olga. "We think you come with us."

We return to our bunks as perplexed as we were in Sergei's apartment. *Who the hell are these guys?* I think, echoing a line from *Butch Cassidy and the Sundance Kid*. Where Butch and Sundance worried about someone tracking them across desert slickrock, I worry about the tracks below us carrying us deeper into Siberia and into a deeper reliance on running a river such as the Bashkaus with complete strangers.

"Why is it that whenever we hear of some new river here, we hear about people dying?" Ben asks. "First, it was the three people Igor saw die on the Bashkaus, and now it's four on the Kitoy."

"Maybe we should stick with the Kalar," Van suggests.

I think of my wife, Denise, back home, alone, and how any of my decisions here could affect her thousands of miles away. The only thing we can agree upon is that we can't make a decision until we reach Barnaul.

Things lighten up later in the evening. Calling us over to his berth, Ramitch pours shots of vodka into cups brought just for that purpose, then breaks out a guitar. It's comforting to see that for someone who has river rapids mapped out on Mylar, Ramitch also has an unregimented artistic side. And that's the way we spend our first night heading toward Siberia—drinking and singing to get to know each other.

The songs are lively and loud. Between verses, Boris tries his best to translate. All the songs hint of a river-running heritage, suggesting rafting has its own folklore here. One song, Boris tells us, is about not being a man unless you survive a trip on the Chulishman River and come home with an oar in your leg and a broken nose. Another is a memorial to whitewater athletes who have died. Another is about the weather and how it can ruin your day, and still another is about building boats. Whether it's the booze, the percussion of the train tracks, or the language they're sung in, the songs capture our collective mood perfectly. A lot of this is likely due to the language. Russian's endless prefixes, suffixes, endings, and vowel alternations give it rhymes that are impossible in other languages. Almost anything you say can turn into a verse or chorus of a song. If artsy types say Shakespeare sounds good in Russian, imagine what the language can do for river songs belted out on a train across Siberia.

Then Ramitch croons a song comparing those who run the Bashkaus to those who walk a tightrope in a circus. Our misgivings continue.

Then they pass the guitar to us. Ramitch requests "The Sound of Silence"; Boris, "Rocky Raccoon"; and Yevgheny, "American Pie." Luckily, we know them. But their fast-paced songs make ours belong in Sunday School. After lulling them, or at least ourselves, nearly asleep, we pass the guitar back for the second set. Though they keep the rest of the car awake, the Latvians pay no mind, cranking out a seemingly endless repertoire of songs that everyone knows the words to. And no one is shy about joining in, least of all Boris, whose hearty baritone carries down the car over the clackity-clack of the train.

Other passengers join in, too. Listening, I stare out the window into the jet-black Siberian darkness. My reverie is interrupted by the slam of a door between the cars. It's the conductress, in her own polite little way letting us know we're being too loud. She reminds me of the school lunch lady busting students for taking too many Tater Tots, or the lifeguard scolding kids for running. I feel like we're always getting under her skin, as if she constantly suspects us of something. Somehow she always knows just when to surface.

Something else surfaces under our own skin the next morning. We awake covered with welts. Van gets the bedbug award for most bites. His back is riddled with red bumps.

Our seat cushions, which fold out into beds, harbor mites—Siberian biting mites that have no trouble protecting their turf with their teeth. To make matters worse, it's hot and muggy, so the bites itch all the more.

Though we can't do anything about the mites, the Latvians have come prepared for dealing with the heat. They stole a key from a Latvian university that fits the window locks, making them, and us by association, the only people on board who can get fresh air. As if she enjoys seeing us swelter in the heat, whenever she finds the windows open, the conductress shuts them with a scowl. The Latvians wait a few minutes until she's gone and open them again.

That afternoon, the Latvians begin packing their food and cigarettes into plastic bags, rationing them with tags for certain days. They're very organized, serious, and disciplined. Plain Sergei stitches a hole in his shoe.

If the Latvians are industrious, they're nothing compared to our first train stop, Omsk, once home to the largest prisoner way station in Siberia. The region is one of the country's top industrial producers, clearly visible in the mile after mile of smokestacked buildings that we pass before we roll to a stop. Fourth biggest in all of Russia, the area's industry centers primarily on chemicals, oil refining, and metallurgy. But with total output now barely 50 percent of its level a scant year ago, it's now in the throes of a deep depression. Instead of a vibrant train station, we are greeted with gloom. Gray skies match the gray buildings, which match the gray moods of the station's pedestrians.

Industry here developed primarily because of this same long train system now taking us toward the Bashkaus. Without transportation, there could be no industry and no town. Until a few years ago, towns like this weren't open to foreigners; tourists were required to take the 5,810-mile Trans-Siberian railroad to the north, the only land route between Western Europe and the Pacific Far East. On a train few Westerners have ever ridden, we're paralleling the famous Trans-Siberian tracks to its south.

Russia's Trans-Siberian system is one of the man-made wonders of the world. It comprises the longest continuous railway on earth, each line covering almost 6,000 miles, 100 degrees of longitude, and seven time zones. For those going the whole way, it's seven straight days on the tracks, watching Mother Russia pass by, resetting your watch at least once daily. Most people make the journey opposite the sun, as we were, traveling rapidly ahead into time, west to east, from Moscow to Vladivostok, where you can continue by ferry to Japan.

Four Trans-Siberian lines make up the nearly 24,000-mile-long system. The Trans-Manchurian follows the Trans-Siberian as far as Tarskaya, east of Lake Baikal, before heading southeast into China. The Trans-Mongolian heads to Ulan-Ude on Lake Baikal before dipping south to Ulaanbaatar and Beijing. In 1984, after fifty years of construction, another route, the Baikal Amur Mainline, was completed farther north, departing the Trans-Siberian a few hundred miles west of Baikal.

As with trains in the United States, the Russian lines were built to connect more populated areas with those just opening up to exploration. When Russia established Vladivostok as the country's first Pacific port in 1860, lack of transportation to the new city was a major concern. In 1891, after Vladivostok existed in relative isolation for thirty years, Czar Alexander III initiated plans for the Trans-Siberian Railway. The continent-spanning project was carried on by his son, Nicholas, and took nearly fifteen years to complete. The route was finished in 1905, barely in time to be put to use for the Russo–Japanese War. The line's current route, including a detour around Baikal, was opened in 1916.

We can only hope that the other Trans-Siberian lines have more accommodating conductresses than we do. Evading her almost becomes a ritual, like dodging the bully at recess.

If Ratchet of the Railways doesn't like us, at least most of the passengers do. Whether because of our moldy-oldie guitar sin-galongs or our blatant naivete on the train, we are adopted, in a way, by most everyone in our car. Our friendliest carmates are a family from Armenia taking a vacation from the Georgian war.

Georgia is located on the Black Sea, the same body of water delaying our kayak-building comrades from joining us on the Kalar. Acquired by Russia in 1829, Georgia was made a Soviet republic in 1921, and later declared its inde-pendence, like Latvia, in 1991. With the country's indepen-dence, however, came hard times, just like those that befell Latvia. In 1992, its citizens rebelled against the existing post-Soviet regime. Other regional republics did the same, until a full-blown civil war erupted. Just a year before we met our Georgian family, Russia stepped in to help the rebellion. The combined forces would ultimately prevail, but right now, the war is still on and the rebellion is what this family is escaping.

The head of the family is wearing a loose yellow muscle shirt. Its unrestricted fit echoes what he is most likely searching for—a life free of restrictions. His sky-blue eyes seem to sparkle with imminent freedom. Perhaps getting away from the war is all he needs to glimpse a safer, more secure future. He asks Sergei the Small to take our picture with his family, a tangible reminder that freedom is indeed possible.

As if we are a commodity or circus attraction, other pas-sengers also go out of their way to accommodate us. Though we've tried hard to blend in as Russians, our secret is obvi-ously out, and they are glad to befriend us, and even protect us: When we get off in Omsk to stretch our rail-weary legs, a woman from the end of our car helps us negotiate a bag of raspberries; though times are as hard in Omsk as they are in the rest of the country, the vendor gives us an extra bag. Another charitable gesture averts a crisis. As we thank the woman for the extra berries, Van wanders across the tracks to a bench at the main platform. Shouts from another train neighbor quickly pierce the air and Van comes scurrying back.

Twenty seconds later, we see the reason for the alarm: another train arrives from the opposite direction, which would have separated Van from ours. With ours leaving momentarily, he would have been stuck passport- and penniless in Omsk.

"That was too close," Boris says once Van is safely back on our side of the tracks. "You stay close to us."

It's hard to imagine spending any more than fifteen minutes here. The sky is monotone gray and all the buildings equally so. A chill commands a jacket. The city looks industrial, polluted, and bleak. Its Communist history is likely equally dismal.

"Imagine living here in the first part of the century," Ben says once we're all safely back on board and heading away. "You'd experience two world wars, a revolution, a civil war, coups, and even oppression from your own government."

"And it was probably still gray like this the whole time," I add.

As we gratefully watch Omsk disappear in the distance, we dig into the the raspberries and pass them around to the Latvians. It's a welcome break to our standard railroad rations. The meals so far have been staple Latvian fare: bread, cucumbers, tomatoes, onions, and some sort of fish spread. They started out interestingly enough, with our curiosity overshadowing the culinary monotony. But as we head farther down the tracks, the meals head farther down the tube. Today's lunch hits an all-time low: a dollop of rice cooked over a single-burner backpacker's stove, and a whole shrunken pickle, plucked from a bag holding fourteen others like it. Already learning the ropes, I try to size up the biggest one before making my selection. Despite the fact that we've yet to commit to join them, they have already included us as members of Team Konkas.

The fare wouldn't be so bad if it was just one meal. But it's like this for breakfast, lunch, and dinner. Though our raspberries help break the repetitiveness, that night we venture through the crowded cars to a restaurant at the end of the train. They can share the surplus of our rejected allotments.

Unable to decipher the menu, we end up with bread and mystery-meat soup. A man sits next to us and tries to make small talk, but his words are as hard to digest as the soup's meat. We do understand—from muscular arms rippling beneath his shirtsleeves and bloodshot eyes trying to hold ours—that we don't want to offend him. Prisoners in Russia gain clout the more tattoos they have. We have just passed the largest prisoner way station in Siberia, and this man has tattoos on all ten fingers. We eat hurriedly and thread our way back to the safety of our more familiar strangers, with a renewed appreciation for their generous inclusion.

For dessert, we break out a bar of chocolate to share with Team Konkas. The chocolate and the cheese we readily ingest serve a dual purpose: we hope its constipating properties will delay the inevitable trip to the latrine at the end of the car. It doesn't, of course, and a half hour later I have to make the walk of doom down the aisle. Inside the latrine, the stench is nauseating. There is no seat, nor would I use it if there were. Instead, antislip footprints mark where you are supposed to squat over the stainless steel rim. Excrement clings to the top rail and sides. I brace against the wall, wobbling with the train. I flush with the foot pump, wash my hands in the stainless steel basin, then stumble, as if drunk, when the train takes a corner. My timing is impeccable—right when I emerge into the hallway, the conductress walks through the adjacent car door and scowls.

Team Konkas breaks out another bottle of vodka that evening. We return the favor with our bottle of duty-free Johnny Walker Red, passing it across the aisle and sharing it with other passengers who join in the celebration. We follow suit, again, with the guitar. This time, Boris leads the charge with more river-related folk songs. We call ourselves whitewater athletes, but so far, the only things getting a workout seem to be our vocal chords and livers.

Boris wakes us in the morning, leaning his scruffy beard over me as I sleep in the lower bunk. "Breakfast is waiting," he says. "Maybe afterward, you will write down words to 'We

Will Rock You?'" He tried playing the song the night before but got hung up on the lyrics after the chorus. I tell him we'll jot them down for him.

After bread and more fish spread, we return to another summit at our seats. Though we didn't have time to visit the river-running library in Moscow, the Latvians are the next best thing. They are a veritable encyclopedia of Russian rivers.

"I wish we had these guys around when we were filling out that grant," Ben says.

"Yeah, but the way these guys travel, you don't even need a grant," Van adds.

"Just a healthy liver," Edge says. "And maybe some earplugs."

We acknowledge that running a first descent here, at least one of any real merit, would be difficult. We've now learned that Russians have been running Siberian rivers recreationally since the early 1960s. It started, in part, when the government commissioned workers to explore the taiga to research flora and fauna, census villages, and survey the topography. Oftentimes, the easiest way back was to float out. This meant building suitable equipment and learning how to paddle it.

As word of these expeditions got out, people followed for fun, using rafts simply to explore the unknown. Whether as a quick escape from the confines of Communism, or simply a vehicle to access inaccessible terrain, the sport grew entirely on its own merits without any further prodding from the government or commercial enterprises. While mountaineering expeditions have long received government support, save for the few early surveying trips, rafting here has always been a private experience. It gained momentum during the so-called Khruschev thaw of the 1960s and '70s, a new era of relative political freedom and an enhanced ability to pursue outdoor activities such as rafting.

Ironically, a sport we often view as the essence of freedom was partly fostered by the Communist political structure. Many Cold War towns were built around industries, from collective farms to mining operations. Most of these factories, as well as certain universities, offered sports or tourist clubs that centered on everything from mountaineering to whitewater. These formed the hubs of citizens' social lives, and they existed on many levels, from district and regional divisions to central clubs in Moscow. At one point, as many as 100 such clubs existed in Moscow alone, one of which, the river-running club, still actively catalogs expedition reports.

Some of the whitewater clubs—many of which were based in Moscow, St. Petersburg, Novosibirsk, and other economic centers—had official commissions that checked equipment and verified skills before trips. Club teams could also get official registration documents, which helped them obtain train or bus tickets, rent vehicles, or secure help from local authorities. In return, the teams were obligated to file reports of their expeditions so the information they gleaned could be shared.

The best thing about the clubs, though, was that everything was free. Staffed by volunteer instructors, a university club might offer classes in the field, with students paying only for trip transportation and their equipment.

When it comes to traveling on the cheap, the Latvians seem molded from this same school—except they don't even pay for their equipment. They make it. If they can get away without paying for transportation, that's just gravy on the Russian dumplings.

CHAPTER FIVE

Decision Time

A typical meal, showcasing fourteen equitable portions of pork fat, dry bread, and sugar cubes.

We try to secure more information from Ramitch on the Kitoy and are again discouraged. While yesterday we learned of four people who drowned after missing a portage, as illustrated by the skull and crossbones on the map, today we learn of another group that perished there while trying to get drinking water.

We return to our bunks on the train both confused and anxious. We still have to decide whether or not to join them on the Bashkaus. I stare out the window at the passing countryside.

Like the roar of a river next to a campsite, the clack-ity-clack of the train going over the tracks fades in and out. Sometimes you notice it, other times you don't. The only time I'm guaranteed to hear it is when I go to bed and there are no other distractions to take my mind off of it. That's when I'm also better able to process the decisions we have to make. Only then, without interruptions, can I think the clearest and assess our options. But even the train doesn't deliver answers. It just delivers its cargo, and right now, that's us, joined at the hip to the Latvians.

A bright side of the whole predicament is our companions. We could be stuck with a far worse group of people. The Latvians we've stumbled onto seem to place a strong emphasis on the concept of team. From forming bucket brigades to load gear onto the bunks to dispersing rations into equitable portions, each member seems a wheel to a greater end, just like those of the train now carrying us deeper into Siberia. Like a chance and unprepared piece of driftwood on the Bashkaus, we're now caught up in the middle of it with them.

As our familiarity with the Latvians grows, so does our familiarity with life aboard the train. In his book *The Big Red Train Ride*, Eric Newby writes, "Railways, like rivers, are difficult subjects for writers because they go on and on." Indeed, oftentimes when you're on either, there seems to be no beginning or end, just a long middle. And our middle is in the middle of Siberia. Newby experienced it in 1977 during the Brezhnev era, training across Russia from Moscow to Khabarovsk with his wife, Wanda. Joining them was a government-sponsored interpreter named Misha and a German photographer named Otto. Even surveillance by the KGB didn't dampen Newby's opinion of the transport. "There is no railway journey of comparable length anywhere in the world," he writes. "The Trans-Siberian is the big train ride. All the rest are peanuts."

Though I appreciate his outlook, and would have appreciated his peanuts even more, with our familiarity comes monotony. There just isn't much to do, apart from read, avoid the bathroom and conductress, scratch bedbug bites, and create and nurse hangovers. It's hour sixty, and Newby's observation that the ride goes on and on rings truer than ever. It delays a decision but doesn't help us reach one.

While we're feeling claustrophobic, the Latvians are anything but. Every year, they'll travel seven days and nights straight just to get to the start of a river trip. Accustomed to easy access to almost everything in our own country, it's difficult to remain patient in this one.

Not only the bedbugs, tight quarters, and language barriers cause consternation; it's also the culture. Like Vladivostok and Moscow's train connection, our cultural lines are miles apart. That afternoon, Van tries to describe to Boris his job as an appraiser in Jackson.

"You know when you buy a house, well, you go to the bank for a loan, see, and they want to find out how much the house is worth before they agree to loan you the money, which has to be amortized over fifteen or thirty years and ... " The attempt to establish an occupational common ground draws a blank stare. Buying a house is more foreign to them than making rafts is to us. Appraising it for a loan is truly alien.

With three hours left until our arrival in Barnaul, a silver lining breaks through the gray Siberian clouds. Somehow, we have finally won over the evil conductress—she actually smiles once when she walks by. We've made it now and she, too, seems glad. Maybe she just wanted us to know that we never fooled her. The real proof comes when she lets Ben use the well-kempt bathroom at the opposite end of the car before we disembark.

"I think she likes you," says Edge when he returns.

Before disembarking, Valeri shuts the train car window for the last time and pockets the key; he'll break it out again on the train ride home.

The best thing about the train ride is that we don't have to deal with our gear for three days. That changes as soon as we arrive in Barnaul, Siberia's second largest city. The Latvians are as methodical while unloading their gear as they were putting it in, forming an instant chain gang that passes everything out in record time. The train moves on with no evidence of our passage on it, or of its passing through the station, except for us and our mound of gear now deposited in the middle of Siberia.

Van and Edge guard our gear while Ben and I follow Olga to the post office to try calling Andre in Moscow. It has been four days since our last attempt, and we are nearly 2,000 miles closer to the Kalar—but 2,000 miles farther from the people with whom we are supposed to be running it. We're glad we aren't on our own. Even with Olga negotiating and cutting corners, the call to Moscow takes four hours. We give the phone attendent a ruble and she places the call while we wait in a crowded lobby. She calls our name about an hour later only to have the line disconnect. We start all over again. On the fourth attempt, we finally get through to Andre's wife. She still has not heard of us, Andre still has not returned from Turkey, and she still has no idea when he'll be back. If Plan A deteriorated in Moscow, Plan B now falls right on its heels. So far, the trip has been one of contingencies and shattered arrangements. First, it was the Manuska. Then the Kalar. Then the Kitoy. Now, if we join the Latvians, we need our own new plan for the Bashkaus. Still, Barnaul is located on the Ob River, the main artery in our original proposal. All things considered, the train tracks have kept our goals more or less on track as well.

"Why don't we just put in here and run the Ob out to the Arctic Ocean?" Van asks. "We have our cataraft." He's serious, and the plan could work.

With no Andre and no boats, we again face the big decision. Back at Mount Gear, Ben and I break the news to Van and Edge.

"We finally got through," Ben says. "But his wife still has no idea when he'll be back."

Van, who has been talking with Ramitch through Boris, revisits the earlier reason for aborting the Kalar.

"Ramitch says the train tracks leading to the Kalar are too buckled by permafrost."

"And we know nothing about the Kitoy, other than that the map has skulls and crossbones all over it," Edge adds.

"And we'd have to do it alone," I add.

As we did in Sergei's apartment, we huddle together as if our fate is still ours to decide. No one likes aborting our plan to run the Kalar. It's what we based our grant on after the Manuska fell through. But we have no real alternative. We feel like all of our planning and logistics have been for naught, other than to put us here at this moment, with these foreigners. We have mixed emotions about it; we are hesitantly excited, but also nervous. We walk over to Boris to announce our news: we have agreed to join the Latvians.

Boris scurries off to tell Ramitch, who nods his head solemnly at our decision. I'm not sure who feels more nervous about our agreement—us or Ramitch. Accepting responsibility for four foreign newcomers on an expedition down the hardest river in the former Soviet Union, an expedition that he has been planning for more than a year, isn't easy. From our perspective, neither is joining a group of strangers we can barely talk with or understand. For better or worse, our lives are now joined with Team Konkas as foreign, junior, innocent, and, admittedly, ignorant, partners.

The colors of people's clothes shine a lone bright spot on the grayness of our collective moods. It's as if through fashion, people here try to make up for where they live by dressing far better than in Moscow, on the train, or in Omsk. A woman in a bright purple shawl and yellow, collared-shirt pauses in front of our gear. Her eyes go from the equipment to us, still grimy from the train and bedbugs. She takes us in and then keeps going on her colorful way.

So do we. Having officially joined the Latvians, we begin shuttling all of our gear a few blocks over to a bus station. After the uncertainty of where we were going, the paranoia caused by the conductress, and the phone debacle, it feels good to be moving again—especially to be walking more than fifty steps without having to open a train car door. Several round-trips later, we've relocated everything from one method of transportation to another. Telling us again to lay low so we won't be charged the steep foreigner's rate, Ramitch strikes a deal with a driver to take us nearly 250 miles south to a town just sixty miles north of Mongolia. His trump card is a letter of support from the river-running library in Moscow.

Once again we play dumb, letting the Latvians carry our gear on board so our new backpacks don't give us away as tourists.

"I think I could get used to this part," Ben says, watching Boris struggle with the weight of his pack.

Boris, realizing his servitude, flashes us a mock scowl.

CHAPTER SiX

The Rest of the Way

Eugene (right) and Edge killing time on one of several long bus rides toward the put-in.

The bus is hardly a Greyhound. It's a private charter, and, unlike on public transportation, the fourteen of us pile atop our gear in the back ten spaces, bending our necks to avoid the ceiling. Despite the tight quarters, we feel good to be moving toward a large range of snowcapped mountains in the distance: the Altais, the tallest in all of Siberia. We get out only once on the cramped six-hour ride for a quick schnitzel lunch at a roadside café.

When we arrive in Gorno-Altaisk, it's easy to tell we're not far from the land of Genghis Khan. At the bus station, a rough-looking redhead wearing baggy brown pants and a black jacket walks by a group of three Asian-looking natives and shakes one of their hands. Then the redhead grabs the cigarette right out of one of the native's mouths and walks on, as if his ancestors had been doing it for eons.

It was almost 800 years ago when Khan began attacking the region from the south, eventually creating the largest contiguous land empire in history. The region he controlled was based on the conquest of more than twenty different kingdoms, and included chunks of modern-day Russia. After Khan's death in 1227, Kievan Rus (today's Russia), continued to be targeted, with the most notorious raids carried out by his grandson Kublai Khan, who destroyed all of the region's major cities except Novgorod and Pskov. He then taxed them as a tribute to the Tatars, whose domain became known as the empire of the Golden Horde.

It was an apt name. With a population of 200,000 mostly Altais, Kazakhs, and Russians, Gorno-Altaisk's main industries are agriculture and mining. The mountains here harbor vast amounts of mercury, iron, and gold. These mineral deposits, we'd later learn, play a big role in the myths of the area's mountains and rivers.

We camp across the river from the village. Local women wash their clothes by hand in the shallow waters in front of us, stealing errant looks as we begin to unpack in their backyard. Soon we wander over for a final logistics meeting with Ramitch. The conclusion, he says, is to run the entire 200-kilometer-long Bashkaus, unless it's too high, in which case we might hike out to the less difficult Chulishman. Talk inevitably turns to our equipment.

"You have too much," he says through Olga.

The Latvians are a tough act to follow. They're able to carry everything they need for a thirty-day raft trip on their backs, including all equipment and food. The plan is to reap everything we can from the land, including equipment in the form of raft frames and paddle shafts, and food acquired by foraging, fishing, and bartering with villagers along the way. But more than just our accessories need paring down.

"Your boat is too big," Ramitch continues through Olga, referring to the lightweight cataraft we had specially made for our expedition by a company called Jack's Plastic Welding and had so painstakingly lugged halfway around the globe. "Too big for the tight slots; and too heavy to carry. We have extra you can paddle."

We're not sure what kind of boat they have for us. We are hesitant to give up our customized oar rig, a style we were accustomed to. In the end, considering the possibly long hike to the put-in and portages ahead, we accede his point. We give in and agree to go Latvian-style. After lugging our raft, frame, and oars to the middle of Siberia, we'll stash them in town tomorrow, hoping to pick them up on the way back. From his Russian tutor, Van learned the word *smutkyi* (pronounced "schmootkie") and uses it to describe our excessive belongings. We like the sound of it and will repeat it often when lugging our gear around.

The Latvians verse us in the art of trimming down our *smutkyi* to what one person can carry. We sort through everything, discarding whatever isn't absolutely essential. We had packed for a Class II to III float down the Kalar. Now we are paring down to run some of the hardest whitewater in all Siberia. With countless steep portages and perhaps a three-day hike in (and possibly a longer hike out), we must go even lighter. The Power Lounger covers for our ground pads are the first to go. Next, we opt for iodine tablets instead of water filters, and root through our clothes. In the end we keep only half of what we brought.

"Better keep these," Edge says, shaking a bottle of ibuprofen. "We'll probably need them at some point."

"Especially for the extra calories from the sugar coating," Ben adds.

Throughout these early travails, we have found humor to be an odd and unassuming ally. With all the hassles and changed plans, oftentimes it's the only thing that keeps us going. There's actually some basis to this. In *Deep Survival* by Laurence Gonzales, a book on who lives, who dies, and why, he quotes Al Siebert, a psychologist and author of *The Survivor Personality*, as saying that "survivors laugh at threats" and that "playing and laughing go together." Playing, Siebert adds, keeps the person in contact with what is happening around him and in touch with his environment, while distracting him from the specifics he can do nothing about. Laughter "makes the feeling of being threatened more manageable" and also releases tension even as it builds. It preserves perspective.

All good survivors, he says, from fighter pilots to Tom Hanks, marooned on an island with Wilson the Volleyball, are good at it. "Laughter stimulates the left prefrontal cortex, an area of the brain that helps us feel good and stay motivated," Siebert notes. "And that stimulation alleviates anxiety and frustration." From expedition partners who never materialized to bedbugs, our evil conductress, and changing itineraries, we've had plenty of both. Technical aspects aside, humor just helps us cope.

"Here, I'll lighten that ibuprofen bottle by taking a couple," Van says before Edge packs it away.

If humor doesn't pick up our spirits, Ben pulls out something that might: real spirits, in the form of beer he bought at the bus station. Unfortunately, just like our humor often is, they are flat. They're also warm. To make matters worse, after he puts the open bottles on a nearby fence post, two children climb up and steal them. Warm and flat would have been better than nothing at all.

"Why, you little urchins!" Ben says, feigning chase.

I decide to break out the motion sensor to guard the rest of our gear. Might as well use it once, I reason, beyond its errant ringing at the airport. We set up our tents as far away from the Latvians as we can. We've been in continuous close quarters with them for almost a week and need our own space. Likely, so do they. While threading our tent poles through the sleeves, I look over to where Valeri is pitching his tent. Apart from hauling their homespun paddles and backpacks around, it's our first real lesson in homemade equipment. While our tents come from sponsor REI, the Latvians' are made from scratch, stitched together from cut-up old parachutes. Valeri's tent is made from the same light-blue parachute as his backpack, making them match perfectly—a coincidence of function as well as fashion. With his blue eyes, jet-black hair, and handsome, chiseled face now sporting a week's growth of stubble, he could be modeling for a J. Crew catalog. Only, it's doubtful they'd have much luck marketing the tent.

Instead of using poles, which mean extra weight, their tents are held up by the paddles they'll use on the river. A paddle is placed vertically on each end, with ropes tied to the ground to provide tension. Though the paddle-as-tent-pole concept appears to work, the tents are hardly freestanding; ours go up far easier. While Sergei the Small struggles to find a suitable sapling, Edge and I methodically put ours up a short distance away from Van and Ben's. Standing out in stark contrast to our slick pop-up dome is Sergei the Small and Andrew's pink parachute tent secured with a hammer-and-sickle paddle on end near the door. A clear piece of plastic, the type you might find in a Dumpster, offers the only rainfly protection from the cloud bank gathering in the distance.

Camp set, we join the Latvians around the fire for dinner. Accustomed to leading expeditions for NOLS, Ben takes the liberty of serving rice from the pot for everyone. But he quickly feels Olga's eyes boring into the back of his head as he doles out rations.

"Too much," she reprimands. "Our boys don't need that much." Next, it's Van's turn to fume when Olga scolds him for putting too much coffee in the pot.

"No one tells me how to make coffee," he says under his breath a few moments later. "If there's one thing I'm good at, it's making coffee."

Olga's coffee is a rude awakening to what might be in store. It's a far cry from the normal-strength coffee trips we've taken down other rivers. Later that night, Van and Ben come to our tent with second thoughts about the whole ordeal. Olga's antics aside, we are all concerned that the Latvians are controlling our destiny. But as we penetrate deeper into Siberia's Altais, we also realize that we'll grow increasingly helpless without them.

"I just have this feeling that we're on a runaway train, and that once it starts, there's no way off," Ben says, huddled by the door.

"And Olga seems a lot like Ratchet of the Railways," I add.

"No one tells me how to make coffee," Van repeats.

We all know we can still jump ship, for the sake of our lives, if nothing else. But then, what would we do? We're nowhere near our intended river and have no one else to turn to.

ﻫﻫﻫ

It's not the first time I've been thrown a curveball by strangers when trying to go paddling. My first stint as a raft guide almost got me as sidetracked as we are now in Siberia. After my sophomore year in college, I was on my way to Alaska for my first summer of guiding; it was the first time I had really ventured out on my own to an unknown job in an unknown land. Before I left, my well-traveled older sister advised me to always take advantage of situations that present themselves while traveling. "You never know where they might lead," she said.

This was certainly true for us now. We had jumped on a situation—Boris greeting us at the airport—and still weren't quite sure where we were going to end up.

College naivete in hand, I took my sister's advice to heart, almost to the point of an abrupt career change. My flight arrived in Seattle the evening before the next morning's ferry. Resting on a patch of grass outside Pike Place Market, I didn't notice the couple approaching me until they were upon me. They seemed friendly enough, asking questions about where I was from and where I was heading. Remembering my sister's words and empty pocketbook, I took them up on their offer for dinner and a place to stay at a house about a mile away.

I didn't get nervous until we sat down. After waltzing through a buffet table filled with rice, chicken, and other foodstuffs that were a far cry from our current fare, I found an empty seat at a table of strangers. I was glad for the free vittles, but a certain uneasiness crept in once dinner was over and all the chairs were repositioned to face the front of the room. Up front was the woman who had invited me to dinner. Behind her, a chalkboard. Before I knew it, she drew a stick figure standing up in a makeshift raft. Underneath it was my name, spelled out in the angled letters you can only achieve on a chalkboard.

"Now, suppose," she addressed the group, "that Eugene decides not to go to Alaska to become a raft guide and decides instead to stay here and follow the Reverend Moon." I cringed, looking left and right to my Moonie neighbors. I began to fidget, picking at my cuticles. Everyone's eyes were on the chalkboard, only after boring through the back of my head.

While the Good Reverend Sun Myung Moon had converted thousands at large-scale recruiting rallies, I was the first to be recruited with the old chalkboard-stick-figure-in-a-raft trick. I was glad when a screen was pulled down over the chalkboard for a slide presentation, which I was not the main character of. I slept fitfully on a cot in the corner, my stick-figured totem hovering above me. At breakfast, after dodging more questions about my future, I hightailed it out of there, sticking to my original plan. I was heading to Alaska, not a commune. Four days later, I saw a similar chalkboard at the guide house in Juneau. Instead of flaunting a poor likeness of my stick figure, it detailed the week's guide schedule. It reminded me of the importance of sticking to one's goal and carefully considering any new paths.

On the first night of our Siberian decision, in our tent, we reassess our options, going over the pros and cons of each decision. Kalar? Bashkaus? After discussing the situation thoroughly, in the end we agree again to continue on with Team Konkas to the Bashkaus. But we vow to establish a firm say in expedition matters and, if necessary, maintain our independence. More importantly, we also vow to always be open with each other regarding our feelings about our situation, the expedition, and its other members. We will always be far more dependent on each other than we are the on the Latvians.

In a way, our newfound resolve makes me think of

Gorbachev's glasnost policy, a Russian word for "publicity" or "openness." While we're commiting to be open with each other, Gorbachev introduced glasnost in 1985 to open dialogue between hard-liners and conservatives to gain support for his reforms. Until glasnost, decisions made in Moscow regarding Soviet republics were beyond reproach. Gorbachev hoped that open communication might bring a better understanding of his ideas. But the press used it to expose the government's problems. Like our plans expanding from a simple float on the Kalar to running the hardest river in the country, glasnost went far beyond what Gorbachev originally intended. Many feel it undermined faith in the system and is what led to the breakdown of the Soviet Union.

Unlike the pre-glasnost republics, Team Konkas, at least, has a willing ear in Ramitch. He makes the decisions, sure, but he also listens, absorbs information, and doesn't hide anything. Invoking our own glasnost, we commit to be open with Ramitch and each other, and to be involved in major expedition decisions. We want freedom of speech, and to actually be heard. It's a bit interesting, I think, that the same policy we're vowing to employ with the Latvians—having a say in expedition matters and not be autocratically governed by a higher authority—is the same one that helped lead to their freedom and to the breakup of the Soviet Union.

Right now, Boris is exercising his right to open communication, singing full force by the campfire. Alone with his guitar, he belts out Queen's "We Will Rock You" at the top of his lungs, each line punctuated by hearty "Hahs!" of self-appreciation. We weren't sure of all the lyrics when we gave them to him on the train, so we made up a few. As he bursts into "Baby, you're a rich man and you've got a suntan!" we look at each other and smile.

"Well, at least we have Boris along," Van says.

CHAPTER SEVEN

Yuri and the Bus

Yuri and his broken-down shuttle rig (note the hose extending upward from the radiator to serve as windshield wiper fluid).

We break camp early. Only one major road, the Chuisky Trakt, traverses the area, stretching from Biysk to Gorno-Altaisk and finally on to the Mongolian border. We are taking it nearly the entire way.

While Ramitch searches for another bus to take us to the village of Ust-Ulagan, twenty-four hours away, we convince the bus station clerk, a pretty, brown-haired girl named Natasha, to let us stash our leftover gear in her office. We leave everything behind that we had so painstakingly packed: boat, frame, breakdown oars, kayak paddles, spray skirts, collapsible water jugs, stove, pots and pans, water filters, personal gear, Edge's guitar. We'll be back, we say, in three to four weeks to pick it up. But who knows if it will still be here.

Truth be told, we aren't exactly sure when we'll be back. Our itinerary is iffy, even before we get to the river. The last time the Latvians were here—three years ago to run the nearby Chuya—they had to wait four days for a bus. For Americans accustomed to quick access and instant gratification, that seems like an eternity. Luckily, Ramitch pulls another coup. A self-proclaimed "tourist agency" official wants 4,500,000 rubles, or $4,500, for the fourteen of us to travel in his "region" for thirty days. Though the Latvians are also visitors here, Ramitch talks him out of the high price, lining up our next bus in the process.

Bright red and without doors—only openings on each side where doors might have been in a former life—it belongs in a *Mad Max* movie. Even there, it would be the demolition model of the lot. No grill covers the front fan, causing its hood to stare out like a one-eyed bandit. A missing front fender scars its left cheek. Like a long earring, a black hose climbs out of the radiator, wraps once around the cracked rearview mirror, and then rises up to the top of the windshield like a giant eyebrow placed too high on a forehead. We'll see the rationale behind it soon enough.

Even in this beat-up, broken-down bucket of bolts, we once again have to play dumb and blend in with the Latvians.

"*Nyet,*" Edge mutters, repeating what has become our mantra, as we climb aboard.

The corrupt official's attitude is not lost on Yevgheny.

"The whole country is like this bus," he laments after we take our seats. "And the government is like the driver."

In front of the vodka-toting driver, a thin-haired and equally thin-bodied man named Yuri Kashtamov, the front hood bangs open, urging me to lean closer to hear him. "The country and government have it all wrong," Yevgheny continues. "Instead of encouraging people to travel and then capitalizing on it by selling them things, they say, 'You can come, but you have to pay.' So no one comes."

The work ethic of a true consumer economy has yet to take hold. People like money, but apart from the tourism "official," not many seem motivated by it yet. Earlier, when we tried to secure return airline tickets from Barnaul to Moscow, the attendant didn't show much interest in trying to help us. Even bribes didn't help. It was just a lack of interest or pure non-chalance. People here seem so accustomed to the Communist umbrella of provisions, and no further choices, that incentive to earn money hasn't entered the picture yet.

Olga is particularly opinionated about the country's lack of a work ethic, exercising no patience for people unaccustomed to having one. In Latvia, she says, people understand that if you work hard, the money will come, and with it some privileges of choice. But in the case of our airline tickets, it took approaching five people up the chain of command before one man finally agreed to help us.

"The first woman should work harder," Olga admonishes.

Yevgheny isn't through with his soliloquy. "If you have a car and opportunity to work tomorrow, you ready your car for work," he adds. "Our driver, like the government, doesn't do that."

As with people's work ethics, our shuttle vehicles also become progressively sketchier the deeper we penetrate into Siberia. First, we luxuriated in the first-class section of Finnair. Then, we endured a bedbug-ridden locals' train. Next, we curled ourselves into a cramped public bus. And now, we hire a backfiring jalopy that belongs in *Sanford and Son*. But it does have its amenities, even if they aren't in the form of an engine, transmission, suspension, or even doors. Above the driver, who is now tapping his hand on the steering wheel to Madonna blaring on the stereo, is an outdated *Playboy* calendar opened to a large-breasted Miss June. Below her stands a statue of the Virgin Mary on the dash. Blue flowered drapes hang from the windows. Apart from the statue, they're the only touch of care evident anywhere. Two rows of seats extend three across; the aisle ends in our pile of gear on the floor in the back.

The bus's mechanical side is as run-down as its cosmetics and music. The front hood flaps up and down and bangs with each bump. By lunch, the bus has already overheated three times. No one can sit in the front row of seats because when it overheats, an Old Faithful–like geyser erupts from the dash-board inside, spewing a boiling-hot fountain two rows back.

"Whew, that one was close," Van says from the back row when the eruption happens for the third time. Once again, we climb down rubber-topped steps below what should be the door to wait for it to cool down. Each of us, privately, is still rethinking our choice to join the Latvians. Unlike our easy egress from the bus, we have no clear exit strategy should we change our minds.

The overheating, of course, is also the reason for the jerry-rigged hose leading from the radiator, around the rearview, and up to the top of the windshield. Not only does this delay the inevitable Old Faithful inside the dash, but it also strategically sloshes out hot water, which serves as wiper fluid for the windshield. It's yet another contraption born of necessity serving a dual purpose. Before it overheats for the fourth time, Yuri turns on the wipers in a Pavlovian response to the anticipated pending splash.

When the bus finally gets going again, the bumpy road takes us by the Chuya River, one of five Siberian classics and the location of Misha's long-running river rally. In the distance, we see a saw blade of snowcapped peaks, the runoff of which is responsible for the area's many canyons.

A short while later, we stop at a Buddhist shrine, a fountain beneath a tree with little white pieces of cloth tied to its branches. Olga insists we throw coins in for good luck on the Bashkaus. We could also use some luck for the bus ride.

The driver, who has been drinking vodka all morning, is now officially drunk. His red eyes match the color of the bus. But it doesn't seem to affect his driving, especially when it comes to dodging cows. As he knows his bus's radiator, he knows his Siberian bovines. He doesn't veer one inch when passing them, anticipating their every movement, just as he does the erupting radiator fluid.

We stop for lunch at a small roadside restaurant. A dilapidated tin roof repels a light rain.

While eating another questionable schnitzel, Van casually asks, "What is it that your sister, Cathy, is studying again?"

He's referring, of course, to her PhD research in nematodes, an intestinal parasite found in pork.

"Worms," I reply between chews.

"That's what I thought," he says, taking another mouthful.

So far, we've been lucky with stomach ailments. Despite the sometimes-suspect food and vulnerable bowels, none of us have gotten overly sick. There were the few close calls with the Exorcist Room on the train, but that's been it. Perhaps this is the meal that will do one of us in?

Deep into his own schnitzel, Yevgheny progresses from politics and parasites to paddling. He tells us that the Bashkaus is one of five multiday Class V to VI runs in the Altai Mountains known as the Altai Bars, meaning "Snow Leopard." If you run all five—the Argut, Chulishman, Chuya, Chulcha, and Bashkaus—you achieve your Snow Leopard. Though the Altais are one of the sole remaining areas where the animal is believed to still exist, the quest is about as difficult and spiritual as sighting the goal of Peter Matthiessen's trek across the Himalayas in his book of the same animal name. The rivers are a testament to the terrain. There are five two- to four-week-long Class V to VI rivers all located within 100 square miles of each other. The Altais are the serious river runner's ultimate dream, like the Himalayas are to mountaineers or Hawaii is to big-wave surfers.

Despite their proximity, however, just as Matthiessen discovered, achieving your Snow Leopard isn't easy. Each river's continuous whitewater makes Idaho look like Ohio. Ramitch and Sergei the Tall have notched three of the coveted runs each, including the Bashkaus. Two more and they will join the most prestigious circle of paddlers in the country.

The problem is that every time we hear about a trip down one of these rivers, a startling truism hits us: with every new river comes new stories of death. Overhearing our discussion of the Altai Bars, Olga interrupts to tell us of a group on the nearby Chulishman that was forced to break camp at gunpoint and put on the river. Four members of that expedition died.

"There is much that can go wrong on our rivers," Olga continues, driving home a point that needs no driving.

Later, when we pass through a village named Inya on the Chuya, Olga shares a story from their last trip here when they spent twenty-nine days on the Argut. They ended up without any food left, she says, and they were forced to buy a sheep from a local farmer and butcher and clean it themselves. Then they again ran out of food and had to beg door-to-door for bread in the village. Ramitch, rail thin to begin with, lost twenty pounds, dropping from 145 to 125. We exchange uneasy glances. No wonder Olga admonished Ben for serving too much rice and Van too much coffee. No wonder she imposes carefully counted equitable portions. Though they will seem and feel like starvation levels, to her and everyone else, they are subsistence. We're not sure this is confidence-lifting news.

The stories are testament to the area's rugged terrain. The Altais lay a broad swath across southwest Siberia and into China and Mongolia. They stretch 1,200 miles along a northwest-to-southeast axis, forming a natural border between the arid steppes of Mongolia and the taiga of southern Siberia. This creates a unique topography of everything from broad steppes, taiga, and desert to snowcapped peaks, tundra, and rollicking rivers, which tumble down from peaks as high as 14,540-foot Mount Belukha. While one region of the range might encompass grass-covered plains, another comes right out of *The Sound of Music*, with towering peaks and glaciers. The region covers 845,000 square kilometers and ripples into four different countries: Russia, Kazakhstan, Mongolia, and China. Because of their castlelike terrain and multicountry area, the Altais are as rich in legend as they are in minerals. Their name comes from the Mongolian word *altan*, meaning "golden."

Olga's stories take a needed turn for the better when she relates one pertaining to the area's rivers. Father Altai, the story goes, had a daughter, Katun, who fell in love with a handsome man named Biya. The father didn't like this, and to stop the two from joining, he threw many stones into the Katun River, creating its many rapids. It didn't work, and the two rivers, Katun and Biya, eventually joined to create a daughter, named the Ob.

Mention of the Ob reminds me again of the Manuska and our original plan. I ask Olga if she knows of it and she, in turn, asks Ramitch. He shakes his head *no*. He has never heard of it. It certainly doesn't show up as a long-forgotten son in Olga's legend. If Ramitch, three-fifths of the way toward achieving his Snow Leopard, hasn't heard of it, no map shows it, and no legend includes it, chances are it really doesn't exist.

Another legend, Olga continues, involves our take-out at Lake Teletskoe. When Father Altai learned of enemies who wanted to take away his riches, he began to throw all of his gold into the river. The ensuing dam created the lake, which is rumored to contain vast amounts of gold.

"Like in Sergei's teeth," she says, causing Sergei the Tall to break into a wide smile.

The drive continues. Hour after hour passes with stories, legends, bumpy reading, guitar playing, sleeping, and watching the passing countryside. We plan on eating dinner at a restaurant Ramitch knows about, but when we arrive, we find it closed, not just for the day, but for an entire year.

"Typical," Edge says. "I've seen 'Back in a few minutes' signs, but 'Back in a year'?"

So we plod on, the bus backfiring its way deeper into Siberia. Despite the lack of ambition we've seen from those at or absent from their work, what we see next surprises us, especially considering where we are. Through the dusty side windows, we see a cross-country ski area where members of the Russian Nordic team are training on roller skis. Five of them are lined up behind one another, making only slightly worse time than we are in the Old Faithful–mobile. A few miles later, we look up to see six hang gliders soaring on thermals in the middle of nowhere.

"Probably homemade also," Edge says.

"Not sure which I'd rather be in," Ben answers. "A

homemade raft on the Bashkaus or a homemade hang glider high on an Altai thermal."

"Or a homemade bus," I add. Still, it's refreshing to see people playing and apparently having fun, and it seemingly contradicts my earlier assessment of people's lack of ambition. Recreation quickly gives way to subsistence again; below the hang gliders a group of women work a field with scythes.

Our lunch is late. We stop in a large, glaciated valley hemmed by the Chuya and a towering cliff on the far bank. Figuring that we have endured the Latvians' foreign foodstuffs long enough, we turn the tables and introduce them to the virtues of peanut butter. They have never tried it before, creamy or crunchy, and they smack their lips like a Siberian husky with a dollop of Jif stuck to the roof of his mouth. They quickly get the upper hand again, however, by enlightening us with slices of dry bread about the size of a quartered bagel. Then they play their trump card—atop each piece of bread quivers a cube of pork fat. About the size of a mini-Snickers you'd get on Halloween, each fat slab glistens in the afternoon sun. It's called *sala* and is a staple on all Russian river trips. It comes either salted or smoked, both sharing the same meatless texture.

Its use in the Russian region arose thanks to Muslim Turks, who, when invading Ukraine, would commandeer all farm animals except for pigs, which religion forbade. So there grew to be an exorbitant number of swine in the region, with no body part overlooked for sustenance. The fat was, and still is, a cheap and concentrated form of energy.

But none of that does anything for its appearance or palatability. We sniff the jiggling fat squares gingerly before trying them. Unable to get past its appalling texture and Siberian-sized cholesterol count, I dish mine off to a readily waiting Boris. Van, however, digs in, swallowing the entire thing in two bites.

When Edge finishes sniffing his, I borrow it for a bite. It takes as much guts as running any rapid on the Bashkaus. Sinking your teeth into pork blubber doesn't come naturally. You don't really feel anything, or feel like you're getting anything out of it. Your teeth just slice into it without any resistance. And that's the first thing you notice about it: an absence of any real substance, of anything you'd even *want* to sink your teeth into.

Weird food is a natural part of traveling, especially when you're outside of the tourist traps. I'd eaten fried ants sold by the bag in Colombia, raw squid in Japan, and crocodile in Africa, all in the name of river running. But at least you knew that those things were good for you—an instant injection of protein, if nothing else. But pork fat, the same stuff you intentionally pick off your bacon or spit out when you get a white lump in your spoonful of Van Camp's Pork and Beans, is another matter. It goes against everything you've ever learned about food. Not that fried ants are commonly served at our family dinner table, but fat is usually something to be discarded rather than savored. You cut it *off* your steak. And if you happen to get a mouthful with your meat, at least it's cooked. And maybe crusty.

Still, without any real texture, its only redeeming quality is that it melts in your mouth, much like an M&M or lump of salty margarine. Well lubricated (as 100 percent fat always is), it then slides easily straight down your throat. But then it plops into your stomach and just sits there, waiting to be digested. Even with stomach acid attacking from all sides, it doesn't yield an inch for the first hour or so until it eventually turns into its destined energy and cholesterol. And therein lies the rationale for its consumption: on the Bashkaus, you want maximum of the former, with minimal carrying weight, and don't really care about the latter—there are plenty of other things that could kill you before cholesterol does. Since it will become our only energy source, we'll eventually learn to devour each piece down to and including its hairy-stubbled rind.

After forcing the rest of his down, Edge strolls over to a nearby field. When he bends over at the waist, I think he might already be purging his stomach of the artery-clogger. Instead, he calls me over.

Setting down my own piece of fat, I get up and follow. Still bent at the waist, he's looking at wild marijuana, or hemp, plants, known here as *cannabis selvia*, about thigh-high and in full bloom.

"Maybe that would help make the pork fat go down," Edge jokes. "You know, give us the munchies."

Though it's only lunchtime, Valeri soon has a raging fire going with a pot for tea dangling from an improvised crossbeam. We decide to take advantage of the heat source by breaking out a bag of popcorn for dessert. As Ben pours some kernels into the pot dangling over the fire, Edge somehow tricks Boris into eating a handful raw. Boris puts them in his mouth and crunches. An odd look comes over his face as he pulverizes them with his molars. "Hrmmph!" he says, surprised at their taste and texture. Apparently, he has never seen popcorn, either.

"You're supposed to let it pop first," Ben admonishes, pouring the bag's contents into the pot.

When the popping starts, Boris and the others listen intently. When it stops, we pass the pot around and they all dig their hands deep inside. We've shown them peanut butter and popcorn all in one meal. Then Ben pulls out a bag of M&Ms, which they've never seen before either. Yevgheny eyeballs them suspiciously and then takes a few, crunching quizzically. A smile sweeps across his face, and he holds out his hand for more.

We pull over to camp eight hours later, around 2:00 A.M. While I head straight to my tent for some much-needed shut-eye, the Latvians go straight to work. Soon, they have another roaring fire, over which dangles a pot for noodles and another for tea. Snug in my sleeping bag, I don't bother to get up when the dinner cry comes. It's the last time I'll forsake food of any sort for twenty-eight days.

I learn my lesson in the morning when two sugar cubes rest atop each of fourteen pieces of rock-hard dry bread. In adjacent tin bowls rest one equally measured dollop of porridge. Rations have begun. Up until now, even with Olga's monitoring, food has been dispensed relatively randomly. The operative word, of course, is "relatively." It still hints of grade-school cafeteria portions, weighed and measured as Ben's rice incident illustrated. But now that we are inching closer to the river, every calorie counts. No one has snacks. You eat when served, or not at all. Team Konkas only allocated its team members 400 grams, or about a half pound, of food per person per day. According to Ben, the usual daily allotment for most expeditions is around two to two and a half pounds. Since they didn't know we'd be joining them until they had packed their rations, to feed us all we would use the rations we brought every seventh day. Still, it's barely enough to sustain us.

In a stroke of genius, Van figures out how to salvage more calories from his porridge bowl by swathing it with leftover tea and then drinking the remains. It also served to clean it, saving him the caloric expenditure of scrubbing.

Then it's back on the backfiring bus, with a red-eyed Yuri at the wheel. The day's first stop is at some pictographs etched into a series of rocks resembling a mini-Stonehenge. The drawings, Yevgheny says, are similar to artwork found in Alaska, adding credence to theory of early man's migration across the Bering Strait at the end of the last Ice Age.

Man's history in the area is as convoluted as the road we're traveling. We pass villages whose residents have blood-lines tracing back to Ghengis Khan, the Tatars, and Turks as well as Huns, Mongols, and early Russian settlers. The region's sparse population has a solid place in human evolution. The Altai area has long been a crossroads of human migration. Near Gorno-Altaisk is a set of cave dwellings called Ulalite that date back to the beginning of the Paleolithic period more than 900,000 years ago. Human ancestors occupied this area well before the South Pacific Java Man, whose 700,000-year-old skullcap and femur are thought to belong to *Homo erectus*.

Countless other excavation sites dot the area as well, showing man in various stages of development here, from the Stone to the Bronze and Iron Ages. The Altais also harbor

Mount Belukha, believed by locals to be the birthplace of the next great civilization.

Despite government-sponsored helicopter drops for mail and supplies, many of today's villagers never liked being part of the Soviet system and remain proud of their independence and traditions. In many places, wool is still spun by hand, logs for homes are hewn by axe, and hay is cut by scythe. They've made-do by themselves for so long that they're resistant to change. The Turks invented hardwood saddles and stirrups in the region in the fourth century. Even music has some beginnings here, with the world's first bowed, stringed instrument, a precursor to today's violin, invented in the Altai region in the fifth century. Some villages still practice traditional Altai throat singing, a guttural sound that makes Boris's rendition of Queen deserve a Grammy.

The discovery of Stone Age cliff paintings in the region shows yet another Altai contribution to society. Dating back to 10,000 B.C., the paintings depict hunters using primitive skis for transportation, the earliest proof of the sport's existence.

It's easy to fathom man's early presence here at our next stop. It's at a tiny village without electricity or running water. Ramitch disappears into a primitive yurt with wood siding leading to a domed roof. The home's architecture is based on the *ger* camps of nomadic Mongolians, whose current political border is just sixty miles south.

Most of the Altai people were nomadic herdsmen up until the twentieth century. Many still are. Used while herding sheep, cattle, camels, and yaks, their portable homes are traditionally made of white felt and heated with coal to ward off the long winters. Just as the surrounding Altai Mountains are steeped in superstition, so, too, are the structures. The doors of traditional yurts always face south, toward the light. Buddhist Mongolians also believe that digging up the ground harms its life, upon which everything depends. For millennia, their culture has relied on their uncultivated steppes of grass. They don't plow fields, plant, or harvest. They don't dig and build foundations under their yurts. It's easier to pack up and move with their herds onto greener pastures on an ongoing and rotating basis. No land gets exhausted. They, their land, and their culture are a long-established and sustaining ecology.

Proper etiquette is encouraged in order to not disrupt the yurts' occupants. Rules to follow include making noise outside to alert occupants of your arrival—no knocking on the door; stepping over (never on) the threshold with your right foot; moving counterclockwise inside if you're a man and clockwise if you're a woman; no whistling inside; and always accepting a host's hospitality, whether it's yak's milk, goat's milk, or tea.

I'm not sure if Ramitch follows these protocols or not, but whatever he does, it works. He soon emerges with two loaves of fresh bread and a jar of homemade strawberry jam. Olga measures out equal portions as we continue along our own wandering way, bouncing farther into Siberia.

The bus chugs fitfully up a steep pass and Edge and I try to relax on the pile of gear in the back of the bus, but it's difficult. The mound is uncomfortable, and so are our feelings as we inch our way closer to the canyon. Edge seems preoccupied.

"The last thing everyone told me was to be careful," he says, summing up our predicament. "And here we are careening down switchbacks on a Siberian pass in a beat-up bus with a group of complete strangers who don't speak English, on our way to run a Class VI river on homemade equipment we've never even seen before. That's careful?"

His words hit home. The lump in my stomach is not pork fat. I'm thinking of Denise, and trying not to. Among all of us, I'm the only one who's left a wife behind.

We are all growing increasingly apprehensive. But unless we part and drive back with Yuri—which might well be more dangerous than running the Bashkaus—we've made our decision and are bound by it. For better or worse, we're part of Team Konkas.

A few hours later, we pull over at a bridge to stretch our legs. The river it spans disappears downstream in a wall of white around a thickly forested corner. For a second I think that it might be the Bashkaus. But it's only one of countless unnamed tributaries to the Ob system. If this is a river of no consequence, we slowly realize what might be in store for us on the Bashkaus. Throwing a piece of wood into it and watching it get swept downstream, Edge and I pine for our kayaks, the precision craft we know best and are most confident in. The closest we come to them are a few four-legged yaks roaming a nearby hillside.

"Something seems to have gotten lost in translation," Edge says as we climb back aboard the bus.

A few hours later, something is also getting lost in translation between Ramitch and a new driver in the village of Ust-Ulagan. He's arguing with the owner of an open-air army truck about how much it will cost to shuttle us farther up the dirt road to the put-in. If necessary, the Latvians are prepared to backpack to the river. They have done so in the past, schlepping their gear for up to four days just to get to where they'd *start* their river trip. But they are not martyrs. If they can finagle a ride and save the calories, so much the better—especially if it can be paid for with vodka they won't then have to carry.

We wait with our gear against a metal railing surrounding a white, two-story building with blue-trimmed windows. Ramitch and the new driver continue arguing. By now, I know to place my bet on Ramitch. The driver shakes his head as Ramitch pulls out half a bottle. Ramitch digs back in his pack and adds another quarter. They have a deal.

The village's name, Ust-Ulagan, meaning "place where the river starts," could also mean "place where the bus stops and driver can drink with reckless abandon." Despite the benign-looking grassy hills just outside of town, the road from here on is too difficult for the Overheatmobile. Ramitch makes arrangements with a red-eyed Yuri to meet us in twenty-eight days at a village at the far end of Lake Teletskoe, which we will paddle into after the Bashkaus joins the Chulishman. Below Lake Teletskoe, the river becomes the Biya, which joins

Father Altai's Katun to become the Ob. After all our itinerary changes, we are not too far from our original proposal for the Manuska. We'll actually be navigating a tributary to the Ob.

Foolhardy or not, none of us have the gumption to resist running the Bashkaus with the Latvians. Just like the river we'll soon be paddling, ever since Moscow, we've gone with the flow of least resistance. With the Latvians' back-of-an-envelope approach to everything we've seen so far, I can't help but think that Shipton and Tilman would be proud.

CHAPTER EIGHT

The Bashkaus Put-In

Andrew (left) and Yevgheny hauling logs from the forest to the put-in to turn into frames for the rafts.

After 182 hours of solid traveling involving three airplanes, five cars, a seventy-three-hour train ride, two buses, and an army truck, the last piece of the puzzle falls into place. Our put-in for the Bashkaus is a broad camp atop a bluff overlooking a sparkling green waterway. Boris, grinning from riding shotgun in the army truck while we were crammed outside in the bed, hops out and unlatches the rear gate. Our four-hour bumpy ride jostling on top of gear is over.

"Come on, guys," he says. "We're here."

We quickly pile out, followed by the rest of the Latvians. Unfortunately, there is no time for stretching. No sooner than their feet touch ground, they set to work. Sergei the Tall and Valeri start a fire to boil soup, Ramitch and Sergei the Small notch logs to place around a fire pit, and Boris secures enough firewood for an army. It seems overkill until we hear it will take three days to build the frames for the rafts.

"So close," Edge says, eyeing the river, "and yet, still so far."

"So far" is right. We're about as far into the boondocks as any of us have ever been. I look downriver for a glimpse of the "fairy landscapes" from the river description but see nothing but rolling, grass-covered hills pocketed with stands of thick forest.

After the confines of the road trip, it's nice to finally be at the river. We've been traveling in close quarters with the Latvians for a week, and the lap of the river and the Siberian air are refreshing. I stroll a few yards from camp to a ten-foot-high cliff overlooking the river. Cobblestones on the far bank lead up to a foot-thick layer of dark green moss, above which lie hundreds of small yellow flowers framing a grassy bench. The bench ends abruptly in a thick forest of larch and pine.

The water is clear and fast, but not dangerously so. Below me, the current has slackened into a green pool, with a large eddy lining a rocky beach. Upstream, the water turns white, where a Class III rapid extends up around the corner. It's bordered by granite cliffs, with boulders constricting the river into a series of drops and folds. Neither the rapid nor water volume looks overly intimidating. I dare an inner smile of joy, before remembering what lurks downstream.

Turning that direction, I try to see where the water goes. But the river is bordered by a thick-walled forest on each side and disappears around a blind bend. I won't know until I'm there and on it, when there's no turning back. When we won the grant to run a river here, we felt luck was on our side. Now I continue to wonder if we are still so lucky after all.

While the Latvians set to work, we unload the gear from the back of the truck and find our packs among the odd assortment of Latvian gear. Separating ours out, we pull out sleeping bags, pads, and other gear, shaking it off from the dusty ride.

When Yevgheny sees us unpacking our slim, compact life jackets, he comes over and holds one up for examination. He then yells to Ramitch, who also comes over to inspect what is our only chance for survival should we swim in the Bashkaus. Turning it over in his hands, Yevgheny squeezes the jacket's

flotation and fusses with the zipper. Then he goes over to his
pack and pulls out his life jacket, beaming.

"Your life jacket, no work," he says, putting on his own.
"This is jacket you need for strong river."

The source of his pride looks cartoonish. A giant inflatable collar rises behind his head like Dracula's cape. Two
twelve-pack-sized rectangles of foam are sewn into each breast,
with two more dangling in front of his stomach. When he finishes buckling his crotch strap he looks more like a motocross
racer than a rafter. Our life jackets pale in comparison, both in
fashion and flotation. Where ours are state-of-the-art kayaking
life jackets made by reputable manufacturers, like their backpacks and tents, the Latvians' are entirely homemade.

Ramitch puts his life jacket on, too. Soon, he is clad in
purple from shoulders to toes like Barney. Ensolite strips are
sewn into every available square inch of surface area for extra
flotation. On his arms, the strips run parallel to his forearms
before switching 90 degrees and running across the elbows
for flexibility. Then, they resume a parallel position along his
upper arms. The same Ensolite flotation pattern holds on the
legs and knees of his purple overalls: parallel along the shin
and femur, and sideways across the kneecap for mobility. He's
so protected, he could survive a Russian hockey game (the
intended purpose of his light-blue helmet). The final piece
of his ensemble is an orange plastic cylinder dangling from
the front of his life jacket. Inside is mandatory survival gear:
matches, fire starter, and, most importantly, cigarettes.

Sergei the Small strides over with his life jacket. He
puts it on over a white-and-maroon flannel shirt and joins
the promenade. It's akin to being at a Paris fashion show, only
we're in the middle of Siberia, the models are hairy-legged,
stubbly-bearded males, and instead of touting delicate bikinis,
they're modeling bulky head-to-toe wardrobes for whitewater.

Sergei's life jacket has a markedly different look from
the others. It's made from six halves of soccer balls, with three
domes protruding proudly along each rib cage. Each dome

has an improvised rubber valve for inflation. He shows us his homemade helmet, an oblong white blob made out of pieces of Styrofoam glued together and shaped in a close approximation of his head.

Boris's life jacket is equally unique. Rather than have the bulk of his flotation on the front like the other jackets, two giant humps rise from his back like Quasimodo's. The jacket matches a pair of bright-orange, flotation-riddled overalls underneath. Andrew's life jacket has a still different approach to flotation— it's made from old wine bladders housed in nylon sleeves.

Everyone's life jacket looks different. Like a coat of arms, each one is decked to the hilt with pride and customized for each wearer—as well they should be. Each creator's life depends upon his or her life jacket in event of a swim in the Bashkaus. But there's also an obvious attention to aesthetics. Colors match and the odd flotation solutions are hidden. Still, I can't help but chuckle. We're about to embark on a multi-week Class V expedition and we're standing in a Halloween party of Draculas, Barneys, Quasimodos, Michelin Men, and assorted cosmonauts. But these aren't costumes. They're our most important pieces of equipment, with function playing a far more important role than fashion.

Just when we think we've seen all the innovations possible in a personal flotation device, Valeri appears. His goes a step beyond merely providing buoyancy: it has an additional breast-pocket housing a homemade parachute. It's designed to pull him out of a Siberian-sized hydraulic should he fall into one. In theory, if he were getting recirculated in a reversal, a rock would fall out of the pocket and deploy a nylon parachute that would grab the faster green water reached by the rock below and pull him to safety. That's the theory, anyway.

"I might worry about those cords wrapping around your neck instead," Ben says after examining the potentially guil-lotining gadget.

We hold our own life jackets up again and suddenly feel inadequate, like showing up to a drag race in a K-car instead of a Trans Am. For the Latvians, the term *life jacket* is a misnomer. Combined with their floatable overalls, the result is a complete life suit of flotation. Despite the animated look of the final package, there's no denying which we would rather be wearing in the heart of the canyon. A new dread for the inadequacy of our preparation hovers over each of us.

The Ensolite serves several other purposes besides lifesaving flotation. Strips of it are taped around each paddle to protect the obvious works of art. If I had invested as much time into the paddles' designs as they have, I, too, would want to ensure that they didn't sink if dropped overboard. Rectangular visors of the foam also adorn everyone's helmet, to ward off the Siberian sun.

"Incredible," Ben observes, only half in jest. "Even the visors add more flotation."

Another purpose for the Ensolite is even more important than flotation or sun protection. After the life jacket parade, Yevgheny strolls up with a piece of string and wraps it around each of us, measuring our waists. Then he heads off toward his tent and comes back fifteen minutes later with four *sidushkas*. Each one is a simple manila envelope–sized piece of foam with an elastic band that you wear around your waist. When you stand up, the butt-sized pad rests out of the way around your lower back. When you sit down, you slide it into place under your derrière for cushioning. Voila! The Latvian answer to the Crazy Creek Power Lounger.

Though we don't know it at the time, we would become addicted to them after our first day of sitting on rocks and logs. Yevgheny has customized his with a roll of tape and large knife hanging from his waist strap. Since he's always wearing his *sidushka*, his knife is always at hand.

"It's a *sidushka*-knife," Edge says.

Van discovers another use for his *sidushka* at dinner. Gathering around the fire, Olga serves us piping-hot bowls of soup. The bowls are actually old tin cans of creamed fish rations, which stack inside each other perfectly for packing.

But the tin radiates heat as fast as the soup is poured in. When he sets his bowl on his lap, Van yelps. Then the lightbulb flashes: he slides his *sidushka* from beneath his butt over his thighs to provide an insulated tray for the scalding bowl.

"Look, a place mat," he says proudly.

"Yeah, but now your butt's not protected," Ben counters. "Hey, Yevgheny, we need another one of those over here!"

We all laugh, and so does Boris, whose English is barely good enough to understand Ben's joke.

Everyone is tired from the week's travel. After the soup, we scatter to set up our tents, our REI domes again going up far easier than the Latvians' homemade parachute shelters. Then we sleep for the first time on the banks of the Bashkaus.

The next morning, we get another glimpse of the Latvians' innovation and the dual purpose of much of their gear. The reason for the two empty slots in the back of Ramitch's life jacket—as well as the perforations in his and Olga's sleeping pads—becomes clear when he folds the ground pads into two compact rectangles and slots them into the two empty sleeves on his life jacket. The pads serve as futon and flotation all in one. While we have to stuff our pads into our packs every day, he simply carries his with him as an integral part of his life jacket.

Some things serve even more than two purposes. Made from simple rectangles of corrugated sheet metal, the spare paddle blades—which will attach to wood shafts still to be hewn from the forest—also serve as Dutch oven lids, serving trays, and cutting boards. If it came down to MacGyver versus any member of Team Konkas, I'd take the Latvian, hands down.

All this improvisation results from the resourcefulness borne of impoverishment, as well as the need to create gear that can be easily carried. There are no outdoor stores in Russia or Latvia where you can buy whatever you need for an expedition. Even if there was, no one could afford to shop there, so everything is made from materials at hand. Where there's a need, there's a creative way. As Ramitch's ground-pad-life-jacket-flotation and the tent pole paddles show, this yields innovations that escape conventional manufacturers.

Such is certainly the case with our rafts, which we begin building after breakfast. Though perhaps even more important than our life jackets, they, too, are homemade. Their airtight bladders are made from old germ-warfare suits. In his chemistry days, Ramitch invented a glue in his kitchen one night that bonds the suits together. With some stitching and reshaping, the end result isn't pretty—much like two giant kielbasa sausages per boat—but it's effective.

Even the foot pump we use to inflate them is homemade, mating the germ-warfare suit material with an old radiator hose. By noon, we've finished inflating the last pontoon. Six green sausages now line the beach above camp. The only things they're missing are butchers' knots at the end of each link. These six tubes will form the basis of three catarafts, with two long pontoons per boat. Two boats are for the Latvians and one is for us. We help stuff the inflated bladders inside casings made from old truck tarps to protect them with an abrasion-resistant outer shell. This turns the sausages from green to gray and gives them the durability they'll need to scrape off rocks, which will be constant in the lower canyon.

The team's boatbuilding improvisation is in their blood. The Slavs of Kievan Rus, as Russia was known in the single-digit centuries, were accomplished boatbuilders. Their major cities, such as Kiev and Novgorod, were built near rivers and lakes along the Vikings-to-Greeks trade route, with boats providing everything from transportation to food. One of the region's first craft was a canoelike vessel propelled by poles. Builders then added oars and sails to make the boats faster, and by the seventh century, the Slavs navigated most of the region's rivers for communication and trade. They also took their boats onto the open sea, sailing as far away as Italy and Crete.

For these longer voyages, they designed lightweight open boats called *lodyas* from hollowed-out oak or linden trees. They topped the hulls with planking for greater depth, and attached oars for rowing and a mast for sailing. Like the boats we'd be paddling, the *lodyas* were also light enough to portage if need be. While our catarafts carry four to five people, the huge *lodyas* could carry forty. They used these, and even larger craft, to launch sea battles against such empires as Constantinople and Byzantium.

The Bashkaus was to be our Byzantium, and we could only hope that our homemade germ-warfare suit and truck-tarp catarafts would withstand a similar beating. Unlike the Slavs' war craft, Ramitch's boat has a diplomatic touch. Its bladders are from an old raft he had named *Ambassador* and a new raft named *Prule*, which means "good at cards." He's named his new cataraft *AmbassaPrule*, loosely translated to mean "a diplomat who's good at cards." On the high-stakes whitewater of the Bashkaus, they both seem like good traits to have.

Like the tubes, the frames are also homemade. We'll reap them right from the land, spending the next two and a half days building giant log-pole squares to hold the tubes together. The first task is searching for suitable timber to strip and dry in the sun. The forest is a jumble of cedar, pine, birch, spruce, fir, and larch. It's the latter, growing closest to the riverbank, that quickly falls prey to the Latvians.

Soon we hear a crash from deep in the forest. It's Boris, felling the first of countless larch trees to be used to build the frames. We hear several more crashes, followed by several more. We look up to see the tops of several trees waver and then plummet to the forest floor. I get the feeling that, given the chance, these guys could decimate an entire forest in days. Soon pairs of paddlers emerge from the forest like ants, carrying logs on their shoulders. Ever the team's übercontributor, Valeri emerges carrying two logs, one set of ends resting atop his broad shoulders and the other dragging behind him along the ground.

To cut the poles down to size, Ramitch pulls a serrated saw blade from his pack and finds a suitable sapling, which he strips and bends into a C-shaped handle. Even the saw handle they use to build the homemade frames to put on the homemade rafts is homemade.

We spend all afternoon hauling logs to the riverbank and stripping them of their bark. Soon I'm sitting in a knee-high mound of light-colored, boomerang-shaped shavings. It reminds me of aboriginal oyster shell middens I'd encountered while sea kayaking in Tasmania, only these won't withstand the test of time. Rather than become an archaeological site, they'll be swept away by the Bashkaus during next year's runoff.

The bark-peeling job isn't rocket science or backbreaking labor. Sit on your *sidushka* and whittle away as if you're peeling carrots. But at least they think we're good enough for it. We're at it for about three hours straight, during which we glance around at our surroundings.

"You certainly don't see this every day," I say to Edge, who is stripping a log next to me.

"*Nyet,*" he replies, exhausting his Russian vocabulary.

It's not the Montana-like forest, rolling mountains, or pristine river coursing by that garners our attention, but the Latvians themselves—a bunch of grown men standing around in only their underwear and butt pads, smoking cigarettes that match their pasty-white skin. It isn't a pretty sight. Nevertheless, they attack their log-chopping, hauling, and stripping chores with the work ethic of bees.

Assuming our ineptitude, or at least lack of experience in felling a forest to make raft frames, Ramitch next assigns us the more harmless task of stripping the bark off of wooden dowels. He and Yevgheny have spent the past hour cutting 300 small wooden dowels the size of long Lincoln Logs. These will be twisted into loops of webbing that will hold the frame joints together like a tourniquet. Perched on the cobblestone bank, we whittle the hot dog–sized frame anchors while watching the Latvians' progress. While Van whistles "Whistle While You Work" from *Sleeping Beauty*, the Latvians are close to being censored by Disney. Stubbed toes and smashed fingers from the log work give rise to a barrage of Russian words I haven't heard before. The exclamations are augmented by the universal body language of pain. All the while they wear nothing but tighty-whiteys, covered on their backsides by *sidushkas.*

By the end of the day, the dowel job is done. And quite well, I might add, with 300 perfectly peeled hot dogs of larch resting in a pile on the beach. We move on to another mundane task matching our competencies. We burn the ends of two-foot-long pieces of frayed webbing with our lighters to prevent them from fraying. These will be used with the dowels to hold the poles together for the frames. Once the ends are fray-proof, we tie the webbing into loops with water knots. While we're tying knots, Yevgheny dams part of the river to create a pool. When we're finished tying the loops, he puts the webbing in the pool to soak overnight. In the morning, we'll wrap them around each frame joint while still wet and then pass a dowel through each loop. Then we'll twist them like a tourniquet, tightening the webbing around the logs before tying the end of each dowel off with another piece of smaller webbing. As the webbing dries, the joints will tighten even more, creating a fastening system as tight as any manufactured metal clamp could accomplish. The only metal at all on these hewn-from-the-land frames are four small triangles used to hold the plastic seats. The aluminum for these seat frames? One guess. It's leftover from the army cots used for the backpacks.

Soon three giant larch squares rest on the cobblestone bank next to the pontoons. They look as if you could run a high-school football drill through them, as coaches did with old tires. One forms a giant *H* with additional cross beams on each end. Another looks like a large *M*, and the third resembles a tic-tac-toe board. They look like giant crisscrosses of lattice, only their role is far more important than shading a patio. They'll hold the homemade rafts together, keeping us afloat and alive on the Bashkaus.

CHAPTER NINE

Final Preparations

Boris lashing the frames together at the put-in (note the use of wooden dowels to secure the joints, and aluminum tripods—the frames' only metal—as seats).

By day two at the put-in, Olga has taken on a motherly role—actually, more of a food clerk's role at a military base. Everything continues to be rationed, sugar cube by sugar cube and spaghetti noodle by spaghetti noodle.

The food's presentation is as foreign to us as the pork fat. No matter the meal, everything down to the last raisin gets divided into fourteen equitable portions. You don't serve yourself from a pot of spaghetti as you would in the states, but take what's allocated to you. With each meal, two sugar cubes rest atop a piece of dry bread to have with tea. Eventually, we learn to pick one set of cubes over another, because their corners might be more intact. Full corners mean extra calories.

Like a kid in high school, I get scolded for having a cup missing from the day's soup lineup. We realize full well by now that everything is ritualistic, especially around mealtime. But this catches us off guard.

"Where is other cup?" Olga yells, noticing the absent

dish. "It was here for breakfast."

Unfortunately, I know right where it is. It's back at my tent site from the night before.

"Where is cup?" Olga shrieks again.

I bolt for the tent and sneak the cup back into the lineup when Olga turns away. I'm not sure if she sees me, but she doesn't have to. Like trying to avoid a college professor when sneaking into a classroom, I feel she knows all the same. Still, harmony is restored as fourteen identical cups await fourteen identical helpings of soup.

Soup, of course, is a misnomer. Especially when, like today's, it involves fish. Like a scene from *The Flintstones*, each day's catch is simply dropped into a pot of boiling water, head, bones, tail, eyeballs, and all. This makes hot fish water—not to be confused with hot fish soup. But it's all calories, and that's what matters. After Olga portions it out, we pull our *sidushkas* down and take a seat on the logs around the fire.

"You lucky," Van says, glancing into my bowl. "You got the eyeball."

If the eyeballs mean extra calories, catching an entire fish is reason to celebrate. Though we stashed most of our equipment at the bus station, Van kept his fly rod. Even though he's continually out-fished by Valeri and his homemade rod and lure, Van contributes to the team—almost to his detriment. After lunch, he nearly breaks his ankle scrambling to land a whopping six-incher, a fish that would have been quickly released back home. Though pride won't let him get his picture taken with them, he lands four tiny grayling and keeps every single one.

I'd been in this situation with him before. Once, on a trip down the Grand Canyon shopped by vegetarians, we tried to single-handedly satisfy our meat craving with our fly rods. We collaborated on every catch, high-fiving each other with each successful landing. It's the same thing here, only we've lowered our expectations. Anything with a heartbeat is a keeper, even though you often burn more calories catching it than you get from consuming it.

To go with that night's hot fish water is, joy of joys, more pork fat. I pass on it once more, again handing the translucent, domino-shaped rectangle to a drooling Boris. But later, stomach growls give me the courage to stomach a piece whole.

We seem to have surprised Boris—he had never met an American before, and we seem to be what he expected, with one exception.

"River runners are the same no matter where they're from," he says, gnawing his rind next to the fire. "But I didn't expect you to eat fat."

We certainly didn't expect to be eating it either, nor making a daily habit of sucking sugar cubes. Like the patties of pork fat, the sugar cubes have become a valuable commodity. They're so cherished that sometimes we stuff them in our pockets to pull out later with tea. The first time I do so, however, Yevgheny busts me. He points and says, "*Zanachka!*" accusingly. Andrew and Sergei the Small laugh and we ask Boris what it means.

"It means 'to squirrel something away,'" he says, adding that it originated in the Soviet Gulags. "Everyone does it, but no one likes to admit to it, or be caught."

The greater problem with *zanachkaing* sugar cubes, I find, is that they rub each other inside your pocket, shaving precious calorie grains off the corners. And that lost energy quickly turns into sticky, lint-gathering goo.

I'm not the only one worried about the cubes. After dinner that night, Van pretends to throw one of his coveted cubes into the fire. The fake thrust draws a shriek of rage from Boris. Van responds by throwing it to Boris's main food rival, Sergei the Small. This gets Boris yelling even louder. "That's worse than throwing it into the fire!" he shouts.

The food's preparation is as regimented as its presentation. Cook detail is broken into teams of two, with each pair responsible for cooking a day's dinner, breakfast, and lunch. With fourteen of us, that means I'm on cook detail once every seven days. Halfway through building the frames it's Edge's and my turn. In keeping with the food-parceling rules, we go strictly by their book, separating everything equally, including two perfectly balanced sugar cubes atop fourteen equal allotments of sweet bread. Dinner is equal portions of freeze-dried vegetables and bulgur, with five dice-sized carrot cubes apiece. But we spice things up for dessert, with fourteen pairs of two jelly beans each lined up in a perfect row.

I can sense Edge's pride in the presentation. We got the beans from the bulk-food bin at NOLS, but never expected to be counting them. We figured it to be the type of snack where you reach your hand into the bag and grab. But not here. If they allocate sugar cubes, we'd better do the same with jelly beans.

"Which color do you think has the most calories?" Edge asks before we call everyone over.

"I don't know," I reply. "I'm going with green."

"Maybe we should sort them so everyone gets the same colors," he says.

He's only half joking. We still don't fully know what to expect.

The next day, we continue the rationing for lunch, this time turning it into an art form. We slice three PowerBars into fifteen pieces. Pork fat meets PowerBars, East meets West. We can't figure out how to divide the three bars into fourteen equitable portions, so we have one piece leftover. We'll teach them how to play Roshambo for the last remaining morsel. Then we put a glob of peanut butter atop each one, and then top that with two vertical jelly beans sticking out like flowers in a vase. The presentation is flawless, the invention worth every inquisitive look on the Latvians' faces.

"What is this?" asks Boris, sinking his teeth into the gummy creation.

"Oh, we eat these all the time," Edge replies. "They're, uh, Colorado gobstoppers."

"Harrumph!" replies Boris, the jelly beans sticking to the peanut butter sticking to his mouth.

When it comes time to play Rock, Paper, Scissors—or

Roshambo-lovich, as Edge puts it in pig-Russian—for the last remaining gobstopper, we call everyone over and teach them. Boris and Sergei the Small are first in line, but Boris quickly gets eliminated. After several rounds, Olga wins, much to the chagrin of runner-up Sergei.

"What do you think the Russian equivalent of this game would be?" Ben asks. "Hammer, Sickle, Wheat?"

We try to come up with suitable hand signals. Hammer and sickle come easily enough, but we get stuck on wheat. We'll soon learn that the Latvians have a similar game, only it involves counting fingers instead of turning them into scissors and paper, and they use it for something far more consequential than an extra Colorado gobstopper. It's how we will determine whose boat will first run rapids on the Bashkaus.

The fact that the gobstopper concoction is foreign to them—in truth, it surprised Ben and Van as well—shouldn't be surprising. It's not something that is reaped from the land, and that's where we'll be getting a substantial portion of our provisions. If they aren't fixing gear or chopping down trees, the Latvians are either fishing or foraging for berries, mushrooms, and onions. After dinner that night, Valeri disappears and then shows up with a tonic made from Altai grasses to mix with vodka. He also pulls out a big sack of fresh-picked mushrooms, which he simmers all night over the fire. The next morning, we have them with oatmeal. It's not bad. We can only trust that they're edible.

"Mmm … oatmeal and mushrooms," Ben says, taking a spoonful. "I'll have to remember this for back home."

Our fears of eating poisonous mushrooms are unfounded. Safety is of paramount concern, as evidenced later that morning by us all taking turns swimming to get a feel for the river's current. The swims also offer practice to those manning the safety throw-ropes below. It's also our first chance to see the Latvians' high-float life jackets in action. When Yevgheny bobs by, he looks like a cork with water wings. Boris gets a quick scolding from Ramitch when he wants to swim the rapid above camp from higher up than anyone else.

"You go here," he says, not wanting to introduce any more risk.

Ramitch's concern is for good reason. We're in the middle of nowhere without any outside communication. Even a minor injury could become deadly or break up the expedition. Adjacent to camp is a cliff dropping into a deep pool. In the desert canyons of Utah, I wouldn't think twice about throwing a backflip off of it. Here, it's different. You don't flip for fun. You concentrate on surviving. There are enough risks to overcome as is. No one takes any additional chances.

Under Ramitch's guidance, everyone has their own little projects today, whether it's sewing a pocket onto a life jacket, fixing a tent fly, helping with the frames, foraging, or fishing. The only thing they all have in common is that they're good for the team. Throughout the trip, we'll all rely on each other and serve the whole.

The Latvians intrinsically seem to know what to do; they don't have to be told. If the team had a flowchart, Ramitch would occupy the top box, with everyone else spaced equally below with no other subsets of leadership. Though Olga likely captures his ear more than anyone else, if there were a second in command, it likely would be Valeri, a seeming master at everything that needs to be done.

In a brief moment when he's not doing something for the team, Valeri glues the sole back onto his black leather boots. They are the only shoes he brought and they'll get drenched every day. He'll paddle in them, portage in them, hike in them, and even get a severe case of trench foot in them by trip's end. In a way, his fixing them is still a team pursuit. Fixed shoes mean less downtime, less chance of getting hurt, and more time to tend to the expedition's needs, be it setting up safety or adding mushrooms to oatmeal. I regret leaving my river sandals at the bus station, but still have twice Valeri's footwear: a pair of wet-suit booties I'll wear every day on the river and lightweight hiking boots for camp.

The same minimalism can't be seen in the Latvians' impact on the forest. It's the exact opposite of low-impact camping. If Leave No Trace is ever in need of examples of what not to do, they could make the Latvians their poster children. Boris returns shouldering another barrel-sized log. He pulls out a hatchet and starts notching it to place around the final night's fire. Edge and I wander into the forest to help Sergei the Small with his contribution. On the way, we joke about building "infrastructure," how "it makes our country strong," and is "good for zee team." But inside, our environmental ethics are fuming.

Back at the fire, Boris is finishing his furniture masterpiece, an ottoman. The project, like the others, is so industrious that he even strips the log of its bark before placing it around the fire as a bench.

"We always have big party night before running river," he says, justifying his new log contribution. "Need more places to sit."

Between the frames, paddle shafts, post-and-beam kitchen construction, saw handles, and enough logs to seat a crowd at Yankee Stadium, the Latvians could destroy an entire forest for just one camp. Every hour, it seems, we hear a loud crack and look up to see a treetop wiggle and then plummet earthward. But that's their philosophy. When they escape the city, they use everything the land so graciously offers.

In our sponsorship proposal to REI, we mentioned that the "Soviets would teach us the conservation ethics and practices of the Soviet Union." I doubt the grant panel would want us picking up any preservation lessons here. Their environmental ethics are as few as Andrew's teeth. Besides felling the forest for bow-saw handles so that they can further fell the forest, the concept of litter escapes them. At dusk, Sergei the Tall throws his video camera's dead batteries in the fire. Our first reaction is to pick them out and put them in the trash, but then we realize that there is no trash. If there were, you'd have to carry it around every portage.

We try to tell Boris that on river trips back home, we pack

everything out. Leaving things such as batteries in fire pits is unacceptable. We draw a blank stare. The stare grows blanker when we tell him that we also carry out our ashes from the fire, and that our fires have to be in self-contained pans so they don't scar the ground.

"No fire on the ground?" he asks, perplexed.

Then we add the clincher, causing his stare to reach its blankest.

"We also have to carry out all our human waste."

"You carry out poop?" he asks incredulously. "Hah, big weight."

He then relates this to Sergei the Tall, sitting next to him, and they both break out in laughter. To them, none of this makes sense. You come here to survive by living off the land, not to carry out your excrement. So few people come here that leaving a trace of your presence is no big deal; those who do come are more focused on surviving than camp aesthetics.

They do have an innate sense of scarcity and purposeful recycling, however. Germ-warfare suits and truck tarps become rafts, parachutes turn into tents, army cots convert to backpacks, and soccer balls and wine bladders float as life jackets. But it's opportunistic, not environmental. Waste is neither disposed nor removed; it's recycled or abandoned. Both of our cultures, it seems, could learn from each other.

"I can just imagine these guys showing up to run the Grand Canyon and getting the customary shakedown by the ranger," says Ben. "Or, 'Can I see your fire pan and shitter?' he'd ask. Before they could answer, he'd see them felling the put-in's only three trees to make seats for the campfire."

But the Grand requires no portages and no hike to the put-in, nor trudge from the take-out.

Edge tries to persuade Boris to publish something in his club's newsletter about carrying out human waste and trash and not trashing campsites. Boris nods his head in understanding, but it's doubtful he will. Campsites aren't heavily or sequentially shared.

From deep in the forest, we hear another "chop, chop, whack, whack," signaling someone else's contribution to the team.

Soon, it starts to rain. While we set up one tarp, the Latvians go to work on another. It's an exercise in culture and style, and turns into an impromptu competition. Schooled by NOLS, Outward Bound, and countless private trips, we use one technique, and the Latvians another. Both tarps get completed at about the same time.

We eat dinner crammed beneath the tarps, rain funneling off the corners to course through camp and join the Bashkaus. Again, it's hot fish water a la eyeball. Then the customary slabs of pork fat for energy. In a breakthrough of sorts, I discover that dicing mine into the soup serves a dual purpose. It makes the fat more palatable, while adding a sense of broth to the hot fish water. But I also learn a downfall of chopping it into your bowl—if you do it before the hot fish water ration is served, your bowl will look fuller than everyone else's once the soup's been added.

Using your own bowl, as I sometimes do by substituting my trusty Salvation Army cup with a folding handle, instead of a team bowl has its pros and cons as well. You know no one else will grab it from the lineup, no matter how much food is piled inside. But since it's hard to eyeball portions into differently sized bowls, you often get the short stick, ending up one eyeball short, if you will. This holds especially true when the server returns to top everyone off; though you might have just as much as everyone else, your bowl might already be full. Then you're out an extra spoonful. Luckily, for coffee anyway, my aluminum Salvation Army cup consistently provides a higher yield than the smaller dishes.

But even extra coffee doesn't help wash down the pork fat nor help you digest it. And if the fat is hard to get down, the hairy-stubbled rinds are worse. Boris, sticking his head out of the tarp to reach the fire, shows us a trick. He skewers his rind with a sharp stick and heats it over the fire.

"It's like cooking a marshmallow," Van says.

The oily sponge cackles and spits over the fire. When we sample it, it still takes fifty chews.

"Kind of like pork-fat chewing gum," Ben assesses.

Edge makes a joke about shaving the whiskers off his rind to make it more palatable and then saving them for Boris.

After straight fat, it's on to straight sugar. When the cubes come atop the night's ration of sweet bread, we eat ours instantly, while the Latvians save theirs for tea. Tonight, at least, we forsake having sweetener for our tea in favor of instant gratification.

For later gratification, and because everything's still so novel, we stage a photo of Edge using his *sidushka* as a place mat. We borrow an extra piece of pork fat from the group rations to place near the bowl as a prop to round out the image. Still chewing on his pork marshmallow, Ben takes the photo.

"Boys, make sure you put fat back," scolds Olga, the food cop.

The rain eases in time for the after-dinner festivities. It's our last night before putting on the river, and reason to celebrate. But there's a ritual to this, too. You don't just grab a beer from the cooler as you would on a trip back home.

Van gets the honor of raising the Latvians' official team drinking flag, a multicolored flap of nylon riddled with several emblems. It's a work of art, with the word *Riga* stenciled above a set of thick clouds hanging above the buildings of a city. Below the buildings is a whitewater athlete stroking through a set of rapids. The word *Konkas* is spelled out in big letters below.

Van hangs it from a branch near the fire and we toast with vodka shots and fresh grass tonic, courtesy of Valeri. The booze is especially soothing for Yevgheny, who at lunch cracked his molar on a piece of dry bread baked a year earlier in Latvia. Talk turns serious when the toasts are through. We discuss river signals and paddle techniques. It's like taking a driver's test for your learner's permit. They ask us what to do in case of a flip and how to rescue a swimmer. We add our own questions and insight, too, comparing techniques. When the more serious topics are covered, Van asks a question that draws a round of laughter once Boris translates: "What do you do if you see three Latvians and one American swimming?"

"Go for the Americanski," Edge answers.

When things settle down, Ramitch turns serious again.

"River not know or care if you are Russian, Latvian, or American," he says. "All she knows is you must be strong to run her."

He also emphasizes that to survive, all must act as a team. Most of Team Konkas has been running rivers together for more than ten years. They know how each other responds in a crisis, their respective strengths and weaknesses, and how each team member handles the stress of "long staying alone in the isolated deep canyon." As do we. But neither team knows the other, and we now must all be an equal part of one team. After another toast, we elect Ben to be trip meteorologist. Unfortunately for Ben, this requires taking water and air temperatures three times a day to monitor weather patterns and rain. If the river warms up, that means it rained upstream. Rain means the river will rise, which can spell trouble in the heart of the canyon. Ben isn't overly excited about this honor. It seems superfluous, an unneeded, calorie-burning task when there are more important ones.

"Talk about being rigid in your ways," he says under his breath as he walks to the river for his first sample. "Reading number one: fifty-eight degrees!" comes his yell a few minutes later.

The water is cold. Hypothermia cold. Since we only have three wetsuits—we counted on one of us rowing our cataraft and staying high and dry on the Kalar—we decide to take equitable turns wearing them. Every four days, one of us will take a turn wearing fleece and rain gear. In return, those wearing the wetsuits will each forfeit a sugar cube as partial compensation for the extra calories expended from the inferior insulation. We, too, are starting to act like a team.

Ramitch helps us track the four days by making everyone synchronize their watches to his. Surprisingly, they didn't bring just one for the team. We're now officially on Ramitch Time, meaning no excuses for being late. Breakfast is served at 8:00 A.M. and dinner at 6:00 P.M. sharp.

At least there's no such schedule—yet, anyway—for Ramitch's guitar. That evening, he breaks into a fast-paced folk song that, with everyone singing, drowns out the roar of the river. We whittle away at the night with more shots and songs, the Latvians' voices echoing off the mountainside.

CHAPTER TEN

Rafting's Roots

(Clockwise from top left) Edge, Van, Eugene, and Ben testing out another group's *ploht* (note the two-shafted oars and handcrafted webbing).

In the morning, we gather around the boats to give them a final inspection. While doing so, another group rows past in a *ploht*, a Land-of-the-Lost-looking craft with three giant, dark-brown pontoons positioned sideways to the current. It's a work of art, as worthy of a museum as a river. Homemade backpacks are fastened neatly in a row across the tubes, as on any well-kempt ship where everything has its place. But it's the tubes that stand out. Each one is massive. If the bladders on our catarafts are sausages, then these are full-on bratwursts, each one at least waist high. The brown tubes stand out in stark contrast to the bleached white of the frame's bark-peeled larch poles holding the three tubes together. The craft is steered with giant sweeper oars, one facing downstream and one upstream, each made of two freshly hewn log poles requiring two standing men to handle.

The shaft poles provide separate handles for each rower, with the four rowers standing on a homemade canvas floor stretching between each set of pontoons. The craft is enormous, like a giant three-bellied alien bug with oars resembling stiff-jointed legs.

The oar blades are simple pieces of sheet metal. They look like they've been cut from a trash-can lid. Attached to the ends of the two-poled oar shafts, the blades jut up at an angle, giving them better purchase in the water. They look like they could double as guillotines should a swimmer accidentally brush up against one. Empty salami cans cover vertical wooden dowels protruding up from the frame to serve as tholes for the oars. The gap between the two-poled oar shafts then slides over the salami cans, allowing each oar to pivot when pushed or pulled by the men straining at the craft's helm. The dowels allow the oars to pivot up and down as well as side to side.

In the United States, the setup is called a *sweeper*. They're not used much, with only small pockets of aficionados on the Snake River near Jackson Hole, the Middle Fork and Main Salmon rivers in Idaho, and a few rivers in Oregon. That a similar craft evolved an ocean away from each other justifies the technique used for getting downriver.

The shortfall of both *ploht*s and sweepers is that they can only move back and forth across the river, dodging obstacles like a wilderness version of the video game *Space Invaders*. They don't allow the craft to speed up by paddling downstream or slow down by backpaddling. They simply go with the flow, allowing you to steer around whatever you have to.

Designs like this came about far differently here than those in the United States. Without private or personal property, and no patents, here there was never any such thing as intellectual property. The designs emerging out of early expeditions were willingly shared and continually changing. Small improvements evolved into the great variety of craft seen today. Aspiring river runners could easily obtain drawings and build a boat on their own. There were even books published on making equipment. Unlike the commercial world of the United States, groups would share hand-drawn designs of everything from boats to life jackets, fostering a unique camaraderie that nourished the sport.

A strong force in the evolution of Russian raft design was and still is the extreme remoteness of the country's whitewater. There aren't any whitewater rivers near population centers. While we enjoy rivers such as the Potomac in Washington, D.C., or the American in California for quick whitewater runs close to home, paddling whitewater here usually means planning a full-scale self-support expedition into either the Urals or Siberia.

The closest, easiest rivers were explored first, with the more remote, difficult rivers attempted as skills and equipment progressed. The first craft used by early Russian river pioneers were simple log rafts, which provided buoyancy but little maneuverability. The craft were also extremely heavy, making them a Russian bear to portage. If paddlers encountered an unrunnable rapid, they simply ditched the old raft and built a new one below. Paddlers also used homemade *baidarkas*, or two-person, wire-frame kayaks. Resembling contemporary Klepper kayaks with an open deck and no inflatable components, the foldable craft were easy to transport and remained a popular mode of river travel in Russia up until 1989. A few people redesigned them to include closed decks, spray skirts, and inflatable balloons for increased flotation, and some of these remain in use today.

As people ran harder rivers, they graduated to Aviation Rescue Boats (LASs), which they acquired from leftover equipment storages or army and government outposts once the craft's serviceability had expired. Wherever these early river runners acquired them, they found them much better suited for the rigors of whitewater than their unwieldy log craft. Another craft seen on the water were inflatable rescue rafts, which were bigger and rounder than the LASs and came with a built-in shelter for overnight expeditions.

Still, nothing was perfect. Even the rescue rafts were hard to transport and couldn't withstand the river's abuse. So Soviets began tinkering with various designs to improve their river worthiness. One of the first boats to come out of this genre was the *ploht*, whose first incarnations had tubes running parallel to the current instead of perpendicular, as the one passing camp today.

In 1976, Sergey Papush invented the four-seat catamaran, which we'll be using. Two paddlers sit opposite each other astride each tube, using canoe paddles to maneuver through rapids. As well as the two-person catamaran invented a few years later, to date, it remains one of the most effective craft for negotiating the region's rivers. As paddlers tinkered with designs, offshoots arose. Some are still around, and others have faded into obscurity. A hybrid of the four-person catamaran and *ploht* surfaced shortly after with the *chester*, a catamaran featuring two front paddlers and one big sweeper oar in the stern. Also developed was a smaller *ploht*. The tubes ran perpendicular to the current, but paddlers sat facing each other.

One of the oddest-looking craft, and one still used today, is 1984's *bublik*. While commendable for its thinking-outside-the-box approach to paddling, it's best likened to two giant donuts standing on end, connected with wooden coffee stirrers. The paddlers sit on each tube beneath a giant inflatable arch. When stuck in a hole, the craft rotates end over end, taking the gerbils strapped inside with it. While this makes the craft unflippable, it also has a hard time staying on course, oftentimes bouncing awkwardly through rapids. It also has a propensity for getting stuck. When caught in the grips of a hydraulic, it can make the riders as nauseous as a Tilt-A-Whirl at an amusement park.

From log rafts, *baidarkas*, and airline rescue boats to *plohts*, catarafts, and *bubliks*, one constant emerged throughout this innovation: a love for exploring rivers and designing specific craft for that purpose. River running here evolved exactly as needed to get the job done.

While all this was occurring in the Soviet Union, rafting in the United States was light-years ahead. The sport's roots in the United States are much deeper. On top of easier accessibility to whitewater, two contributing factors are the government's involvement in continental exploration and expansion, and paid, commercial recreation.

Huck Finn proclaimed, "There warn't no home like a raft," in Mark Twain's *The Adventures of Huckleberry Finn* back in 1885, but river exploration started well before that. It began in earnest with the government commission of Lewis and Clark to find a waterway leading to the Pacific in 1803. Their Voyage of Discovery lasted three years, covered 9,046 miles, and tested the water worthiness of more than twenty different boats, including a keelboat, two pirogues, a variety of canoes, skin boats, and log craft. They would have especially appreciated the Russian's going-light approach during a twenty-five-day portage around the Great Falls of the Missouri in today's Montana.

River travel took a step forward in 1842 when U.S. Army Lieutenant John Frémont and businessman Horace Day invented the rubber raft to aid their explorations of the Great Plains and Rocky Mountains. Day secured a patent for the design—a square boat with four separate cylindrical chambers—in 1846. The government became involved again in 1869, backing John Wesley Powell's exploration of the Grand Canyon. Graduating from Lewis and Clark's canoes, his expedition used decked, wooden oar boats and the only method known to navigate whitewater at the time: they rowed the craft downstream, with their backs toward the rapids. Unable to see or maneuver, the pilots often broached, capsized, or wrecked their boats.

All of that changed in 1896 when Utah's Nathaniel Galloway turned the seat around and looked downstream, allowing him to row upstream and slow the craft down. This "upstream ferry" afforded him more time to see oncoming rapids and maneuver around them. It also led to the first commercial whitewater trip in 1909—more than fifty years before the Russians began running rivers recreationally—when Julius Stone charged money to take clients down the Grand Canyon.

Day's rubber-raft concept reappeared when the military

began experimenting with them as airplane life rafts during World Wars I and II. But it wasn't until 1938 that they were used again for whitewater, when Amos Burg took an inflatable named *Charlie* down Idaho's Middle Fork of the Salmon River and Grand Canyon. Fitted with rowing frames, these army-surplus rafts then became popular among recreational river runners.

The sport's commercial industry also gave it a jump in innovation. Bus Hatch acquired the country's first recreational concession from the government in 1952, spawning more design improvements. Pioneers such as Georgie White collaborated with manufacturers to create whitewater-worthy craft such as the G-rig, a giant three-pontooned raft made specifically for the Grand Canyon. The J-rig followed, as did other more conventional craft throughout the 1960s—right when the sport was just starting in the Soviet Union. The great leap forward came in the early 1980s with self-bailing rafts, which utilized a laced-in inflatable floor enabling water to drain out. This opened the door to harder runs as guides no longer had to worry about water weight making the craft unwieldy, or forcing paying passengers to continuously bail.

The bailing problem never arose in Russia as their catarafts lack floors. More importantly, unlike the commercial operations in the United States, river runners never relied on a paid stranger to guide them. They all chipped in to help an expedition succeed, fostering today's emphasis on teamwork.

We scramble downstream for a closer look at the *ploht* when it pulls over below our camp. On board is a family: one woman, a teenager, four men, and a dog wearing a homemade harness and life jacket. In Russian river-running circles, it's a small world, even in Siberia—this is the same group the Latvians met a year earlier while running the Kitoy. Ramitch talks with them, probably mentioning Americans, and then gives one of the men a big hug. We watch them push off and head downstream. Though the craft looks like a beast to portage, Olga says that oftentimes they'll simply throw the bulk of the frame away and then build another one if necessary.

When I ask about the dog, she says the group is not running the entire Bashkaus. They'll hike out to the nearest village just upstream of the lower canyon. "It is not a place for a family," she says.

During a break in preparation back at camp, I discover why. The river description Ramitch picked up in the Moscow river library says the river is runnable only in July and August, and that it drops 4,143 feet before reaching the take-out 130 miles later. Where the Grand Canyon drops an average of eight feet per mile, the Bashkaus drops thirty-two, most of it in the lower canyon. Most trips take twenty-two to twenty-five days, the majority, like the river's gradient, spent in the thirty-mile lower canyon. Not that there are river gauges anywhere remotely close, but the ideal flow is about 2,800 cubic feet per second, about the same as our town run during peak flow in Steamboat Springs. Combine this with the isolation of Siberia, an average gradient four times that of the Grand Canyon (and easily twenty times that in the lower canyon), homemade equipment, and complete strangers you can't talk to, and the reality of our imminent journey again hits home.

Squatting by the river, Ramitch looks across at a rock on the far side. The river is quite a bit higher than when he first ran it, he says. While on that trip, another expedition had two deaths.

Though the lower gorge occupies our thoughts, here, the terrain is unassuming. Undulating, forested mountains evoke Idaho and Montana, though at fifty-three degrees latitude, we're about ten degrees farther north. From here, the Bashkaus snakes northward for 130 miles before joining the Chulishman. The upper reaches traverse rolling, pine-covered peaks flanked by grassy hills where nomadic herdsmen allow their sheep to graze. Occasional gorges harbor sporadic Class IV and V rapids, and then the terrain broadens again. But then comes the tight-walled lower canyon, where the river expends its last gasp before emptying into the Chulishman and Lake Teletskoe.

High clouds hint of rain and a brisk breeze sneaks

through my wool pants. Before we officially begin the expedition, we carry the catarafts upstream for a trial run through the rapid above camp. Even without gear, the boats are heavy, due largely to their wooden frames. Once above the rapid, we put on our river gear for the first time. Van, Ben, and Edge don wetsuits, while I wear a green one-piece fleece suit that makes me look like a giant frog. Over that I wear blue rain pants and a teal dry top. I haven't received my extra sugar cubes yet, but plan to at lunch. Our life jackets, low flotation by Latvian standards, snug everything tight to our chests and add yet another element of color to our moveable, paddling palette. Capping it all are our helmets—two red, one yellow, and one gold.

We're a colorful ensemble atop the gray rafts and under the gray skies, much more so than the Latvians, whose gear is more worn and subdued. But how we look on the water is not nearly as important as how we look paddling it. Everyone is curious to see how we, experienced river runners from the United States, will fare in our first rapid on homemade Latvian equipment. All eyes are on us as we ready for our inaugural run. Though we four share similar river-running experience, I have the loudest voice and am elected to take the guide position, for day one at least. We'll trade off as the trip progresses, but for our maiden voyage in front of our newfound peers, I'll call the shots while kneeling on the back right of the craft.

ॡॡॡ

Rafting, especially paddle rafting, where everyone depends on each other for a clean line, is quite different from kayaking, where a sole paddler controls his own craft. Kayaks are also lighter and far more maneuverable, and give you the parachute of an Eskimo roll to get back upright should it flip. Tip over in a raft and everyone swims.

I got my first real taste of rafting as an eight-year-old on a family trip down Colorado's Yampa Canyon. I don't remember much, save for the guide making up some lie that scared the heck out of me about a whirlpool under Tiger Wall, and giving a bouquet of Indian paintbrush to my mom and one of the female guides, who embarrassed me by saying how cute I was. But it was an indelible experience, one that helped shape who and where I am today.

A few other family trips, including one on the Colorado River's Cataract Canyon in high school, planted the seed deep enough that my sophomore summer of college found me—thanks to a mukluk-in-the-door recommendation from Van—guiding rafts in Alaska. After narrowly escaping the Moonies, my first guiding job was on Juneau's Mendenhall River, where we'd pile ten 300-pound passengers straight off cruise ships onto an oar boat, give them worthless ponchos, and then row them upwind in the rain across an ice-studded lake to the start of the river. Then we'd dodge rocks, ply our passengers full of smoked salmon, havarti cheese, and a combination of peach brandy, apple cider, and champagne (called Mendenhall Madness), and send them on their way two hours later. On a busy day, you'd guide four trips at a salary of thirty-five bucks a pop and hope for tips to blow at the Red Dawg Saloon.

Eventually, I was shipped off to the Anchorage area to guide rafts on such runs as the Eagle, Portage, and Kenai rivers. I was still working primarily with oar boats, but occasionally we'd give the passengers paddles. You couldn't count on them really helping, but it introduced me to the art of yelling commands. We explored several other runs in the area during our time off, including the Matanuska, Nenana, and Chickaloon rivers, and by the end of the summer, I had a solid grasp of guiding.

I picked up some paddle-boat skills the next summer while guiding on Colorado's Arkansas River, the most popular commercial rafting river in the world. I broached and dumped passengers into the river on some days and had clean lines on others. We punched through river-wide holes such as Seidel's Suckhole, slalomed through such rapids as Pinball, Three Rocks, and Big Drop, and careened down wave trains such as the Seven Staircases and Zoom Flume. All the successes and swims helped me garner the intricacies of paddle rafting—how a team is only as strong as its weakest paddler, and how a coordinated, petite woman can contribute more than a weight lifter. The key is working as a team, and individuals avoiding second-guessing where they think the craft should go, trusting the guide to call the shots.

Most paddle rafts don't have the rigidity of frames to stop them from buckling, nor the reliance on a sole expert at the oars. But if executed correctly, they offer more power and maneuverability than oar boats. Though I graduated to kayaking shortly thereafter, another year of guiding in Alaska—and organizing private trips on such runs as the Grand Canyon, Middle Fork of the Salmon, and Selway—gave me a solid understanding of how rafts handle. But I'd never paddled inflatable germ-warfare suits before and had no idea what to expect.

"Remember," Ben says, as we cinch the thigh straps over our knees, "you don't get a second chance to make a first impression."

Unfortunately, I've already blown it. I don't realize the triangular saddle I'm straddling in the stern right position is upside down until Boris tells me to stand up. I thought it felt funny, but I wasn't sure how it was supposed to feel.

"Nice first impression, captain," Edge congratulates as he straddles another triangular frame diagonally across from me in the bow left position.

Ben takes stern left across from me, and Van bow right, in front of me. Inside shoulder to inside shoulder, Edge and Ben are three feet away from Van and me, about the distance of an aisle in an airplane. The frame spans the water between us. The kneeling position is awkward at first, with weight spread equally between knees and butt. But it's also effective, allowing us to rise up and reach far over the water for draw and pry strokes. The kneeling position also provides leverage for full-bodied power when paddling forward.

It's different than the sitting position maintained while

kayaking or guiding a conventional oar or paddle raft. It's like whitewater canoeing, where you kneel on the bottom of your boat while resting your butt on a seat, keeping your weight low and your leverage strong.

The strange craft feels odd, and we practice with the Latvians' homemade paddles in an eddy before we get ready to peel out into the current. The thigh straps fit snug against my groin, holding me fast to the boat even when I lean over the water to grab for better purchase in the water.

"Right side back, left side forward!" I yell, lining us up to get out of the eddy. "All forward."

The boat turns right and into a proper ferry angle to exit the eddy. Despite its Stone Age appearance, it handles surprisingly well.

We cross the eddy line and feel the current of the Bashkaus grab and turn us downriver. We're off.

"Left side back, right side forward," I yell to turn us away from an undercut wall approaching on the right.

The boat reacts perfectly, as if we've always paddled this type of craft together. Then we straighten out and with synchronized and balanced strokes, we punch through a wave train leading to the eddy below camp. The Latvians line the bank, curious to see how we'll fare. Some are at the put-in, others are atop the cliff near camp, and others are near the take-out. We pass by with the flying colors of our life jackets and helmets and take our first real step toward being accepted as equals.

After everyone's pilot runs, we regroup at the eddy below camp for lunch. Fourteen portions of dry bread and pork fat are lined up perfectly as our reward, compliments of Olga.

"Nothing like pork fat to help you paddle," Ben says, giddy from the success of our run. "Hell, we could probably even use the rinds to patch the raft if we needed to."

We're all in good spirits. After all these days, we're finally on the river, and the boat handles well.

After lunch, we load the boats with gear, topping them with dry bags, backpacks, and bags of food housed in homemade canvas sacks lined with garbage bags. We put the weight as low as possible to keep the craft from being top-heavy. We put two backpacks on each pontoon between the two paddlers, and lash two more to the poles spanning the water. We secure them with an assortment of ropes and straps using trucker's hitches for knots. Providing a mechanical advantage, the knots draw an appreciative look from Valeri, who is tying gear onto his own boat.

The fourteen of us are in three boats. Ramitch and Sergei's rafts have five people each. They put more gear in the center for the fifth person, a passenger, to ride atop. On Ramitch's boat, this passenger is always Olga. On Sergei the Small's boat, the passenger rotates each day. We don't have an extra passenger on ours, but given our unfamiliarity with the craft, that's probably for the best. We'll all have an equal hand in our fate.

Ramitch comes by each boat and gives it a final look, as if inspecting troops before battle. We keep our stomachs in and chests out as best as our motion-limiting life jackets allow. Nodding his head in approval, he returns to his own craft, and we push off.

We're not exactly an armada, just fourteen people who barely know each other paddling homemade equipment on the hardest multiday whitewater trip in the former Soviet Union. But like the pork fat coursing through our arteries, we've gelled as a team and feel prepared for whatever struggles the Bashkaus might throw our way.

CHAPTER ELEVEN

On the Bashkaus

Approaching the narrowing walls of the upper canyon's first Class V.

It feels good to finally be on the familiar current of a river. We've endured sufficient hardship to get here, from the planes, trains, buses, and trucks, to trying to communicate with the Latvians. But now, the language of whitewater takes over. On the river, we're all equals. Though our alphabets might be different, we all read water the same. It's our bodies that do the talking, through hand signals and paddle strokes. There's no more negotiating with bus drivers, hiding from conductresses, or wondering what the group is laughing about around the fire. None of that matters once pontoons touch water. It's just us and the current. We are full of confidence and on our own again. For now, at least on today's calmer stretch, we don't have to rely on anyone else—a marked contrast to the past week spent with the Latvians.

A few token Class IIIs and one Class IV test our maneuvering, but, for the most part, we're able to watch the rolling countryside pass by. Still, we realize that each stroke is taking us farther and deeper into the unknown. And while we relied on our expedition partners for simple travel logistics earlier, soon it will be for our lives.

One rapid causes us to dig in hard to avoid a large boulder. From our kneeling positions on the pontoons, we're able to lean far out over the river, hunched over at the waist until our torsos are parallel with the water. Still learning what we can get away with, we reach as far forward as our bodies will allow us to gain an extra inch of purchase on our paddle blades. We plant our blades and pull, not so much forcing the blade through the water, but pulling the boat to the blade. We stop our strokes at our sides, not pulling them inefficiently behind us, but picking the blades up again and reaching forward in order to regain the most powerful portion of each stroke.

We stroke quickly, about once per second. It doesn't take many to miss the obstacle.

"Hold up!" I yell once we've cleared it.

It's important not to overshoot an obstacle, but miss it by just enough to set up for the next one. Overshoot and you might careen toward another. Undershoot and you'll hit it. We practice more on the flats until we feel completely confident that we understand how the craft responds. With the gear, the boat is heavier now than it was during our trial run above camp. But that just means we have to react sooner, and it gives the craft better momentum to punch through waves and holes.

Soon the river narrows into a more turbulent, tight inner gorge of black basalt. Cliffs on both sides are capped with grassy meadows leading to rippling hillsides. It's John Wayne country, the type where you could gallop from horizon line to horizon line, slowing to a trot only when you hit a patch of forest. Higher peaks rise in the distance, the year's first snowfall clinging to their jagged ridges.

At the narrowest part of the gorge, we pass under an old wooden bridge. It's built from logs stacked one on top of the other, farther and farther apart until the gap is linked by one final log spanning the opening. The technique is copied in another set of parallel logs, creating two support beams crossed with shorter horizontal planks for walking.

"All forward," I call out, not wanting to be underneath it if it collapses.

The boat responds perfectly as we accelerate faster than the current. At 5:00 P.M. Ramitch Time, we pull over to camp. We've made about eight miles. We unload and, acting like termites, the Latvians immediately set to work surrounding a fire pit with freshly felled and notched logs. We help them span the fire ring with another post-and-beam cooking structure to hang billy pots for soup and tea.

Our stew that night contains a surprise: freshly butchered sheep. Before leaving the put-in this morning, Ramitch traded a liter of grain alcohol to several armed horsemen for one of their flock. They'd tell their boss that the sheep got taken by a bear. Ramitch had brought along twelve liters of booze for such bartering. So far, it had only been used for shuttles. Coincidence or not, the horsemen waited to trade until the day after we raised the drinking flag. Maybe they knew they might get a better deal when Ramitch was hungover.

The meat is dark red, contrasting sharply with the silver of the spare-paddle-blade-turned-cutting-board. Andrew chops the mutton with precision, the white bone and red meat matching the plaid of his flannel shirt. I help by chopping a small onion Valeri found near camp. It's about what I'd use on a hamburger at home, but here, it's enough for fourteen people. I don't bother chopping it, or a lone clove of garlic, too fine. In the middle of Siberia, it's not worth losing a finger over a perfectly diced onion. I also take care to only peel off the outermost crinkly yellow layer of skin. Even every onion calorie counts. Seeing that we're having stew, Ben introduces the Latvians to dehydrated green peppers. Then he shows them brewer's yeast, which he uses to bake rolls, using the spare-paddle-blade cutting board as a Dutch oven lid. Now, a simple piece of sheet metal has served three distinct purposes on the trip

Though it would quickly end up in the dog dish back

home, we readily swallow the stew's gristle, the chunks of which are allocated as carefully as the meat. In fact, there seems to be more gristle than actual meat.

"Mmm ... gristle stew," Ben says between mouthfuls. "Hey, trade you two pieces of gristle for one piece of meat."

No one, not even Boris, takes him up on his offer, even though the transaction might mean coming out ahead in calories.

"Hah, wery funny," he says. "I like meat more."

His answer prompts us to continue asking him questions that have answers starting with the letter *V*, just to hear him pronounce it.

"What's his name again?" Ben asks, pointing to Valeri.

"Waleri," answers Boris.

"Where do people live around here?" Van asks nonchalantly.

"We have wery, wery much willages here," answers Boris.

The concept of "willages" prompts Edge to make a remark about tax dollars, which draws a blank stare.

"Taxes?" Boris asks. "What are taxes? They come from willages?"

We explain as best we can, but even after a week of traveling together, our cultural and political gaps are as wide as ever.

The trip dynamics follow the Soviet economic philosophy: from each according to his ability, to each according to his need. Instead of the market economy we're accustomed to, where prices link supply and demand, here, as on any long wilderness trip, supply is limited and relatively fixed, with no relationship to demand. As we well understand by now, this holds especially true for food. Shortages and excesses are all dispersed evenly. Communism's arguments play out easily on the river.

I doubt Karl Marx and Friedrich Engels envisioned their *Communist Manifesto* applying to food rations on the Bashkaus. Written in 1848 for the Communist League, an organization of German émigré workers living in Western Europe, it formed the basis of the modern Soviet Union's Communist party.

Among its tenets are premises that "the history of all hitherto existing society is the history of class struggles" and "society as a whole is more and more splitting up into two great hostile camps, into two great classes directly facing each other— bourgeoisie and proletariat." The immediate aim of Communists, it continues, is the "formation of the proletariat into a class, overthrow of the bourgeoisie supremacy and conquest of political power by the proletariat." Its final line sums up both the party's vision for the government as well our own for getting down the river: "Working men of all countries unite!"

Contributing to the team, or basic civic humanism, comes naturally for all of us and we all chip in equally. All chores are for the betterment of the whole—whether it's fishing, foraging, or felling trees—and we gravitate to the ones we're best at. For Valeri, it's fishing. For Boris, it's chopping wood. Olga tends to cuts and bruises, and monitors food supplies. Andrew has taken to monitoring each raft's air retention. Ben takes the air and river temperatures.

Putting the community over the individual is common to both our values and theirs. As modern Americans, we may have lost some of this ethos through our rampant individualism, but a return to nature quickly restores it. All it takes is being thrust into a situation of shared benefit and burden, with a common desired outcome. For all of us, that outcome is getting down the river.

Edge and I continue to do our part the next evening by gathering strawberries.

"It makes our country strong," Edge says, reciting what has become our mantra.

Then he stoops over to pick an impossibly tiny berry, burning more calories stooping over than anyone would get from eating it. If, like the *Manifesto*, we gave each according to his need, we'd be in for a lot of picking. Our knack for finding them is marginal, and each one picked is the size of a pebble. I feel guilty about pilfering a few from the group's rations, but I live with the remorse.

We're beginning to appreciate the rituals in their lives. The Latvians have never had the choices that come with personal freedom and have learned instead to put the needs of the team ahead of the individual. This is evident on and off the river. Instead of getting to camp and unwinding, they keep their wet clothes on and immediately set about tasks for the common good. There is no relaxing or worrying about personal affairs until team needs have been met. On a river trip back home, people often scatter to claim premium camp positions as soon as they touch the bank. Here, it's the opposite. Wetsuits stay on until the fire is blazing and benches are built. Even drinking is a ritual, requiring the raising of the official drinking flag. You don't just pop open a can of beer and break out the horseshoes. Everything is as rigid as the frames holding our rafts together.

In the morning, I wake everyone up by cupping my hands and blowing "Taps." The sound carries through the crisp morning air, wafting through camp, and then continues on over the river until it joins the Siberian breeze. Since I know they can't understand me, I follow with my best drill sergeant impersonation: "Let's go you maggots! Up and at 'em!" Sergei the Small is the first to poke his head out of his billowing parachute. He saunters over for a cup of tea, where we have sugar cubes balanced perfectly on dry bread, and oatmeal—with minimal picked-for-the-team strawberries—dispersed in fourteen equitable portions.

After breakfast, Olga asks our trip meteorologist what the temperature was earlier in the morning. Ben, who shirked his duties and hadn't bothered checking yet, turns around, slyly pulls the thermometer from his pocket, and replies, "Thirty-eight degrees."

It's cold for rafting, but our arms loosen after a few miles of easy water and casual paddling. The banks pass by, water giving way to cobblestones, the cobblestones capped with moss, and the moss eventually swallowed up by grass leading into thick forests.

We learn the Latvian version of Rock, Paper, Scissors at our first Class IV rapid. We christen the game Russian Roshambo. For the more straightforward rapids, only the guide from each raft gets out to scout. It saves calories. The others stay behind to rest, taking the scouter's word and stroke calls for the correct line. To see who has to run the drop first, the three scouters throw out between zero and five fingers each. Ramitch then adds them up and, starting with the rapid, counts around in a circle to his left. Whoever his count ends up on has to go first. It's a quick way to whittle a field of contestants down to a single person. If the stakes are an extra piece of pork fat, that person is a winner. In the case of having to run a rapid first, the person it lands on is a loser for his whole boat, and a gift for the others who will be watching how the first craft fares.

Though the macro side of our trip is relatively authoritarian—Ramitch calls the shots, whether it's lining up a truck or bartering for sheep—this dynamic changes on the river. Here, it's more of a democracy. Everyone is free to make his own decision about whether to run a certain rapid, and everyone's opinion is taken into account about which route to take. Each person is free to make up his own mind to paddle or walk.

During the scout, ideas are discussed and shared, potential routes and consequences identified, and the concluding action respected. On easy rapids, the process might take a few seconds, with a positive report back to the calorie-saving paddlers waiting in the raft. On more difficult drops, everyone will get out and discuss the options, with nicotine easing the Latvians' stress. But there comes a point when talk amongst scouts is as cheap as the cigarettes and you have to make up your own mind. Then you vote among your raft mates and stick with your decision. Save for the guide, one person changing his mind midstream would prove disastrous. Each successful decision strengthens your faith in both the system and your abilities as a team. It also strengthens the bond and respect between the different rafts.

Assuming everything goes according to plan, it's usually more energy efficient to run a rapid than it is to portage around it. And that's where the fingers game comes in. It's the great equalizer, indifferent to a team's strengths or weaknesses. While running a rapid always is a game of chance, the risk is tempered with calculated strokes, ferry angles, and positions. But the Latvians leave the run order to Lady Luck.

It doesn't take long to see why. During the first fingers game, I throw out a three, Ramitch a two, and Sergei the Small a four. The count to nine ends on me. I lose the trip's inaugural game of chance and report the bad news back to Van, Ben, and Edge. The Americans have to go first. The main disadvantage is that we don't have anyone else to watch before our run. It helps to have a probe. When scouting big rapids kayaking, oftentimes you'll throw a stick into the river to confirm your eye and better determine where the current is likely to take you. But an actual boat is an even better gauge. Now, we're that boat. If we go one way and get worked, team two will learn from our mistake and go a different way.

Luckily, it's a relatively straightforward rapid and we nail the run, sliding easily between two boulders constricting the river at the rapid's bottom. Ramitch and Sergei follow with equally successful lines.

It would have been an interesting day to check my horoscope. I go on to lose the Russian Roshambo game three more times, each time forcing us to run first. We begin to get a sneaking suspicion that this might not be mere coincidence. When I return to our raft for the third time with the news that once again we're to run first, Van's eyebrows raise.

"Isn't it funny that we have to go first at every drop?" he asks. "You ever think that maybe they're changing the rules on you?"

We'll never know. When it's just Ramitch, Sergei the Small, and me, without Boris or Olga to translate, everything happens quickly and I can't understand a word they're saying. Fingers are thrown and counted rapidly and you live with the consequences.

On this rapid, we opt for the left channel, hit a rock, and get spun backward, ad-libbing the rest of the run. Sergei, who took second in the fingers game, absorbs our data, reconsiders, and opts to go right. He fares only slightly better. After seeing both of our botched lines, Ramitch runs down the middle perfectly. Of course, sometimes there is only one possible route and no number of fingers can help.

That the Latvians prevail at the fingers game could be attributed to the fact that they play it all the time to distribute rewards and benefits, as well as risk and hardships. Equal participation in chance, rather than invented notions of merit that separate people into unequal individuals, determines everything from the allocation of extra pork rinds and sugar cubes to the order of running rapids. The Latvians even use it for more consequential items. In 1989, they played it to see who got to join Yevgheny at an international rafting event in North Carolina. Ramitch, Andrew, and Sergei the Tall won, teaming up with the Nantahala Outdoor Center's John Kennedy to take eleventh in a field of twenty-three international teams. Their team even placed first in a few individual events.

In keeping with their team spirit of shared equality, they didn't play the fingers game to see who would sit in the two first-class seats on the flight over. They split the flight time into equal portions, just as they did food for the river. They also took turns rotating between first and economy class to take full advantage of the food and drinks. As soon as one of them finished a meal, he ran back and swapped places with someone else. I can only imagine the flight attendant's double take, a hungry and toothless Andrew smiling up at her when moments before it was Sergei the Tall.

Instead of scrambling from seat to seat on an airplane, we're now scrambling from rock to rock on the bank, trying to get a better view of the next rapid. Below, the river cascades over a series of ledges and funnels through a tight slot on the left. If we don't make it there, we'll end up in a boulder-strewn maelstrom on the right, with potentially lethal consequences.

It's a solid Class IV rapid, our hardest of the trip so far.

Rapids are universally graded on a scale from I to VI, with Class I being little more than flat, moving water of no real consequence, and VI being technically unrunnable. The classifications have been slowly downgraded over the years as more people, with more technology and better equipment, run harder and harder rapids—similar to what is happening in the sport of climbing. But the stakes have remained very much the same. And these stakes get upped when the rapid is in an inaccessible place like Siberia, compared to a roadside run with evacuation and hospitals close at hand.

That's where scouting comes in. But even that isn't foolproof. Applying what you see to the reality of running the river is often as much a gamble as the fingers game. If someone's been down the river before, that helps. He can point out the correct route. But listening to Ramitch isn't necessarily black-and-white. The only English he knows as far as running the river is "left bank," "right bank," "camp place," "big stone," "carry things," and "big stop." Sometimes while staring at a rapid, he'll use them all in the same sentence, hand gestures providing the only real clue as to what he's talking about: "Camp place," he'll say, pointing to the bank below a rapid. "Big stone, right bank, big stop, carry things." The "big stop, carry things" comments are the most unnerving. They usually mean a mandatory portage, where a screwup could prove disastrous.

Deciphering his mutterings is harder than winning the fingers game. Asking if he means ferrying above a certain log, then cutting left above a hole before running a slot on the right, is futile. "Big stop, camp place, carry things," he responds without inflection. I have to take his word for it and realize that those are the main points to remember. The rest is up to our eyes and judgment.

The "carry things" command carries extra connotations. It means burning energy that could otherwise have been saved by paddling, where the pontoons carry the weight rather than our backs. With limited rations, Newton's law of conservation of energy has become paramount. Like it or not, life is revolving around calories. One day, a bite of soup happens to have a fly in it. At home, I would have discarded it instantly and thrown out the soup. Here, I am grateful, swallowing it without a second thought. It's extra calories.

Of course, I don't eat all the bugs I see. Siberia is big, and so are its insects, from army ants that walk away with pork rinds (unless thwarted by Sergei the Small or Boris) to bees and horseflies that can puncture a raft. If one of the horseflies buzzing around camp had fallen into my soup, I wouldn't have been so quick to ingest it. The spiders are also of Communist proportions, often spinning webs that detour entire portages. But they're just trying to catch food, as are we.

We've developed certain tricks of the trade for doing this. Employing Van's technique from the bus ride, every morning we all wash our porridge bowls with tea and then drink the combined sludge. Pots and pans get scraped clean by the dishwashers, the extra calories a perk of the job. We're also careful with unnecessary expenditures. We don't go hiking for the scenery, and we don't scout or, worse, portage, unless absolutely necessary. All our energy is saved for getting downstream as efficiently as possible. Van jokingly wonders aloud one morning how many calories there are in the sand in your eyes. He then rubs his eye and tries some.

"A little salty," he says, pursing his lips. "But not too bad. Anyone want to try some?"

No one accepts his offer, not even Boris.

My journal entry on river day five sums our caloric deprivation: "Pork fat, pork fat, my kingdom for some pork fat."

My kingdom for some pork fat. I never thought I'd see the day when I muttered that, let alone write it down. But we're all starting to look forward to our daily allocations of lard.

Today, Olga loses the lens cap to my camera while taking pictures from a cliff above a rapid. But I end up ahead as she slips me her pork fat at lunch and again at dinner as compensation. She feels guilty, and this is the best way she can think of to make it up to me. Unfortunately, that's also when I find out that three pieces is my stomach's threshold. Piece number four brings a gut-wrenching convulsion.

The Latvians' diet and lifestyle would make the American Heart Association cringe. They're living on salted pork fat, sugar, caffeine, nicotine, and grain alcohol, all the while stressing out about running Class V rapids. If the whitewater doesn't get them, the lifestyle will. The foodstuffs I can understand, if not appreciate. And the caffeine and alcohol seem mandatory as well. As for the nicotine, which comes in the form of hand-rolled cigarettes, it's just their way. Like being at war, they have enough problems in their life, be it running Class V rapids or surviving in a poor economy, that smoking is the least of their worries.

"We smoke because life is so hard," admits Olga one night. "Here and in the city."

It's almost as if they make running rapids an excuse for smoking. They smoke before, after, and even during rapids. On one rapid, Valeri keeps a burning butt in his mouth for the whole run. A hidden benefit is that the cigarettes assuage hunger. When smoking, you're not thinking about eating. But there is no replenishing them once they're gone. So they smoke each one down until the butt burns the tips of their callused fingers, and sometimes even lips.

There is occasional opportunity to replenish food besides by fishing and foraging. We get a break from the pork fat a day later when Ramitch again barters for another sheep. In a clandestine arrangement, he met with several horsemen the night before outside of camp, agreeing upon a drop site farther down the river. Soon, we pull over at the prearranged spot, marked by the *ploht* group's campsite. They are taking out here and hiking out to the nearest village, rather than braving the quickening currents pulling everything toward the lower canyon. The *ploht* has already been disassembled, its tubes seeming grossly out of place in the forest. They lean like giant punching bags against the trees.

In what should come as no surprise, the group's tent is

equally large, a huge orange and pink dome with a lightning rod–like support pole rising from its center to hold guywires to keep the structure rigid. It looks like it belongs in Barnum and Bailey's more than on the Bashkaus. Between the tree-dwarfing *ploht* tubes, and the tent that could house the Bolsheviks, everything is Siberian supersized.

Right now, however, there's giant-sized tension—and not just in the cords holding up the tent. An armed horseman, wearing jeans, black boots, and a black jacket matching a crop of jet-black hair, rides into camp, rifle slung down across his back shoulder. An additional jacket and leather pack is tied behind his saddle, above a well-worn pair of tan leather saddle bags. His horse's slow gait projects his confidence.

He dismounts and a surreal meeting ensues, armed horseman versus Ramitch in his Barney-colored life jacket. But it's serious business. Though Ramitch's flotation might save him on the Bashkaus, it is no match for a bullet. The negotiation is tense. Ramitch finds that the horsemen—there are two others lurking in the forest—have only brought two hind quarters instead of the agreed-upon full carcass. So Ramitch docks their pay, only giving them half a bottle of booze. An argument ensues and voices rise. The horseman's hands remain in his pockets, his hunched shoulders indicating his tense mood. Ramitch's head is bowed down, looking at the ground. Neither makes direct eye contact.

Boris tells us to stand back and try not to look like Americans. The bargaining price would escalate should they discover that they aren't just dealing with "Russians." Luckily, by now, we're getting good at it.

"*Nyet*," Edge whispers, as if on cue.

Ramitch hurriedly walks back over to us. With the sternest voice I've heard yet, he tells us to get back on the boats quickly. Now. We do as we are told and shove off instantly, hind quarters in tow. No more scouting, discussion, or even the fingers game.

The gunmen's hostility could well be traced back to

Russians' lukewarm demeanor toward Latvians. Though the Altai region was taken over by Russia in the late 1800s, Latvia didn't become part of the mother country until 1941. Ramitch and company pride themselves on being Latvians instead of Russians, and this can fuel resentment. We saw the difficulty they had getting bus and train tickets at the Russian rate, and their dealings with the horsemen might also have been influenced by this prejudice.

We are nervous the rest of the afternoon, fearing potshots from the bank as in *Deliverance*. For good reason. That night, Boris tells us of a trip he took on the nearby Chulishman three years earlier when drunken horsemen tore through camp, trampling tents and cutting down tarps before he managed to beat them away with a paddle.

The problem, it seems, as with that of many Native Americans in the United States, revolves around the body's tolerance for alcohol—or lack thereof. The indigenous people here are Altaitsi, named for the Altai Mountains. Because of their contemporary penchant for alcohol, and unpredictable and aggressive behavior when drunk, the Altaitsi face a ban by the Soviet government prohibiting alcohol in the region during the spring and summer agriculture seasons. Though this gives us ammunition for bartering, the natives are the ones with ammo in their guns. And as the American Prohibition showed, banning alcohol often creates more problems than it solves.

With Olga's help, Boris recalls what happened:

There is famous place, a waterfall on the Chulcha River, which most of the teams paddling the Bashkaus or Chulishman are eager to see. The confluence of Chulcha and Chulishman is a regular camping place, and we stopped there and took a hiking trip to the waterfall in August of 1990. In the evening, we began to cook our last farewell dinner and prepare for the feast. The dinner was long and turned into singing fest around the campfire. It was late and dark when two horsemen came into the ring of light cast by the fire. From our previous experience dealing with them, we knew these people had an enormous passion for alcohol and took it very bad. So we never gave them alcohol, fearing their reaction. Naturally, the horsemen quickly asked for a drink. But we had already consumed what little we had at the end of a three-week-long trip. There was no chance for them to have it. They became restless and asked for tea. We gave them a pack of black tea, which was a great mistake! They made *tchefir*—an extremely strong tea using one pack of tea per mug of hot water—and drank it and got crazy in minutes.

Before we knew it, they jumped on their horses and attacked us. It was so unexpected and abrupt that we ran for our lives to the nearest trees and boulders. Several guys were sleeping in the tent and had to cut their way through with a knife to get out quickly—just in time to avoid being run over by horses. The horsemen whipped those unlucky with rough ropes. Finally, when all of us hid from them, they pretended to calm down, jumped down from their horses, and called us back to the camp. Reluctantly, we left our cover and returned to disordered camp. But the rascals cheated us! Once we got back, they started to fight. The bigger of the two punched one of our guys while his companion stood near with a knife. The situation became critical. Our leader tried his best to calm the horsemen down, but they spun out of control. Noticing Rita, the only woman in our team, the big guy moved toward her. Then I had enough of him, grabbed a paddle, and attacked him from the back, trying to knock him unconscious. But the guy felt the danger and ducked at the very last moment, so the paddle hit his shoulder rather than head. I hit him several times, which had a calming effect on him. The guy settled down, started to whine, and then asked for help because his shoulder was severely injured. We administered first aid and made a bandage. After that, he jumped on the horse and the two of them rode away saying, "We'll be back soon with our rifles!"

At this point, we prepared for urgent evacuation. The boats were inflated in minutes, we hurriedly packed camp, and in no time we started down the river in complete darkness! It was some paddling. Thank God there were no rapids down there. But still some boulders, toppled trees, and undercuts were present. And there was zero visibility. As it got light we saw the two horsemen following us along the river bank. Luckily, they did not have any rifles.

All this eventually finished good. We paddled into the Teletskoe Lake, took apart our boats, and got away safe and sound, except for several bruises and a black eye for unlucky Victor.

When they finish, Olga recounts the story about another Chulishman group that was forced to put-in on the river at gunpoint in the middle of the night. The aggressors in this instance were also fueled by alcohol, but this story didn't end as well.

A team running the Chulishman in May of 1992 (two years after Boris's brush with the horsemen and just barely a year before our trip) employed some native men to help them get to the upper part of the river. After they got there and paid them partially with alcohol (sure that they would have gotten drunk somewhere anyway), they set up camp and began building their boats. One man stayed with them in the camp, continuing to drink, and finally getting very aggressive and starting to fight.

The group had no choice but to tie him down to a tree until he sobered up and calmed down. But his horse went home alone and the others worried about his absence. So they returned to the camp and saw him tied down and got angry and began to shoot. The team was forced to jump on their boats and paddle down the river. But the men shot one of the boats and it deflated, and the other raft flipped. As a result, four people in the group drowned. A giant cross is now erected at that same spot in the river in the memory of those who perished there.

The stories would have been captivating anywhere, but they are even more so here, just one ridge away from the Chulishman on a day on which we had already skirmished with gunmen over booze. I stir the coals in the fire and begin to question the idea of giving the horsemen vodka for one of their sheep. At the same time, my growling stomach relishes the fruits of the negotiation.

CHAPTER TWELVE

Penetrating Deeper

A family who resupplied us with fermented goat's milk, fresh bread, and strawberry jelly at one stop along the way.

We have a different sort of negotiation to deal with later in the evening. Thankfully, it only involves us Americans. Around the fire, Olga tells us that since our raft is new and this is the first time it has been on the water, they want us to name it. We huddle up, tossing around corny ideas that sound as though they could be racehorse names: *Capitalist Cataraft*, *Americraft*, *Cold War Champs*, *Democraft*. Eventually, we settle on *Team Cowboyshka*, a play on our Western roles and the word *boyshka*, which means "hole" or "hydraulic" in Russian. Just before we turn in for the night, Boris has the rest of the Latvians in stitches. We don't think it's at our expense, but we aren't sure.

The trip meteorologist clocks the temperature at forty-two degrees the next morning. It's also raining hard, which he doesn't have to tell us. But he does anyway.

"Cold and rainy," Ben says confidently. "Perfect day for rafting in Siberia."

Even with only three wetsuits, we're better prepared for

the elements than the Latvians. As with the catarafts' pontoon casings, the Latvians' rain jackets are made from truck tarps. They're not fashionable—Boris, draped in gray, looks like a walking Christmas tree skirt—but they work. We, meanwhile, are sporting the latest Gore-Tex rain jackets and pants.

In the end, it doesn't really matter. By early afternoon, everyone is shivering. So Ramitch heads to shore where we partake in the Latvian hypothermia cure: shots of vodka. Though technically it induces the opposite desired effect on our core body temperature, it does provide instant gratification, burning down our throats and into our stomachs.

After drinking Ramitch's spirits, our own are lightened further when we stop again at a riverside village to barter for bread. While some people remain with the boats, Edge, Van, Ben, and I follow Ramitch, Olga, and Boris into the village. Scattered yurts and log cabins dot a grassy meadow bisected by a lone dirt road. Smoke rises from chimneys atop domed roofs. Stacks of firewood already poke out of sheds in preparation for the coming winter. Some yurts have deer-hide roofs; others, simple tar paper tacked down with uneven boards. Still, even in the isolation of Siberia, attention is given to aesthetics, with intricate bright-blue window frames augmented with white hand-carved flowers.

We pass a woman carrying two buckets of water dangling from a pole across her shoulders. Continuing down the road, we finally stop outside a home. Ramitch strikes up a conversation with a man wearing a wool hat, tweed jacket, and collared shirt, and we're invited inside. The man's clothes seem fancy considering where we are and compared to our river attire. The yurt is dark and smoky, but yellow- and blue-flowered tapestries lining the walls and Christmas cards perched on a long shelf give it a homey, cheerful feel. So does a bed in the corner with a thick pink blanket and fluffy pillows that look much more comfortable than our mattresses of rock. Large wood beams extend up to the top of the domed ceiling above a fire pit in the center. We end up with four loaves of fresh bread, a jar of homemade strawberry jam, and a taste of yak butter and lip-puckering fermented buttermilk.

When we try to pay, the family turns their backs—they are too proud to receive anything in return. It's a far cry from our dealings with the armed horsemen. Before we leave, they only ask us to take their picture. Two months, later I'll mail a photo to them, hoping it will wind up on the mantle with the other cards. I am reminded that neither capitalism's profit incentives nor Communism's compelled sharing can usurp simple human generosity. Our only reciprocation is complete gratitude.

Back on the water, we continue downstream. It's still cold and raining, but our muscles have loosened up with the gifts, the booze, and the day. An hour later, they tighten up again while waiting to patch Sergei the Small's raft, which was punctured on a midstream rock. Thankfully, Ramitch the chemist's kitchen glue works and the boat is quickly fixed. Sergei the Small suffers similar ill fortune the next day when he briefly pins on another rock, breaking his frame. But it's no big deal. We simply pull over, fell a tree, and make a replacement pole.

Despite these minor setbacks, the boats continue to handle well, perfectly suited for the rigors of Siberia's rivers. They're better suited for it, at least, than our bodies are. Our main complaint concerns our knees. Each day is like doing a hurdler's stretch inside a freezer for eight solid hours. We should have lined up Bengay as a sponsor.

Whether it's the colder temperatures, deepening canyon, and narrowing sky, or the fact that we're losing sunlight daily, tonight Ramitch has everyone reset their watches to yet a new Ramitch Time to take better advantage of the diminishing sun. We initiate our own daylight savings by setting our watches an hour ahead. This is to trick us into waking up and getting going earlier. If we're normally up at 6:30 A.M., daylight-wise it will now be 5:30, giving us another hour of light to get down the canyon.

Ramitch has become somewhat of a shamanic time guardian, but his desire to control such things as time shows his grasp of the immensity of both the canyon and our undertaking to get down it. It takes militarylike discipline to run it successfully, and nothing connotes discipline like time. Our primary disciplinarian is the decreasing sunlight of late summer.

Time here takes on many faces. The river changes daily due to snowmelt and rain. Carry these variances through millions of years, and the canyon it carves pierces deep into the history of the Earth. On that scale, what happens to the river day to day, or even year to year, becomes immaterial. So does an afternoon's attempt to navigate a lone rapid. In the cycle of the river, our month-long visit here is truly insignificant. Except that our lives depend upon what we do each moment we're on it. This time conundrum also surfaces in our day-to-day activities. Let the raft get stuck in a hole and the two-minute ride lasts an eternity, while the week between cooking duty flies by instantly. Scouting a rapid often takes forever, while a night singing around the campfire passes before it began. Ramitch, it seems, recognizes that we're in touch with the cosmos of time on every level here.

Knowing the stress we're under, he also recognizes when it's time to open the portal and cut loose. We don't always just eat our fat and go to sleep, which calorie-wise would be the best thing to do. When he feels the opportunity is right, Ramitch raises the drinking flag and—Presto!—it's officially party time. Then he breaks out the guitar, encouraging us to release pent-up emotions that might otherwise spill out as discontent. It seems to keep everyone in check. Frustration yields to acceptance, and fear of what lies ahead softens the day's accomplishments. More important, errors committed earlier are now harmless and lead to laughter. We become alive with the river when all day we have been fighting it. It's a great tension breaker. Ramitch is a general boosting his troops' morale, but only when the time is right.

It's the same everywhere. Music, much like basic human generosity, still survives even when life is reduced to its basics. Perhaps merely recognizing and appreciating our own existence is what causes us to exalt into song. Life is precious here, and we all realize it. So we might as well sing it out loud. Alive, safe once more on the banks of a charging river, how can we not? I certainly feel more like singing here than I do after a long day at work. Our passing the guitar around puts us in touch with ourselves and our surroundings. Boris belting out "Gogia," a song telling Georgians to go home, brings the same inner satisfaction to us as Gregorian chants likely did to our forbearers. Music softens everything—the river, the hunger, and the assorted aches and pains. Our spirits strengthen for the next day. Releasing our inhibitions at night helps us do so on the river.

When Boris finishes "Gogia," Ben asks him how to play it. Boris says it's simple—it only has one chord, the "H" chord, which is strummed differently throughout the melody. We all look at each other, knowing full well there is no "H" chord.

Ramitch grabs the guitar and plays another fast-paced song. The rest of the Latvians join in for the chorus, and remain appropriately silent during each verse while he solos. The river supplies background percussion, the breeze a crescendoing melody overhead, and the larch trees a swaying dance. Feeling synchronized with life's rhythms, we feel safe to be here.

As Ramitch knew, we need all of our paddling rhythm—and Ramitch Time's extra daylight—the next day. After an hour on the water, we see his boat in the lead tied up on the right. We squeeze into the eddy next to him. Below, a distinct horizon line hides our first Russian Class V. Edge jumps out and ties our raft to a large tree on the bank, and then we all scamper down the side of the river atop a bowling alley of giant boulders. It doesn't take long to realize that our version of Class V and theirs is markedly similar.

So far, we've faced rapids rated up to Class IV. Everything's been pretty manageable. But the ante's been upped on this one. Four gigantic holes litter a hundred-yard-long ribbon of white, squeezed between steep canyon walls. Interspersed, like pepper spilled onto a table of salt, are giant boulders, rounded from the Bashkaus's continual pounding. Hit one of the boulders and you'd flip in a blink, hopefully washing downstream instead of getting pinned. Hit one of the four holes, especially sideways or without momentum, and over you'd go again, all paddlers in the drink and at the mercy of the current—and that's only if the hole's hydraulic decided to let you go. Unless Valeri's rock and parachute deployed from his life jacket as it was supposed to, a spin cycle in each one could churn you until you ended up like the yak butter we sampled in the yurt. You might get spit out too late, too weak, and too out of breath to afford your own rescue. Then, of course, are the smaller holes, waves, and rocks that in an instant could ruin a perfectly planned line.

The vertical drop of each hydraulic is a good basketball hoop's height from top to bottom. The entire rapid covers maybe fifty feet of elevation loss in about 200 feet. Its first hole causes us the most concern. Not only are its consequences the most severe, but, due to its location, it's also the hardest to avoid. Get by it safely to the left and then a path exists that, if everything else goes right, can carry you through away from the other holes. It still requires some precise rock-dodging moves, but barring some other unforeseen events, the raft, and, more importantly, passengers, could emerge unscathed.

Back at the boats, Boris is already unloading his gear. Portage time, at least for the equipment. Though the gear's extra weight helps provide momentum to punch through holes, we can't afford to lose any food or equipment, in event of a flip, this deep in Siberia. So, together, we all carry it down to the first adequate and achievable eddy, about a half mile down-river. Then we hike back up and do it all over again, making two complete trips, scrambling over uneven boulders and bush-whacking through tight foliage. Portage time completed, next comes showtime for the rafts.

Since the Latvians came here to run whitewater, and the route to the left of the top hole looks possible enough to for-sake the caloric expenditure of carrying the boats down, we play Russian Roshambo to see who attempts the maelstrom first. The final finger count is ten. Starting with the rapid as one, and then going to Sergei the Small on his left, and then me, Ramitch counts in a circle of three. With quick, Darwin-esque math skills, Sergei and I realize the counting will end up on Ramitch before he's even halfway done. In a serendipitous turn of events, Ramitch, the only one who has run it before, finishes counting and loses.

He accepts his fate willingly. His crew, Boris and Sergei the Tall up front and Valeri across the frame to his left, piles in. Ben and Sergei the Small walk back downstream and man the safety throw-ropes for rescue. Olga, who usually rides atop the pile of gear strapped to the frame, wisely stays off and hikes downstream. Ramitch pushes off. Without gear strapped to the frame, the boats are considerably more maneuverable. Strokes that had little effect before now force the craft to respond quickly and nimbly. And in the event of a flip, there's no gear to lose or chase down. It's all safe, waiting to be picked up at the end of the rapid.

Despite the added maneuverability, Ramitch's team clips the first hole on the far side and barely makes the ferry over to the safer passage on the left. Then we watch an out-of-control pinball game of reaction and response the rest of the way. His team nearly flips again when they brush too close to a pillow of water rebounding off a rock, but they manage to stay away from the rest of the danger. Eventually, they arrive safely down-stream. All in all, it was a good run, despite the shaky lead.

We're boat two, now a good position since Ramitch's boat is safe and we've had the benefit of watching their run. We climb into our thigh straps, cinching them tight so we can lean out and dig in with all our might. Van unties the bowline and jumps onto the pontoon in front of me. Catty-corner from me is Edge, and across to my left is Ben, taking the rear position behind him. We breathe in together.

"All back!" I yell. The boat responds quickly and we ease out of the eddy. "Left side back, right side forward!" The raft turns to the left as the current grabs us. "Forward hard!" I yell a final time, hoping to avoid the mistake Ramitch made.

We keep our angle pointed to the left and dig in deep with our blades. Though not quite a thoroughbred springing out of the gate, the boat reacts and we gain on our goal to clear the left side of the massive boulder dividing the current in two. Once there, with the first major hole safely to our right, we dig even harder to punch into a wave train protecting the safer passage. We keep it straight and don't get thrown off course until we glance a smaller rock halfway down. But it only veers us slightly off course. We soon join Ramitch in the eddy at the bottom.

Having learned from his route, our run was cleaner. But this is not a competition against each other or the river. Compete against the river, and eventually all lose. Cooperate, and all can win. The river is not out to get us; it's indifferent. We've come to it and have to accept its terms.

"You don't beat the river," Lewis, played by Burt Reynolds, told his paddling partners in the movie version of James Dickey's *Deliverance*. You accept it for what it is, assess its risks, and then use your skills to make a given plan a reality. That's what river running is all about. It's not testing the river, other paddlers, or other rafts. Only yourself, and in the case of paddle rafts, your crew. When success, or worse, failure, depends on the response, power, and improvisational skills of three other crewmates, additional variables are introduced beyond what's anticipated from the water. Therein lies the greater beauty of team paddling. It's a chess game with countless more outcomes, more profound achievements, and more consequential failures.

"Good run," grins Boris. "You miss hole, unlike us."

Sergei the Small's boat pushes off last. Now in the best position, thanks to watching Ramitch's and our run, they clear the top hole and then zigzag their way downstream. Halfway down, however, the boat somehow gets thrown close to the other holes. They correct and straighten out quickly enough to ride past them on a rooster tail of current to the left. Soon, all three boats are pulled up onshore in the eddy, and we start reloading and tying down the gear. A spiderweb of trucker's hitches secures it, and we're soon underway again. Our first

Siberian Class V disappears behind us.

That night, Boris again breaks out the guitar—but no drinking flag. We don't need it. We all feel good. A light rain is still falling, so we cram underneath a tarp. The fire is ten feet away, too far to throw off any heat, but close enough for psychological comfort. The song he plays tonight, he says, is often played on Latvian radio. The writer is also a river runner and the lyrics portray the Latvians' approach to paddling. Olga translates as Boris's rich baritone echoes off the canyon walls: "You know you've been to the river when you have a broken nose and broken oar," she says. We exchange glances. After today, we know too well we are nearing the lower canyon.

Boris passes the guitar to me after he's finished. His is a tough act to follow, especially with such a captive audience. The song was raucous and entertaining. Plus, he's damn good. I'm not. My F-chord skills are a lot like my tennis backhand and hockey slap shot—I never bothered picking up the fundamentals, but rather just jumped in hoping for results.

By no coincidence, I picked up the guitar about the same time I started rafting. To this day, I play more around a river campfire than anywhere else. I have an Ibanez at home, but it rarely leaves its perch atop the piano. It's too nice to bring on river trips, and I rarely play otherwise. So I bring my beater, which, stuffed inside a dry bag, has parted waves on the bow of a sea kayak in Glacier Bay and has a ski-tip hole in its side from a mishap on a hut skiing trip.

Luckily, what genetics failed to provide me in instrument mastery it made up for with an ability to memorize and ad-lib lyrics. Sometimes, of course, this lands me in trouble. My first river guitar was broken over my head one night on Idaho's Bruneau River due to a drunk paddler fed up with my crooning. Forget about Boris's broken nose and oar—you're not a real man until you've had *that* happen.

On a later trip down the Grand Canyon, tripmates took my guitar from Lees Ferry to Phantom Ranch, where I hiked in to meet them. It didn't have a case, so I strapped one to my pack on the hike down. It was Halloween and, for reasons known only to twenty-four-year-olds, I donned a long, dark-haired wig for the hike. Canyon tourists thought I was escaping civilization to find musical inspiration in the canyon, little knowing I was wearing a wig and carrying only an empty case. Camp was just upstream of Phantom Ranch, where my friends had left me a kayak to paddle to camp. Wig on and guitar case strapped to my back, I kayaked up to a raging beach party, as if I had just come from a Grateful Dead show. While my limited playing ability took its toll on captive listeners, the trip itself took its toll on the guitar. By trip's end, it had fishing line in place of its high E string and a wedge of bark serving as a bridge.

Edge and I debated which one of our guitars to take to Siberia. We knew we'd want one, we reasoned, for the downtime on the Kalar. His won out for both aesthetics and acoustics, but as part of our paring down we stashed it at the bus station in Gorno-Altaisk.

Now the group waits expectantly for me to play. Comfortable with my *sidushka*, if not my song selection, I grab the neck and start strumming, seeing what will come. First it's the Rolling Stones and then The Monkees. The songs don't hold a torch to the Latvians' offerings, but they're adamant about us contributing. Then I butcher "American Pie" without any fear of the lyrical exposure I'd get back home—they can't understand me anyway, so I can fake it. Then I slow things down even more with The Eagles' "Peaceful Easy Feeling." For the first time ever while behind guitar, I feel I can do no wrong.

Thanks to Edge's sheet music, which we're sharing like the Latvians' book pages, I've learned two new songs on the trip so far—The Talking Heads' "Burning Down the House" and Jerry Jeff Walker's "Mr. Bojangles." Even though practicing isn't exactly a group pursuit, I figure you're still providing for the team as long as you play the songs around the campfire.

A better song to learn might have been John Fogerty's "Have You Ever Seen the Rain?" The drizzle stays for three long, cold days, progressively dampening our spirits. More importantly, it causes the river to rise—as evidenced by the trip meteorologist's higher water temperature reports. The water is already higher than when Ramitch was last here, and we all remember Igor's story when he witnessed three people die in the lower canyon because of high water. I consider if their obsession with "American Pie" somehow revolves around the song's final lyric ...

If there are a lot of clouds, at least there's a better chance of silver linings. Today's comes in the form of food, the diversity a welcome break to the monotony of pork fat. Breakfast is beans with fresh onions and mushrooms; lunch is hot fish water, but augmented with fresh bread and jam; and dinner is mutton stew and rice pudding.

On the third day of rain, we pass under a bridge leading to a village, which means food. A few kids try to pelt us with rocks as we paddle under it, but not accustomed to moving targets, they miss us and we pass unharmed. The brush with the perils of civilization is worth it, as Sergei secures nine more loaves of bread.

We proceed slowly deeper into the canyon. The rain, layers of gray darkness between cloud and wall shadows, and dwindling rations are wearing on us. Today is the coldest yet. Fresh snow has blanketed the surrounding peaks, and the morning dawns rainy and unseasonably cold. If misery loves company, it's a good thing there are fourteen of us. We dub the night's camp Camp Glum for our miserableness. It's cold and wet, with no tent sites that don't require a visit to the chiropractor afterward. We turn in early. Even with dismal, wet, rocky sleeping arrangements, morning comes far too soon, and with it the harsh realization that we have to greet another day just like it. The first thing Edge says when he wakes up next to me is "Faachck." It's more a statement than anything else, a simple exclamation grieving the start of another cold, wet, and uncertain day.

Our gear is still wet, but we have no choice but to put it on. After a quick breakfast of dry bread and pork fat at Camp

Glum, I notice that my left knee is swollen from kneeling on the catarafts. I had it orthoscoped after playing four years of college lacrosse. (A friend in the geology department turned the removed cartilage into a necklace pendant, now residing in my river ammo can at home.) Bending it like a pretzel day after day is taking its toll. I savor the extra calories I get from the ibuprofens' sugar coating.

We stop after an hour at the last village before the river careens into the lower canyon. There, we barter for three packages of reindeer meat, which Van and Ben make into spaghetti sauce that night. More than beard growth or the nicks and bruises gaining on our skin's uninjured areas, cook detail has become our only real barometer of time. Edge and I have been on it twice so far, meaning we've been on the river for at least fourteen days. Apart from estimating strokes required, counting in Russian Roshambo, and triangulating your way through rapids, cooking duty turns are one of the only uses for mathematics on the trip. We practice the basics—counting to fourteen three times each day—dividing up breakfast, lunch, and dinner.

The next day, we see another group on the river, our first since the *ploht* group departed. They backpacked into the upper Bashkaus and plan to hike over to the lower Chulishman at an upcoming drainage rather than brave the lower canyon. If rafting has a sister sport in Siberia, it's backpacking. The two go hand in hand here, with rafting as reliant on backpacking as surfing is on swimming.

Tonight is Sergei the Small's birthday. Ben uses the Dutch oven to bake him his first birthday cake in his thirty-two years. Compliments of Valeri the forager, it comes with fresh currant icing. Then Ramitch raises the drinking flag. Though its artwork is a tough act to follow, as celebration cohosts we create our own as well, marking a pair of Van's white boxer shorts with the name of our raft, *Team Cowboyshka*. For an emblem, we draw a cowboy hat above a pair of crossed oars.

Soon, it's hanging high in the trees next to the Latvian's

libation flag. But it's not our artwork that gets their attention. It's the bottle of duty-free tequila Ben breaks out. I also play my trump card for the party: a six-pack of dehydrated beer. Just add iodized water from the Bashkaus.

"Hah, it is beer," Boris says, grinning and gulping. His comrades watch him as the foam sticks to his beard. He wipes it off with the back of his hand, licks it, nods, and smacks his lips. The others follow suit. There's no booze in it—that would be a miracle of science—just the taste. But it doesn't matter. There's plenty being poured into fourteen equitable cups by Ramitch. He uses an old stump as a table. I'm thankful no one felled the tree just for this purpose, but I wouldn't put it past them.

Sergei, thirty-two, is a professional dancer by trade. Wearing a blue-and-white horizontally striped shirt beneath a ratty-looking orange and teal nylon jacket with torn sleeves, he stands up and sings a song about his mother wondering when he'll find a girl and settle down. His voice is high, but he hits all his notes behind a sheepish grin. He kicks up his legs and dances around the fire like a leprechaun. My knees hurt just watching him, but I am moved by his agility and natural sweetness. For lack of any better idea, Van and I follow suit with "Camptown Ladies." But no leaps, no dance. The melody holds its own, and no one besides us, Boris, and Olga realizes the "doo-dahs" have no real meaning.

The birthday boy is in hog heaven today—literally. For lunch, five people slipped him extra pieces of pork fat. I had three after Olga's lens cap escapade and my stomach churned like the lower canyon. Sergei wolfs down seven without even batting an intestine, stopping to nibble each rind. When the fourteen pieces of bread are lined up at dinner, his is the only one topped with a sliver of salami capping two sugar cubes. We also have the special dessert of Ben's currant cake.

After Sergei finishes licking the dessert bowl—his prerogative this time around, not a result of the fingers game—Ramitch passes out fourteen shot glasses on one of the spare blades. The simple pieces of metal have now had four uses on the trip—paddle blade, cutting board, Dutch oven lid, and serving tray. Each shot is filled with grain alcohol that makes the vodka taste like water. The only thing toning it down is fresh currant juice leftover from the icing. Ramitch stands up and makes a toast through Olga: "This trip is special," he says. "It is our first time with American river runners and food has been strong."

If the food has been strong on this trip, I'd hate to see when it's weak. But it's the second part of the toast that's more disconcerting.

"We also toast to running the strongest rapid any of us have ever run," he continues through Olga.

It's a gutsy call. First off, these guys have run rivers all over Siberia—a fine pedigree to try and upstage on this trip. Second, Ramitch has been down the Bashkaus before. Does that mean he's planning to run harder rapids than he did then? Or has the rain made the rapids harder? Third, for better or worse, we're stuck at the hip with them. If they run something, chances are, we will also. Either that or hold up the team's progress while they wait to watch us labor through a portage.

The toast is no idle boast. They mean business. Their original plan was all whitewater: they had planned to raft the upper Chulishman and then hike for four days over to the lower Bashkaus, getting the cream of the whitewater crop on each run. But with the American monkey wrench thrown in, and what Olga describes as "not too strong of a crew" this year from Latvia, the plans changed. It's just the Bashkaus—as if that's some consolation. Ramitch and company are serious about running the river's whitewater. They plan to spend another two weeks in the Bashkaus's thirty-kilometer-long lower canyon, averaging just two kilometers a day. The time will be spent scouting, running rapids, and portaging where necessary. On desert runs of the southwest United States, making twenty miles a day is easy. Here, we're planning to make only 5 percent of that—for two weeks straight. Either they're planning to look long and hard at each rapid before running it, the portages are more treacherous than we thought, or the entire canyon is on a scale none of us has ever seen. All three will prove to be true.

Later, after Sergei has retired and the celebration has died down, we ask Boris about Ramitch's toast.

"For us, back home, there is no way to prove yourself," he explains. "Here you can prove yourself by running strong water. I like to prove myself a real man by running the hardest water I can."

None of us on Team Cowboyshka has this real-man complex. We like challenging ourselves, sure, but not proving ourselves to a river. And certainly not when the stakes are our lives, so far away from home. The issue is mortality itself as much as fear.

The next day dawns sedately, partly from the tequila and 180-proof currant libations, and partly from Ramitch's toast and our proximity to the lower canyon. Ironically, during the previous night's merrymaking, my dehydrated beer was the only thing that hydrated us.

The river, however, is having no problem with water loss. In fact, it's looking more hydrated than ever, running more swollen and faster than the day before. Everyone's pensiveness is caused by the rising water level. The last few days' rains have caused the river to rise twenty-one centimeters overnight. And only one river day separates us from the lower canyon. As Igor discovered during his two four-day hikes out, once you enter it, there is no easy way to leave. When Ramitch was here last, the river was three feet lower and he witnessed two deaths while watching it rise. He knows what's ahead.

 invalid 2 2 2

A river's unpredictability is a constant in river running. That's largely what makes paddling whitewater so interesting. The same way weather can't be controlled on a mountain climb, water levels can't be controlled on a river. It can only be measured. If it wants to rise, it will. Conversely, if it feels like showing its shallower side, those on it have to live with that, too. But a flood is far more consequential than an ebb. All you can do is be prepared to anticipate it.

I learned this lesson early, just a few years after I took up kayaking, on a trip down Peru's Tambopata River. The river cuts through some of the most remote rainforest in the world. Once on it, there's no way out but down. Halfway through what was supposed to be a ten-day Class III to IV trip, our trip leader, a Peruvian named Toni Ugarte, went down to check the rafts. If the rafts were moist with condensation, it meant all the water is down low and so it wouldn't rain. But that night, the rafts were bone dry, meaning the moisture was all up in the clouds, waiting to come down in Amazonian sheets.

Sure enough, the downpour started around 10:00 P.M. It wasn't so much as sheets, but Peruvian handwoven blankets. Enough so you couldn't even talk to your tent mate. Enough that creeks began flowing beneath our tents. In the morning, Jaguar Ravine, a side stream across from camp that we hiked up earlier, had become a raging torrent. Another side creek quickly ate away our campsite. We skipped breakfast and swiftly put on the rapidly rising river, keeping our eyes out for a Class IV rapid named Monster lurking somewhere below. We paddled hard all day. Finally, as the jungle's darkness lowered and nightfall took hold again, we pulled over on the only thread of beach butting up against the jungle wall. We took turns on watch duty all night, rotating in shifts to monitor the river's unceasing rise.

The cry came at 4:00 A.M.: "Let's go! Get the tents on the boat! Quick!" Groggy and drenched, we broke camp and bushwhacked with machetes up into the impenetrable jungle. We hauled the rafts up as high as we could, and then yanked some more before running their bowlines high into the surrounding trees and tying them nose up. Then we waited in the drenching rain. One, two, three days, the rain kept falling and the river kept rising. What was once a Class III stretch was now raging jungle-wall-to-jungle-wall Class VI. Huge uprooted trees careened downstream. While sitting on a tied-up raft with a guide named Pepe Lopez, a giant root ball surfaced just five feet away, like a hand rising from the depths to take us away. It would've been suicide to put rafts on the river at this level. Swim—either from missing a roll in your kayak, or, worse, dump-trucking a raft—and that would be the end of it. There would be no safety set up, and no way for rescuers to reach you. You'd be swept alone downstream faster than the approach of the storm that started it all. If you were lucky enough to somehow get to shore somewhere—a big *if*—you'd then be walled in by the densest rain forest in the world. Alone.

After seventy-two hours of bivouacking in the jungle, the river eventually dropped enough for us to continue on. But its high-and-rising-water lesson remains with me.

Now, on the Bashkaus, we decide to lay over where we are to see if the water level will drop, or at least stabilize, before entering the lower canyon. Two groups pass us while we do. One is the group we saw before, paddling two similarly sized catarafts. They plan to hike out at the next drainage instead of running the lower canyon. They look wet, tired, and haggard, but wave as they paddle by. Perhaps they're happy because they know they're leaving.

The second group, consisting of a cataraft and a *ploht*, is headed by Vladimir Vinogradov, at forty-six considered a John Wesley Powell of Russian river running and one of the most experienced *ploht* captains in all of Russia. Three other men ride the *ploht* with him. They're all standing, two on each end facing downstream, commanding the craft's two giant oars. That it takes two full-grown men to handle each oar is testament to the craft's size. The raft is huge and sluggish looking, a Winnebago without brakes or an engine. All it can do is move from side to side to avoid obstacles. But it's big enough that holes that would swallow our catarafts can barely bite onto it. It just plods on through. What it gains in size and momentum, however, it loses in mobility. While we've had to dart this way and that to avoid obstacles, I can't imagine how this unwieldy craft has negotiated the river so far. A lot of it, I guess, has to do with the man calling the shots at the helm.

Vladimir is wearing a faded blue nylon coat beneath a homemade life jacket. Gray wool pants cover his legs. He, too, looks wet. Short compared to the man wrestling the oar next to him, and with a stubby beard complementing the gray of his wool trousers, he flashes us a toothy grin as he passes by our camp. And why shouldn't he? This is his fourth time down the Bashkaus and he's come back to Siberia's hardest with one goal: this time, to run every rapid on the river.

Like us, he is worried about the rising water. Ramitch yells something to him while he's still within earshot.

"What'd he say?" I ask Boris.

"He asked him what he thought of the water," Boris replies.

"What'd he say?"

"That it's high."

Unfortunately, there's only one ten-foot-long campsite at the mouth of the canyon, and it looks like Vladimir has the jump on us for first sleeping rights. We decide together to lay over another day so the camp will be clear. But it also gives us another day to watch the water rise still higher and worry about what's down there.

CHAPTER THiRTEEN

The Lower Canyon

Contributing to the team: illustrating how anything with a heartbeat is a keeper. (Photo by Van Wombwell)

Guarding the canyon like a sentry, a rapid called Unpopulated marks the beginning of the lower gorge. It's an apt name. Not many people in their right mind would pass here. A large waterfall cascades into the river on the left and two large boulders force the river into a narrow slot on the right, barely wider than our catarafts. Then the river just disappears. I've never seen a sharper horizon line. The drop is so abrupt and long that we can't even see the mist rising from below.

A trick to running rapids on a raft is to stand up to get a better view of what lurks downstream. On conventional oar and paddle rafts, you can stand on the raft's floor, or even tubes or frame, to see farther downstream beyond the horizon line. In a kayak, that advantage disappears, but increased maneuverability and the ability to Eskimo roll make up for it. Kneeling on a floorless cataraft affords a slightly better vantage than sitting in a kayak, but not much.

The horizon line is bookended by steep canyon walls. It

141

feels like the walls are closing in on us, blocking all but a sliver of the sky. Downstream, the gorge walls give way to steep scree slopes falling down the mountainsides. Between these are avalanche paths that funnel cracked snowfields from high above down to the canyon floor. The slopes are bare of everything save for Siberian grass still clinging to their snow-ravaged flanks.

We laid over to give Vladimir's *ploht* and the other cataraft group time to get through this entrance rapid. But the cataraft team is still camped at the only available site at the top of the rapid. So after scouting long and carefully, and then lunch—another hearty bowl of hot fish water and pork fat—we decide to push downward first and leapfrog them. The rapid itself looks easier than the Class V we negotiated earlier, but it's more forbidding, flanked by the towering walls of the lower canyon. It's also far more consequential. A flip here doesn't ultimately deliver the swimmers into a nice quiet eddy. The current careens relentlessly toward the next horizon line and potentially lethal drop below.

We scout it for about an hour. By choice, Ramitch's raft goes first without him even playing the fingers game. Perhaps he remembers the rapid from his earlier trip, or otherwise knows something we don't and can show us. Their raft hits the slot and then jogs left, paralleling a diagonal line of boulders placed in a row like bowling pins. The boulders hide sieves, places where the water passes through but not less permeable items such as, say, bodies. Sieves are among the deadliest obstacles to be encountered on a river. I've had paddling acquaintances killed by them. Float into one and you're nothing more than a noodle plastered to a colander. That's why they call them "strainers." Still, these look easy enough to miss if you get through the slot correctly. Ramitch's boat does just that, and he pulls over to wait below the rapid.

Second boat again, we peel out of the eddy and dig hard for the slot, paddling harder than we have all trip. Once there, we spin at the brink to straighten out so we'll fit through. Then we plunge down the giant, narrow ramp into the lower canyon.

If linebackers embrace rookies into the National Football League with a voracious hit, this is the Bashkaus's welcome mat. The hole at the bottom of the slot buries us, only our homemade frame keeping our raft from buckling. Where the earlier Class V had us paddling straight forward to maintain momentum, here, we can not. Once through the hole, we employ a variety of strokes to zigzag our way past the maze of boulders. Faster than I can call for it, Edge throws in a draw stroke at the perfect time to bring our bow around a rock while Ben simultaneously executes a reverse sweep stroke, fanning his paddle blade in a wide C shape across the surface to help turn the boat. Without relying on my commands, everyone intrinsically knows immediately what to do and does it. We're a great team. In a series of tight, well-executed moves, we waterbug our way down and complete the run without mishap.

"Nice line, guys," Edge says in the calmer water below, as we high-five our accomplishment.

"Yeah, nice Lugbill you threw in there," I add, referring to Olympic slalom paddler Jon Lugbill, known for contorting his body into a pretzel when making a difficult stroke. We all made the right moves in the right instant, in perfect coordination, and we know it. Fear activated us, together. At this moment, our commitment to stay with Team Konkas feels right. We breathe hard, satisfied.

Our commendations are short lived, however. Little do we know, we're fast approaching our first taste of Portage Hell.

Almost as soon as we put back on, the next horizon line, marking the entrance to Barricade Rapid, confronts us. We did not anticipate it. We're barely through Unpopulated Rapid when more mist rises from a cataract below. We eddy out above it on the right and see Ramitch's raft. Soon, Sergei's craft pulls up and joins us. It's all we would do today.

"Camp place, carry things," says Ramitch.

We unpack and carry our gear a half mile downstream to camp. Barricade's thunderous roar drowns out our curses as we stumble over the loose boulders.

It's not much of a camp, if it can be called that at all. It's our tightest quarters yet. About thirty feet long and five feet wide, there's barely two feet of width apiece for fourteen sleeping bodies. Worse, it's interspersed with uneven rocks. Worse still, we're sharing it with the six members of the first *ploht* team we met, the ones hiking out at the next major drainage. Even though they're taking the easy way out—at least as far as adrenaline goes—by hiking over to the Chulishman, they still have to get through several more Class Vs, including Barricade, to reach salvation. Vladimir's group is nowhere to be seen. With him at the helm, they must have pushed through quickly and kept going.

Ramitch shows me a boulder ten feet away from my ground pad that tumbled down when he was camped here three years ago. A trail of snapped trees, like broken toothpicks, leads to its former home in the cliffs. Welcome to the lower gorge. If the starvation or rapids don't get you, the rockfall might.

I try to relax by settling into Fyodor Dostoyevsky's *The Brothers Karamazov*, a not-so-easy-to-follow tale about four brothers who become involved in the murder of their father. It's easier to read, at least, than the complicated waters of the Bashkaus. As much as I appreciate Dostoyevsky's work, it does little to settle my nerves. Sentences flow into each other like scattered, random currents, and run on like a piece of driftwood with nowhere else to go. Nothing like a little easy-to-digest Russian literature to take your mind off a Class V drop you hear all night and have to run the next day.

Though the reading does take my mind off the rapid, it doesn't do much about the tree-snapping boulder resting just ten feet away from my head. Buried in shadows, it hunches there like a gargoyle, ready to pounce at any moment. I can almost feel it mocking my insignificance. "I'm only ten feet away," it snickers. "And I have plenty of brothers in the dark still waiting over you, higher up." Unable to concentrate on *The Brothers Karamazov* over thoughts of the rock and the river's roar, I finally fall asleep with the book open on my chest. Thankfully, the river drowns out the nearby snores.

The next morning, Yevgheny is down by the river whit-tling a small, two-foot cataraft out of wood. But it's no toy. He ties a rope with an adjustable toggle knot to one end of the peculiar craft and then heads farther down shore with a coil of rope over his shoulder. He calls it the Little Ship, or *Korablik*, and it's yet another homemade invention, this time a rescue system. He uses it to ferry a rescue rope across the river, much like flying a kite. Putting the boat in the water, he gives it a shove and then feeds out some line. Held fast by the rope, the boat ferries out into the current as if powered by remote control. The result is a taut line extending across the river for rescue, but one that isn't tied off at both ends to create a strainer. Feeding out line and constantly adjusting the boat's angle, Yevgheny positions it at the bottom of Barricade as a final safety net.

It's the most impressive of their inventions that I've seen yet. Better than the boats made from germ-warfare suits, the backpacks from army cots, the tents from parachutes, Valeri's rock-deploying safety device, or even Ramitch's sleeping-pad-life-jacket-flotation. And the innovation goes beyond Yevgheny's Little Ship, offering a rope to a passing swimmer. Attached now to the bottom of each cataraft is a new wooden pole. One end is tied with a long piece of rope to the frame, and the other is attached to a carabiner. If you flip, you can try to crawl up on the overturned raft, grab the pole, and try to clip the carabiner through the rope ferried out by the Little Ship. When it catches, the Little Ship's rope slides through the carabiner until the carabiner snags on the Little Ship. Then the whole contraption—pole, Little Ship, cataraft, and you—pendulums to shore and safety. It's an ingenious system, but one we hopefully won't have to rely upon.

Ramitch gives us an hour to decide if we'll run Barricade or portage. It's a decision for each boat crew and not necessarily the team as a whole. In a kayak, on a less remote run, it would be within my capabilities. On a homemade cataraft miles from civilization, it's another story. There is talk of following the other group, bailing out, and hiking over to the easier Chulishman at the next camp. But that's still several Class V–plus drops away. And these rapids are not one-move wonders. In Barricade, I count eight specific maneuvers needed to get through safely. Three cups of American-style coffee with an extra handful of grounds snuck in by Van do little to settle my nerves.

Neither does the fact that we spend hours contemplating whether or not we're going to run it, letting the cocoon of our stomachs hatch full-grown butterflies. Again, the Latvians' approach to river running reminds me of their political roots. There seems to be no incentive to do things fast or efficiently. For us, time equals money. The more time you waste, the more money you or your company wastes. Not so with their upbringing. While we stew, the Latvians mill about aimlessly smoking cigarettes before we make our decision. After watching the other group nearly flip in the top move, we all wisely decide to portage the entry and put in right below. The games of Russian Roshambo have now gotten far more crucial than they ever were for leftover pork rinds. Ramitch, Sergei, and I throw out fingers. The total is eleven, and I'm standing to Ramitch's left. He starts counting with the rapid and then moves to me before counting around in a circle. By the time he counts eight, I know it's going to land on me. Again, I was caught standing in the wrong place or throwing the wrong finger. We're first.

Still unsure of the myriad choices of poor routes through the holes, sieves, and boulders, I ask Ramitch which way he's going to go. He doesn't need to speak English to explain. "I watch you," he says with simple, universal sign language, pointing to his chest, eyes, and then me in successive order. It's communication at its most basic, and the message comes across loud and clear. Before hiking back up to the boats for our run, I put my *sidushka* around my chest for extra flotation.

Keeping our gear down at camp, we hike back up and

paddle out of the eddy just below the deadly sieve. We make the ferry to the left okay, but then clip a hole with our right pontoon and spin off line. We're now in what Edge refers to as "read it and eat it" mode, paddling by instinct, reacting to whatever happens. It's a life-or-death game of chance, stimulus, and response, and taking things as they come. A wave stalls us and turns us sideways. Van reaches out over the water and digs in with his paddle blade. We react together with a right turn to straighten out.

It's a difficult, adrenaline-filled run, but we make it through still upright and, most importantly, safely. I can't imagine what might have happened had we run the upper portion. Finished with "I watch you," Ramitch's and Sergei's crews carry their boats down and put in even lower than we did. Their runs pass without mishap.

After scouting the next Class V immediately downstream, Ben tells me to throw out an odd number in the next fingers game. We don't want to run first again. It works, and this time first-run fate falls on Sergei the Small. I am glad to watch because the rapid looks absolutely heinous.

We portage our gear again, this time over a minefield of ankle-breaking talus. The fateful fingers say we'll run the top portion second and the bottom rapid third. There is a small pool between them where we hope to regroup. Unfortunately, waning daylight now enters the picture for the second half. Ramitch goes first this time and has a clean run, save for a near flip and surf in the bottom hole. To swim here would be nightmarish. Both rapids compose a half mile of solid Class V, and both are too long to plan, manage, and hold a line. Any run through them would have to be instinctive, relying solely on reaction.

Ramitch's close call psyches out some of us. Van and Ben don't want to run it. Neither do several of the Latvians. The cigarettes come out in droves. The shadows grow longer. They mill around some more. Sergei the Small's crew then decides to give it a go and pushes off into what quickly becomes a predicament of Tolstoyan proportions.

After getting knocked sideways a few times before the main drop, their raft hits the bottom hole without any momentum and surfs out of control for a solid minute. Valeri forces his paddle deep on the downstream side in an attempt to pull the craft out of the hydraulic's clutches. When the upstream tube gets sucked under, poor Plain Sergei gets flushed out and swims.

Actually, swimming has nothing to do with it. He is at the mercy of the current, helplessly carried along as if in an avalanche. He pounds into rocks and gets smothered in hydraulics. We're positioned downstream with throw-ropes but can offer no help. The current is too fast and he is too far away. All the throws either miss him or are just out of arm's reach. His only salvation: Yevgheny's Little Ship, faithfully holding its course farther downstream, above an even more frightful plunge. Like a puppeteer operating a marionette, Yevgheny is in control onshore, continually adjusting the rope's angle so the Little Ship stays in place. Sergei grabs onto the ship's line as a last resort. Lo and behold, it works. When the line grows taught, Sergei pendulums to the safety of the right bank where Yevgheny reaches out a hand and helps him ashore. His crew of three is waiting downstream, having managed to paddle their boat safely to shore without him.

Since it's getting dark and cold, we line the remaining boat down to the gear, using ropes to keep it close to shore. Once everyone is regrouped, we brave three separate death ferries across to a lone, makeshift campsite on river left. It's an adrenaline-pumping climax to an epic day. Everyone is exhausted and depleted. We'll continue piecing together the puzzle in the morning.

Despite the soul-searching swim that nearly drowned him, Sergei doesn't escape cooking duty. And tonight, everyone is as hungry as Boris. Despite the increasing challenges of getting down the river, food continues to occupy our thoughts as much as the rapids. The portions don't. For all we're going through, they remain dismally small, much like our rafts in the lower canyon.

I've been this hungry before. On a twenty-three-day
Outward Bound course during high school, in Colorado's San
Juan Mountains, our patrol had to fast for three days during a
"solo." We were left by ourselves with only a tarp, sleeping bag,
water bottle, and journal. Each day, we had to build a cairn
of rocks at a designated spot and the instructor, if that's what
you call him, would come by at night and knock them over. In
the morning, we'd have to rebuild it. That's how he knew we
were still okay. Rock pile means we're surviving. No rock pile
means he'd better go check. I got through day one okay, but
by day two, it was hard to keep my mind off my stomach. That
afternoon, I found three shriveled raspberries, smaller, even,
than the strawberries Edge and I picked for the team. Instead
of simply eating them, I opted to savor them, dropping them
in my water bottle to make a smoothie. The tactic failed miser-
ably. Our hot fish water had more flavor. Revisiting my journal
from that seventy-two-hour fast (actually eighty by the time
our instructor rounded us all up again) shows drawings of the
perfect cheeseburger and wedges of pizza, as well as descrip-
tions of the ideal Thanksgiving dinner.

I can't decide if that eightieth hour or now is worse. It's
different here on the Bashkaus. We actually have some food.
But back then, at least I knew it was a finite arrangement. And I
had no life-or-death decisions to make, no responsibilities, and
no effort to put out. I simply busied myself counting the tiny
squares stitched into my tarp. My journal noted 1,800 of them.

Here, there is no instructor checking in on us, and no
guarantee it will end anytime soon. Worse, rather than being
encouraged to stay put to save energy, we're expending it at
an accelerating pace. We have to make progress to get out.
Doing so means expending energy, psychologically and physi-
cally, at an alarming rate. "High psychological tenseness of
the long staying alone in the isolated, deep canyon" is a bland
understatement.

Between pork fat rinds, Van shares his secret of warding
off hunger.

"I just focus on making it to lunch," he says. "Then after that, I focus on dinner. Just take it one meal span at a time."

When Boris hears our conversation, he, too, chimes in.

"We are used to being hungry on our river trips," he says between lone mouthfuls. "Russians get hungry, too."

Then he shares his secret for dealing with it.

"The only way to prevent hunger," he says, "is by being sleepy."

Boris's advice is comforting, but offers little caloric value. Not that we regularly supersize orders back home, but the Latvians are better prepared to handle caloric deprivation. Especially Yevgheny, who laments that he'll never lose weight on this trip if he keeps eating as well as he has. Then he rattles off the occasional smorgasbords we've had of sheep, mushrooms, strawberries, onions, and bread from the villages. We can only exchange glances. We are famished, with none of us having many reserves to begin with.

"I'm staying close to Yevgheny from here on out," Van proclaims. "Better chance for handouts."

Knowing what faces us tomorrow, that's the extent of tonight's celebration for making it through the day. Fueled only by adrenaline, now long depleted, sleep comes easier than food.

Part of our food predicament owes itself to the trip's length. With the portages and rapids—and streamlined packing in case we had to hike to the put-in—it's impossible to carry all the provisions needed for twenty-eight river days. It takes time to scout, line, portage, and run the rapids safely. And if time equals money back home, here, it equals food.

In kayaks and with the right team, the thirty-kilometer-long lower canyon could probably be run in three to four days. It will take us two weeks, more if the water rises. I think about our snail-like two-kilometer-a-day pace in the morning while I sip my two-sugar-cube coffee. While doing so, Vladimir, whom we passed earlier the day before, floats by in his *ploht*. He and the other three oarsmen have looks of stark concentration. Not that it helps. Even with the *ploht*'s large pontoons punching through drops that stopped ours dead, they, too, have trouble. In the same drop where Sergei tested the Little Ship, Vladimir broaches in a narrow slot. But like everything we've seen of Russian river running, he has backup. He immediately grabs a long log pole strapped to the frame for just such a purpose and, with water careening over his tubes, pries the boat free.

After the entertainment, I grab a pole of my own to help provide for the team. I promptly land a three-and-a-half-inch lunker and skewer it through the gills with a stick. When I hold it up next to my face for a picture, it runs from my eyebrows to my chin. Everyone laughs when I bring it back to camp.

"Wait until I cut it into fourteen equitable portions," I answer.

While doing so, half in jest and half to gain my fair share of its appropriated calories, I nick my finger with the knife. It's just a small cut, but adds to a growing list of annoyances. Olga is the de facto trip doctor. Usually, this just means a dousing of iodine and coating whatever cuts we have with an antiseptic glue. But like the side canyons nicked into the lower gorge, our ailments are becoming more and more noticeable the deeper we penetrate into the lower canyon. Everyone has them, as well as assorted bumps and bruises.

So far, mine are relatively trivial. The most painful, perhaps, and one I hate to admit to, is an ingrown toenail on my right foot. It sounds feeble complaining of something so dorky on a Class V canyon in Siberia, but damn it, it hurts! My other injuries are more serious, and I notice both as I pack my gear. My left knee is still swollen from kneeling and carrying hernia-inducing loads over rock-strewn portages. My right thigh smarts from spilling hot water on it the night before at camp. I also have token cuts on both hands, including a pus-filled knuckle wound that simply refuses to heal.

"Good morning, fester-knuckle," Edge says daily. Or worse, "How's your fester-knuckle cluster?"

My only other real noticeable ailments are three rope-burn blisters from letting the rope slip through my hands while lining our raft through the top section of Barricade. Perhaps most odd and troublesome is that my armpit is sore. I'd like to think it's from my lifesaving paddle strokes, but Ben has another explanation.

"I'm getting it, too," he says. "It's probably our lymph glands working overtime, storing up infected white blood cells that have retreated from battling various wounds all over our bodies."

Comforting, I think. They can retreat from their battles, but we can't. We're stuck on the Bashkaus with no way out but down.

Ben's right. When you get a cut, no matter how many visits you make to Dr. Olga, it doesn't stand a chance. Cuts get infected immediately, probably because of the sanitary habits of the booze-for-sheep villagers upstream and the crud they dispose of in the river. Between the iodine tablets we drop into our drinking water, the iodine Olga sloshes onto our nicks and cuts, and the iodine in the salted pork fat, we've never had more iodine in our systems in our lives. I'm waiting for my urine to turn iodine red.

When the Latvians first noticed us dropping the tiny iodine tablets into our water bottles, they thought we were adding drugs. They whispered behind our backs about it. It's another example of preconceived notions and cultural stereo-types. We only found out about their suspicions through Boris halfway through the trip and quickly clarified the issue, much to their relief and the redemption of their impression of Americans. The Latvians, meanwhile, drink straight from the river, and somehow it doesn't seem to faze them.

No matter the form, an iodine overdose seems a small price to pay considering the alternatives. And despite my own ailments and what we've endured so far, I feel I'm surviving pretty well. At least better than that three-and-a-half-inch fish now diced into fourteen portions.

Sugar cubes and quarter-inch fish morsels in our collec-tive systems, we ferry our boats back over to river right to scout,

ponder, play the fingers game, and ultimately run a rapid appropriately named Steepness. Because it's one of the most dangerous drops yet, Edge and I borrow two Latvian life jackets for
extra flotation. I use Ramitch's, complete with its dual sleeping-
pad compartments and air hoses controlling different chambers.

The run goes better than Barricade. After a series of more
backbreaking gear shuttles and close calls in the river, we pull
over to camp at a small side creek on river right. The group
we've been leapfrogging uses the creek as a corridor to hike out,
opting for a four-day slog to the nearest village rather than run
the rest of the lower canyon.

We face something new tonight as well. The Latvians surprise us with a river sauna. While we're accustomed to building
riverside saunas back home, where a small, enclosed shelter traps
warmth from rocks heated in a fire, we're not prepared for the
industrial scope of their project. Its scale oozes Communism.

"Euge, you have to come see the size of the tree these guys
are leveling," Van says, pulling my arm to follow him.

I trail him up a small path just in time to see a fifty-foot
pine tree topple to the ground. It shouldn't come as a surprise.
If these guys can demolish a forest for a simple campsite, it's
no telling what they'll do when they actually build a structure.
Their mantra: "When in doubt, hatchet it out."

While the wood collectors are gathering fuel, others build
a Stonehenge-like pile of rocks into a hollowed-out cave. It's the
opposite of how we do it: We build a fire and then place rocks
around it; they build a pile of rocks and build a fire inside it.
Joining the tree-fellers and rock-stackers are the hut-builders,
who find and strip saplings over each other into three giant
arches making a perfect dome. A huge bench waits inside.

Where we cram eight people into one tiny structure for
efficiency, they put a maximum of four people inside at a time.
Hence the large fire, rock pile, and time frame for the ordeal.
The project takes so long that we end up laying over a day just
so everyone can partake of it.

"Nice infrastructure," Edge sums up when he sees the

completed edifice. "It makes our country strong."

Before I climb in, Yevgheny hands me a fan of branches. Its purpose becomes clear inside. Two tarps create a large, airtight dome that traps heat from the rocks inside. The floor is covered with pine boughs and the fifty-footer they felled has been turned into a series of benches surrounding a pile of rocks in the center. As Yevgheny dabs water onto them and the first blast of steam rises, I flinch. Not from the meteoric rise in temperature, but because something whisks my back. It's Yevgheny, flogging me with his fan of branches. It stings at first, but then actually becomes relaxing.

The steam penetrates deep into our pores, cleansing us of all the train, bus, and truck grime, pork fat grease, and soot from the fires that the Bashkaus hasn't already washed away. When we emerge, we cannonball into the side creek, leaving our skin spine-tingling clean. I feel as refreshed as I've felt since the hot facial towels on Finnair. Adding to our pleasure, a member of Vladimir's group downstream hikes up and invites us down to their camp. But the invitation comes with a caveat: "And bring something to have with tea." They have no problem sharing tea bags, but food is scarce for both parties.

"It sounds like a sneaky way to try and weasel some food out of us," Ben says.

Boris grabs an all-too-familiar bag from one of the kitchen duffels, cementing our suspicions.

"Let's go, guys," he says. "Time to eat fat."

Our pores don't stay clean for long.

CHAPTER FOURTEEN

The Bashkaus Memorials

Contemplating a run down the Key in the heart of the lower canyon.

It's a good thing we ate the extra fat. Our first of several cruxes greets us the next morning and we need all the energy we can get. Soon after putting on, we pass a memorial for a rafter who died exactly where Sergei was dumped. A quarter mile farther is another for a rafter who died on a rapid called the Key, which we face at the end of the day. The memorial is bolted on the sheer cliff walls above the high-water mark ten feet overhead. These reminders of death are ominous and silently affect each of us.

I'm not a stranger to death on the river. As a kayaker, and editor of a magazine about the sport, I've known, been with, and attended funerals of too many people who have died paddling rivers. I read annual accident reports and catch wind of rafting and kayaking deaths throughout the United States. Up to now, thankfully, they haven't involved anyone really close (a fact that would change within a few years of my return home). Friends of friends, primarily, but still close enough to make me realize that the sport, like many others, can be lethal at its highest levels. A climbing fall doesn't jeopardize your airway. Make a mistake, or simply suffer a weird twist of fate, in white-water and your lungs' livelihood pay the price.

My first close-hand experience came my first year guiding in Alaska, when I was nineteen. In the middle of recounting some tip-encouraging, Alaskan bear story to a boatful of passengers, we came around a corner to find a woman waving frantically onshore. I pulled on the oars to catch an eddy behind a rock and jumped out into thigh-deep water to see what was wrong.

"He's gone!" she cried. "He disappeared!"

They had been canoeing and their boat capsized after hitting a rock in the quickening waters leading up to a Class III rapid. While the woman swam to shore, her husband simply vanished. I dove into the shoulder-deep water behind the rock that pinned the canoe. The glacial cold of the river meant slim survival time. After searching the area for a half hour and feeling with my hands around the canoe and rock to make sure he wasn't trapped there, we brought the distraught woman onto our raft and rowed her to our take-out, where the police were waiting. The next morning, a story in the Anchorage paper confirmed our fears. His body was found in Cook Inlet, twenty miles downstream.

My next encounter was more personal.

It was in Colombia, on a trip run by an outfitter called Rios y Canoas, exploring rivers for potential commercial use. We were on the Negro, the first of five rivers we were to run, when the accident occurred.

The night before the run, touring Bogotá with a friend who lived there, I saw two dead bodies—one a victim of a hit-and-run and another a transvestite killed by a prostitute. I little imagined the count would rise to three within a twenty-four- hour period. El Niño had dried up a Class III to IV river called La Miel outside of Bogotá, so we were forced into an alternate plan of driving five hours south to run a first descent of the Rio Negro.

It was 4:00 A.M. on the Colombian holiday Diá del Amor y la Amistad (Love and Friendship Day) when we departed Bogotá for the drive south to the river. The outfitter, Javier Gomez Rueda, hadn't seen it but was relying on the scouting report of his friend, Rodrigo, who lived on a palm-oil plantation near Villavicencio and had seen the river on his drives back and forth to Bogotá. There were three of us in kayaks—John Kudrna, a safety kayaker from Montana, Dr. Warren Sattler, from Salt Lake City, and myself—and two paddle rafts, one of which was guided by the company's operations manager, Jorge. The run was a gem, with nonstop Class III to IVs rounding every corner and flowered jungle walls framing countless ribbons of white. We caught eddies filled with bobbing oranges falling straight from trees along the jungle wall. Above the wall towered green mountains as if drawn by Dr. Seuss.

It was a first descent, so we were especially careful around each blind corner, always eddying out and scouting if we couldn't already see to the next safety zone, and pointing our paddles for the route the rafts should take.

Rodrigo told us to keep a lookout for a side waterfall near the cars signaling the take-out. We would see the cars, he explained, and then we should take-out immediately. Lulled perhaps by the countless graceful Class III corners upstream, we came around one and saw the river quicken. This time, the current careened into a series of boulders choking the passage. Rodrigo's raft was already too far along to pull over and disappeared over the horizon line. From the low-to-the-water vantage point of my kayak, I saw his raft flip and then disappear into unknown waters below. With the other raft safely eddied out above, John and I ran a slot on the left to give chase. Paddlers were strewn all over atop midstream rocks and on the opposite shore, and we hurriedly towed them to safety. Below the missed take-out, the river disappeared around another blind corner, and it was no longer Class III to IV.

"Where's Jorge?" asked Rodrigo. Everyone was accounted

for except him. Then someone onshore saw him washed up on some rocks in the middle of the river about 100 yards farther downstream. We gave chase quickly. John got there first, and even from my low perch in the water I could see his shoulders moving up and down in the universal sign of cardiopulmonary resuscitation. By now, we were in a Class V rapid. I joined him as quickly as I could, picking my way through shallow rocks off the narrow, twisting, right-hand channel. Warren arrived about ten minutes later, and the three of us continued CPR for another half hour. Vomit spewed from Jorge's mouth and still we pressed our mouths to his.

With darkness descending in the already dark jungle, Warren was the first to speak. "Guys," he said, "we have a serious decision to make. Now, I'm a doctor and can pronounce him dead. We did all we could. It's getting dark and we have to get out of here." His words hit home. We were with a dead body, in the middle of a Class V rapid, in the middle of an unknown river, in the middle of Colombia. We didn't want to be here in the middle of the night as well. After a half hour, we really had done all we could. So we tied Jorge's body up where it was, on the rock in the middle of the rapid, looping throw-ropes and straps through his life jacket and around his ankles and then fastening the opposite ends to other rocks. If the river rose overnight, we wanted his body to stay put. We would return in the morning to retrieve him. Silently, in the river's roar, through the fading twilight, we somberly ferried one by one through the rocky rapid back to shore and hiked up through a dark, steep-walled jungle to the rest of the group waiting upstream. I hiked barefoot, as I had given my shoes to one of the other swimmers I rescued.

The humid air thickened with our despondency on the drive to Rodrigo's plantation that evening. Jorge's death weighed heavily on everyone's minds. The sudden rapid had caught all of us by surprise. Because of this, Jorge was dead, leaving behind his wife and two small children. With the help of the local Red Cross unit, we retrieved the body the next morning. The Red Cross arranged to transport him back to his hometown of San Gil, and he was buried the next day. While driving to the Rio Fonce a few days later for a memorial float in Jorge's honor, we learned from the autopsy that he had indeed drowned. He hadn't hit his head against a rock or suffered a heart attack. He drowned—from being pulled sight unseen over a horizon line.

We're now on the much harder water of the Bashkaus on far worse equipment. Instead of being within easy reach of a take-out, as we were on the Negro, we're in the middle of an impenetrable canyon in Siberia. I don't want to become one of the memorials. None of us do.

Still, from everything I've seen of the Russian approach to river running—the stories of disaster, the songs about whitewater athletes who died—river runners here seem to treat death as an inherent part of the sport, much like matadors might in bull fighting. It's not that they take death lightly—they don't. Everyone here who has experienced a death on the river has likely been just as touched by it as I have. But the Lativians carry an almost casual or fatalistic attitude toward it, nonchalantly accepting the possibility as integral to both the sport and their free choice of being here in the first place. Perhaps that's what makes river running so appealing to them. When they come back from a trip like the Bashkaus, the mundane stress of day-to-day living in an uncertain economy in a politically changing city is easier to bear. Yet, we too are here by our own choice. Like them, we too have consented to put our lives at stake on the river for whatever we'll gain from it. Beyond our different backgrounds, we share this in common.

In the afternoon, we reach another abrupt, sharp horizon line signaling the start of the Key. The rapid is so named because it represents the "key" to the lower canyon. Pick your way through the maze of jagged boulders straining the torrent and you open the lock blocking passage to the inner gorge. With memorials lining the walls above and absolute maelstrom in the river, we're about to enter the bowels of the Bashkaus.

Since we can't line the boats through it, we get our first taste of what is involved in portaging our catarafts across a loose scree field. We have as much of a taste for it as we do the pork fat. It takes several sweat-filled trips back and forth to get all the boats and gear down.

White and frothy, and with a gradient that looks like that of an avalanched ski slope, the full force of the river is blocked by the canyon wall. There, it takes a sharp right-hand turn. It is immediately blocked again by five fangs of granite that have toppled into the river from far above. After portaging as far as we can until we're blocked by a cliff, we have no choice but to put back in on the rapid. It's as if we are dropping into Tolkien's Mordor. Dark, forbidding boulders dwarf our rafts. It's a jigsaw puzzle to work through, every bit as hard to figure out as a Rubik's Cube or the prisoner's dilemma. Only there's no right answer—just wrong ones, or those with less dire consequences.

Sergei's crew goes first again and has a rough go in the bottom part of the rapid. Slightly off line, his crew has no choice but to backpaddle hard to get away from a row of jagged, tube-puncturing rocks. Without enough time to turn their boat around and paddle away from the row of rocks, they continue to face it, powerfully paddling against the current to slowly, but surely, back away, with their boat facing the rocks at an angle. Six synchronized strokes later, their raft moves backward just enough to clear the rocks and let them pass on their way.

We fare only slightly better, also clipping the hole that threw them off line on the side. But we have enough momentum that it only stalls us briefly, and we make it through the maze. Eventually, everyone does. We're now clear to proceed ever deeper into the heart of the canyon.

If we're being conservative with our route selection, the conservation ends there. At the day's final rapid, called Grinder, I realize the Latvians' conservation ethics—or lack thereof—have rubbed off on us. As the last one leaving the downstream safety position, I glance down while hiking and see an empty cigarette pack left by Olga. I leave it there. It's not that I'd expend extra calories stooping over to pick it up, but the realization that when you're focused on survival, something like this doesn't really matter. Not many people come here, and the landscape is likely to take care of it through a flood or landslide well before it disturbs anyone's wilderness experience.

"They probably don't even bum out about it if they do see something like that," Edge says, kneeling back on the raft. "It probably never even crosses their minds."

We don't have to worry about anyone's trash at our camp tonight. It's in the middle of a boulder garden, and after an hour straight of moving rocks, we manage to clear out an area barely big enough for fourteen bodies to lie side by side. With bumps and lumps in all the wrong places, it's doubtful anyone has ever camped here before, yet our Latvian friends look accustomed to such accommodations. Yevgheny pounds sticks into cracks in the cliff to serve as pitons for anchoring a tarp against an impending storm. Sergei the Small somehow fluffs a rock as a pillow. I strategically place my sleeping bag as far away as possible from Yevgheny, whose snores put the Bashkaus's roar to shame.

We only made one kilometer today, less than our planned average, but we're dead tired. The scouting, lining, portaging, and paddling are taking their toll. With back-and-forth portages and setting up downstream safety, we walked much farther today than we traveled by raft.

While I rig Van's fishing rod, Ramitch tells us that a few years ago, a group hiked out across the river here, scaling vertical Yosemite-like walls rather than face the rest of the river. I crane my neck and stare at the cliffs, having a hard time discerning their route. I return to the fire just before dark with four fish for the group, my best day yet; they're all dreadfully small, but that's still nearly a third of a fish apiece.

"Way to provide for the team," Edge says.

"And me," Boris adds.

My contribution is nothing compared to Valeri's; he is

emerging as the trip's unsung hero. Not only is he one of the group's strongest paddlers, digging in strokes exactly when needed, but he's active and accurate in rescues, made a spare paddle shaft for Sergei at dinner, was instrumental in the sauna building, and always catches the biggest fish on a homemade rod. We don't get to know him well because of the language barrier, but we all would like to. He is a vital cog in the Team Konkas whitewater wheel.

Later, while whittling down by the river, I watch him cast his line into the water and pull out a fish. While I am simply passing the time creating a pile of shavings that will soon be washed away, he is still contributing to our larger good.

Oftentimes, I find myself whittling for no other purpose than because I can. Apart from the dowels for the frames at the put-in, I never make anything in particular, but rather am just content to shrink something down from its original size. In a way, it's a lot like what the Bashkaus is doing to us. We might have come in with grandiose expectations and bravado, feeling our past experience could get us through anything. Humbled now, we realize how little we mean to the river or canyon. We have been turned into man at his simplest, struggling only to survive.

The Latvians' cigarette smoking is akin to my whittling. While I aimlessly strip a stick away until nothing is left, they smoke their cigarettes down to shadows of their former size for no other reason than because they're there. There's no underlying value to either pastime other than they distract from the anxiety and uncertainty of what lies ahead. They calm the nerves and encourage introspection. We fully appreciate our surroundings and our roles and limitations in it. Turning away from Valeri, I wonder what would happen if I smoked a cigarette while I whittled. It might offer double contentment for the buck. But I might also be so contentedly sidetracked that I put the stick in my lips and shave the cigarette.

When I wake up the next morning, despite our depressing rock-strewn camp, I've never been so content or comfortable.

Somehow, I managed to wedge my ground pad in between a series of rocks to create a perfect cocoon. It's only good for one position, curled on my side, but it's much better than what awaits us.

It's hard to straighten and stand to face the day—especially knowing what it entails. Today, we'll encounter four consecutive Class V to V-plus twisted and rock-strewn drops, most of which will likely have to be portaged in part or full. In other words, it's another day of portage hell. The day's only upside: tonight is Van and Ben's turn to cook dinner, which means larger portions.

We try to get an early start to beat the other group to the lone campsite at the end of the day—if that's what you call another jumbled pile of rocks. While we are scouting, however, the other group storms ahead like Boris and Sergei the Small at mealtime. Russian chess champion Garry Kasparov couldn't have played a better move. After the day's portage fest, we get stuck on a rock ledge fifty feet above Kamikaze rapid, a sieve-filled drop littered with fallen boulders from a huge landslide. Like last night's camp, it's a far cry from the Hilton.

If we're not comfortable tonight, neither are we the next day when we pass four more riverside memorials. One pays tribute to a forty-three-year-old and a twenty-five-year-old who died on the same day, August 10, 1990. Red, blue, and yellow plastic flowers are stuck in the crack between the plaque and cliff wall where the memorial is mounted. Another is for a twenty-seven-year-old who died on August 10, 1977, somewhere between the Key and Kamikaze. His body was found downstream five weeks after he died. His memorial is more ornate and permanent, with metal flowers etched into the plaque. Yesterday's memorial below Steepness was also dated August 10. I look at my watch. Today is August 9. Tomorrow is the date on most of the memorials and tomorrow we face the toughest rapids on the trip. Ever since a bad day on the river a few years ago, the Latvians have always laid over on August 13. With the coincidence of the memorials, I'd vote we take it tomorrow.

The memorials commemorate the victims' lives. Beyond that, they suggest other things, and perhaps even offer a lesson or two. Do they mean the party in question suffered bad luck? Poor planning? Pilot error? A loss of attention or focus? They could also simply reflect bad judgment, a failure to act appropriately, or something as innocuous as a right act being overwhelmed by a larger force of nature. Or perhaps just sheer random and indifferent chance? What are accidents in these circumstances where so much is so far from being certain?

If nothing else, they are a tangible reminder that life is as fragile and impermanent as the small yellow buttercups lining the bank, a reminder of the mortality every being on this planet shares, no matter the culture, religion, nationality, or political structure. They're also a reminder that here, the potential for death is always beneath the surface, just a small pontoon and breath of air away.

As I ponder the memorials' implications, the bigger question lurking in the back of my mind moves front and center: are we brave souls or fools for being here, or somewhere in between?

The next day, August 10, the date of death on four of the markers, gives new meaning to the term Memorial Day. We're on the river only a half hour before we consolidate everything into four gargantuan portage loads. Finally wising up, we keep our hiking boots handy, swapping them with our more slippery wet-suit booties. We lug our gear in one backbreaking trip a mile downstream to another makeshift camp. It's another day where we spend more time walking than paddling. And the portages aren't just a stroll in Gorky Park. One traverse takes us on a ledge over a boiling maelstrom, and our overloaded packs turtle our balance riverward. One slip adds you to the August 10 memorials.

Halfway through the portage, we pause to cool off at the mouth of a cave. Inside is a layer of icy permafrost. The wind coming off of it provides a welcome reprieve from the heat of the portage. Remains from other rafting teams are everywhere. We stumble upon broken frames, bent aluminum, and a pile of tube material, as if we're at a junkyard for catarafts.

"Nice foreshadowing," Edge observes, sweating his way through the portage behind me.

For the third night in a row, we camp in an area just big enough for our tarp. A faint trail leads to an alcove in the cliff, which houses yet another memorial on a rock ledge, complete with a tiny jar of vodka, a stale piece of bread, two slices of salami, and a letter from the victim's mother searching for news of her son. The memorial is the most primitive one yet: a piece of sheet metal in the shape of a paddle blade, with an inscription pecked in with some sort of chisel. Here a simple, lightweight piece of equipment has a fifth use: paddle blade, Dutch oven lid, cutting board, serving tray, and, if things go wrong, memorial plaque. A rusted upside-down can had been wired to its top, the semblance of a head, with triangles of bailing wire protruding out from below as shoulders. The paddle blade plaque has become a torso, and two branch sticks resembling fingers poke out at odd angles from the wires, giving the entire sculpture the look of a scarecrow.

Right now, I'm the one who is scared. The water's roar alone seems to make the memorial vibrate as if alive. Starved as I am, the memorial's food offerings look tempting. Not wanting to tempt karma, I leave the offerings intact. I can only wonder if they'll still be here after Boris pays his respects.

Just above camp, I find a register with entries from other parties who have run the lower canyon. For the most part, it has only seen one or two trips a year. Last year, there were three. Since not everyone files trip reports with the library in Moscow or fills out the register, tracing the river's paddling history is difficult.

Between 1969 and 1981, there were seventeen recorded descents on various portions of the river. The upper section was first run in 1969 in a *ploht* by Vladimir Dvoryashin, followed by Alexey Fomin and another *ploht* team in 1971, which made it down part of the river's lower section. In 1974, Alexander Deminsky and Vladimir Kuznetsov ran the upper and middle sections in an open-decked *baidarka*, with *ploht* captain Alexey Voznyuk offering gear support. One of the leaders on that team was Vladimir Krasnikov, a founder of Russia's popular TVT movement, a Russian acronym for "Whitewater Paddling Skills." That same year, a team under Grigory Geyn ran the upper section down to the lower gorge before hiking out to Ust-Ulagan. The next reported trip didn't occur until 1976, when Sergey Papush led a team to Moskovsky Creek using modified *baidarka*s.

One of the Bashkaus's foremost pioneers, Papush returned with *baidarka*s and catamarans in 1978 in the most heralded attempt on the lower gorge. They made it all the way down Troglodite Rapid before hiking out due to high water. A group led by Victor Semenov returned in 1981, tackling the river with folding, wire-frame inflatable kayaks. A flood forced them to abort their mission as well. In 1988, another group brought a lightweight, alpine-style approach to the expedition; paddling homemade catarafts like us, they pierced the inner gorge to an isolated rapid named Trap before expedition member Alexander Ro drowned. Part of the team hiked out while the rest continued down with another group led by Aleksander Izmaylov.

Thumbing through the journal, my eyes land on a lone English entry. It's by Jib Ellison of the United States. His entry is from his trip here in 1988, the same year Alexander Ro drowned: "The *ploht* made it through Meat Grinder okay, but missed the eddy and ended up on river right sleeping on stones. But it was okay because we had the spirits and the only woman on our side."

Jib was part of the first American team to ever experience Russian-style rafting. In 1987, he and a group of eleven other American guides came to Siberia to join the first ever Soviet-American rafting expedition. He ended up cofounding with Mike Grant an organization called Project RAFT—Russians and Americans for Teamwork.

As the first group of Westerners to be granted such permission, they came at the invitation of Mikhail "Misha" Yurevich

Kolchevnikov, a Russian rafting pioneer with a long list of Siberian first descents. He took them to the Katun River, opening the Americans' eyes to a completely different style of river running.

"We dragged our gear halfway around the world based on a one-line telex," Jib wrote about the expedition. "It said, 'Please remit $1,200 per person for expedition on Katun. Visas will be issued.'" They sent in their money and after days of traveling, they ended up at the foot of Mount Belukha and the headwaters of the Katun high in the Altai Mountains. "It felt like meeting a Martian," he wrote of meeting Misha. "We didn't expect to find anyone in Siberia who had even considered running Class V, much less a rafting pioneer like him. But there he was, disheveled, with thick, cracked glasses, and chewing on a well-worn cigarette. If he was surprised at our rafting knowledge, we were equally surprised at his. We spent most of the time in awe of how different our equipment was, but how our love for the sport was similar."

That universal love fostered an exchange of ideas about equipment and technique. The Cold War barely over, the meeting had a profound impact on both parties. "We built trust, camaraderie and teamwork, not only between ourselves and our Soviet companions, but symbolically between our two nations," wrote California outfitter Bill McGinnis in a story on the exchange in now-defunct *River Runner* magazine. "It was an incredible coming together of our two cultures. They had an amazingly evolved do-it-yourself style of rafting which was ingeniously adapted to their social and geographic circumstances. Armed with little more than daring, resourcefulness and knowledge of hunting and edible plants, they'd carve out a life on an unknown river."

Even more remarkable, he noted, was their acceptance of risk and death—something we have now seen firsthand. Death seemed to be fairly common on their trips," he wrote. "It was accepted as inherent to the sport."

Bill had already tried to raft in the Soviet Union, but was turned away. A year before joining Jib's trip, he tried crossing the Russian border after running rivers in Norway, Sweden, and Poland. But the government wouldn't let his group enter the Union of Soviet Socialist Republics with rafts. With Misha handling the government hurdle, a new world opened up to him and the others through Project RAFT.

Just as on our trip, however, despite a mutual love of rivers, bridging the cultural gap wasn't easy—especially when it came to language barriers. To compensate, the two early groups adopted a neutral language of paddle commands based on sounds from both Russian and English. *Fot* meant "forward" and *zad* meant "backpaddle."

At the time, Misha estimated that more than 50,000 Soviets took to the country's rivers each year, stitching, riveting, and gluing together their own gear. By comparison, Colorado's Arkansas River sees seven times that each year. The Outdoor Industry Association estimates that more than 12 million Americans go rafting annually. Most of this occurs on commercial trips, sustaining an entire industry all but missing in the former Soviet Union.

Misha, an engineer from Barnaul, got his start—and helped launch rafting in Russia—in 1967 on homemade wooden rafts, with life jackets "borrowed" from the Soviet airline Aeroflot. Twelve years later, after authoring several Soviet guidebooks and designing various rubber rafts, he founded the Chuya Rally, an annual river festival on the Chuya River that, at its peak ten years later, would see more than 300 participants.

It was the Chuya Rally that brought Jib and several other Americans back in 1988 after running the Katun. Where the year before they met Misha's circle of river runners, this time they interacted with rafting teams from all over the Soviet Union at a sort of Woodstock on water, featuring everything from sprint and slalom races to discussions on safety and paddling technique.

Their real lessons, however, began after the rally. That's when they learned firsthand what goes into putting together a

Siberian rafting expedition. They joined Misha on a high-water trip on the Katun again, and then another on the Chulishman, both of which were filmed for ABC's *Spirit of Adventure* series. Since the lower Bashkaus was too high that summer, Jib's group ran the first Western descent of the upper Bashkaus. That same year, Project RAFT also formed a "citizen diplomacy" expedition to the Katun, and began a youth exchange that would bring Russians over to the Grand Canyon and Americans to the Katun.

With the word out on Russian river running, that same summer, another group of Westerners, a commercial exploratory organized by California's Sobek Expeditions, scouted the lower Bashkaus by helicopter and became the first group of Westerners to paddle it. Doing so wasn't easy. While Misha couldn't join the expedition, he provided logistical support by lining up the helicopters for the scout and shuttle. He tried to convince them to run the easier Chulishman, even going so far as to divert the helicopter en route to the easier drainage. Only after the trip leader signed a contract stating that any evacuation would be paid for by the Americans did Misha relent and take them to the lower Bashkaus.

The trip consisted of oar-boat guides Charlie Ross and Todd Brownell; three kayakers—John Armstrong, Bob McDougal, and Agi Orsi; three commercial clients who paid $6,000 each; and three Russians who paddled a Soviet-style cataraft. Differences in boating styles surfaced immediately, mostly revolving around equipment. While the Americans brought mounds of gear that had to be portaged around rapids, the Russians went light and compact. Their boat was also easier to carry, showing the cataraft better suited for that particular river. It was river-equipment Darwinism, with the Soviets coming out on top.

"We have too heavy of boats," admits Todd in a film of the expedition entitled *Hard Labor in Siberia* that aired on the Discovery Channel. "The Soviets are shaking their heads on the amount of gear we have." Adds Charlie: "Our raft is the wrong vehicle for this river. The Russians seem to have the right idea of going light and fast. They can portage easier."

Still, even Soviet equipment didn't make the trip easy. They were on the river at the same time that Alexander Ro drowned just upstream of them. This made eight deaths on the river in the twenty-two or so attempts since the lower gorge was first run. Not exactly a stellar average—a death on more than a third of the trips.

The lower canyon's second Western descent occurred later that summer when Jib returned with Misha and five other Russians. Apart from eating only soup, dried bread, and pork fat, he calls it the "most dangerous river I've ever rafted."

We are the third group of Westerners to run the lower canyon, and the first to ever link it with the upper section. We are also the first Westerners to paddle it self-contained in our own Russian-style cataraft.

As on our trip, Jib's experiences here fostered a deep feeling of comradeship—so much so that in 1989, Misha took his Chuya Rally international. The event hosted rafters from thirteen countries competing in slalom and downriver races, and even safety exercises. The event was so successful, it later spawned biannual Project RAFT events in North Carolina, Costa Rica, and Turkey. (It was the Project RAFT event in Turkey that waylaid our Russian partner, Andre, who was supposed to meet us in Moscow.)

The sport's more competitive sides were also getting acquainted around this time. With whitewater slalom fighting for an Olympic berth in 1992 for the first time in twenty years, U.S. Canoe and Kayak Team coach Bill Endicott hosted a training camp in the Soviet Union to involve its Republics and help the sport's chances of earning inclusion in the Olympics. In 1988, he flew an all-star cast of paddlers over to Moscow and Soviet Georgia. Included in the group was one boat from each class vying for Olympic inclusion—single kayak for men and women, and single and double canoe for the men. "We wanted to get the Soviet Union back into the fold to help slalom get back into the Olympics," says Bill, who had studied Russian history and language for years. "It was designed as a training camp, but ended up as a sharing of ideas, equipment and technique."

Putting the trip together wasn't easy. Bill had tried for years to breach the Soviet wall with an exchange proposal, but got nowhere. His plan wasn't approved until a friend in the U.S. embassy, Paul Schelp, took it to the top. Luckily, the Soviet dignitary at the head of the reception table was the same C-2 paddler Bill had rescued eighteen years earlier during a 1971 World Cup event. "He recognized me immediately," says Bill, "so things got off to a good start. He sort of owed me one."

The U.S. team's indoctrination into Soviet paddling started much like ours did—obligatory vodka toasts out of goat horns. But once on the water, like the Project RAFT exchange, they found a group of dedicated paddlers making do with what they had. They also found that paddling can supersede political differences. "We hadn't seen their style of paddling for years," says Bill, who coached the U.S. team from 1977 to 1993. "Their equipment was the same as it was in the 1972 Olympics. But it was their attitude that stood out."

Behind the exchange, they found true confirmation that paddlers are paddlers no matter where you are, and that with river running as a common denominator, cultural differences evaporate.

Realizing this, and with the seeds of glasnost emerging and new laws legalizing certain private enterprises, Misha turned his rafting-as-cultural-exchange concept into a business. He founded Altour in 1991, the Soviet Union's first commercial rafting operation, eighty-two years after the first commercial trip down the Grand Canyon in the United States.

If the country had an uphill battle embracing a post-Soviet economy, getting his rafting business up and running was like scaling Mount Everest. Food ration coupons restricted allocations to just 300 grams of noodles per month—not exactly the gourmet fare provided on U.S. trips. And he couldn't just go to a store to augment his rations—stores were often simply empty. There was also the problem of logistics. Shuttle trucks, which he tried to line up with authorities beforehand, sometimes just didn't show up, forcing him to improvise solutions in front of clients. Even chartered flights would be missing in action. And, of course, there were problems with gear. He couldn't go to a store or order from a catalog to get what he needed. For life jackets, he'd make a deal with a factory for material, and then another with someone else to sew them.

This same resourcefulness is evident in Team Konkas, but they're doing it just for themselves, not commercial clients. Misha's entrepreneurial spirit is admirable, but perhaps navigating rivers such as the Bashkaus is better left to teams, not clients.

CHAPTER FiFTEEN

The Dreams

(Clockwise from top left) Ramitch, Boris, Sergei the Tall, and Valeri punching one of countless hydraulics in the lower canyon.

Edge strolls up to Boris and I at the register and pens our entry: "We came to Siberia to run a 'first Western descent' of the Kalar River until we ran into a group of Latvian yahoos in Moscow who convinced us over a bottle of vodka that we should run a 'real' river. So we ended up on the Bashkaus, wishing we had our kayaks, and have been living on pork fat ever since." It's an apt summary.

Boris points out Igor's entry from a few years earlier when he witnessed three of the August 10 memorial deaths on the river. He arrived here on August 8 and camped in the same place for ten days while waiting for the water to drop. As he narrated back in his apartment, eventually, his group managed to hike out to a village on the Chulishman. Then he returned to lead another group out. I try to pick out his escape route and can't. The walls are too steep from here to discern any obvious paths.

Boris then reads us an entry from Vladimir Krasnikov, one of the early Bashkaus pioneers. "Every man who runs the

Bashkaus is like man who walks the tightrope," he says. "One mistake means death." We leave Boris alone to scan other entries. When he returns to camp, he looks sullen. "Let's just say there are a lot more deaths than there are memorials," he says, adding only that a lot of the entries involve flips, swims, and deaths. Ramitch's entry this time will describe how Americans are paddling their own Russian cataraft down the Bashkaus for the first time.

The rapid adjacent to camp is a sheer horror to look at. Dark metamorphic rock has seemingly oozed up from the earthen depths to pinch the full might of the river into a chaotic chasm. It's as if the canyon—its walls polished marble smooth by the relentless force of the river—is so deep that it reaches down to the very core of the earth. Our only saving grace is the knowledge that we're not going to run it. But we still have to figure out how to portage around it and put in on the more manageable waters below. The section we will run is simply the lesser of two evils. And we have to camp right next to it, hearing its guttural roar even in our dreams.

The next day, after a series of portages and paddles around the top rapid, we carry our gear yet again down to another camp. We're like mountain climbers ascending a Himalayan peak by establishing a series of base camps. Only we're establishing them to lose elevation, not gain it. Then we hike back up to the top of yet another Class V, this time with the full intent of running it. Fate is with us this time. The fingers game has us running third. Silently, I'm glad I left the food offering intact at the scarecrow memorial. Perhaps the scarecrow has become my totem and will stay with me throughout the lower canyon.

Ramitch's boat goes first without problem and eddies out on the left. Sergei's crew, however, gets nervous about the first move required. They spend two precious hours talking and scouting before lining their boat down the first drop. Finally, they push off below the first obstacle and make it down to join Ramitch. With verbal communication impossible, we signal to Ramitch on the far bank that we'll stay on the right and hike back down to camp. Aside from us and Olga, everyone else is on the opposite shore, but without any gear. It's eerily reminiscent of Jib's entry in the register.

Ramitch's plan all along was to build a Tyrolean traverse to shuttle the boats and people back across to our side of the river, rather than carrying our rafts all the way down to camp. Through sign language, we help him rig a rope high above the raging cataract. The event is like a classic Russian novel: tedious, complex, and time-consuming, hardly going anywhere. There is a lot of unnecessary milling around as everyone pitches in their two rubles about how to prepare the ropes.

"More like a Tylenol headache than a Tyrolean traverse," Ben says. "Makes me wish I brought along a copy of *War and Peace*."

If Tolstoy's 1,472-page tome about early nineteenth-century aristocrats during the Napoleonic wars takes time to digest, so does the Latvians' way of doing things. While we decide and act upon things quickly—looking at a rapid, deciding if it's runnable, and then either paddling or portaging—they'll mill about smoking cigarettes as if they have all the time in the world. Away from the industrial confines of civilization, perhaps they do. And perhaps they're in no hurry to return. But it's not efficient, and, more importantly, it burns extra calories. Now entering our fourth week on the river, we, meanwhile, are becoming anxious to return home.

"That's not how you make your country strong," Edge sums up.

The milling around, however, doesn't mean they're lazy. Their work ethic rivals that of ants. It's easy to see how the Soviets became the first nation to put a man in space. But now, they're simply trying to get across a river, not the stratosphere. Still, it's not so simple. Ramitch has everyone busy, save for Plain Sergei and Valeri, who absentmindedly kill time by hitting sticks against rocks. Their frustration at the ordeal—and perhaps knowledge that they'll soon have to play Sputnik and trust their lives to a thread spanning a cataract—is obvious.

Worse, there's nothing either can do to contribute to the team.

"Ramitch will definitely hear about this from the boys once they get back home," Olga says, happy to be on our side of the river. "They won't say anything here on the river because he is still the chief."

Thankfully, the tension isn't enough to warrant a revolution like that of the Bolsheviks in 1917. But the 1991 coup is still fresh in everyone's minds. Just two years earlier, rebellion leaders felt Gorbachev's reform program had given too much power to the republics. On August 19, almost two years to the day they stormed Red Square and assumed control of the country—just a day before Gorbachev was to sign a treaty making republics independent, with a common military—the Latvians are trusting their lives to a line spanning the Bashkaus, .

While he was still chief, Gorbachev was placed under house arrest at his *dacha* and was replaced by Soviet Vice President Gennady Yanayev. Demonstrations ensued, loyalites divided like the Bashkaus around a boulder, and the political system became as tangled as Ramitch's ropes. Hopefully, the Tyrolean traverse would have more staying power as the rebellion collapsed in three days. Four months later, all fifteen Soviet republics declared their independence. On December 25, 1991, Gorbachev resigned and the Soviet Union ceased to exist.

We can only hope that no one ceases to exist after trusting their lives to the line spanning the river. Akin, in a way, to the republics joining forces against the hardliners, the cataraft group leapfrogging us stops on river left to help out. But they only add to the quagmire. We can't understand what they're saying, but we don't have to. Their slaps to the forehead display the stress of the situation.

Later, it's a different stress load I'm worrying about. It's Sputnik time. After Ramitch looks over the jerry-rigged rope bridge, Sergei the Tall becomes our trip's version of Yuri Gagarin, in 1961 the first man in space. Only, Sergei is far from weightless. Placing his life on a small thread of rope spanning the Bashkaus, he dangles upside down in an improvised harness and sags the line immediately, dangerously close to the rapid below. Drenched by its spray, he quickly hauls himself hand over hand across the river. Three-quarters of the way across, once he realizes he's almost safe, he pauses and looks down into instant death. Then, he carefully continues to pull himself across the chasm. We applaud his safe landing. Next, they hook up Ramitch and Sergei the Small's rafts to the line and we help haul them across to our side of the river.

With the weight of the frames, the catarafts cause the line to bob even closer to the roiling rapid. The stern of the first one touches the water, placing more torque on the rope. If we lose a boat now, we'd either have to pile everyone onto the two remaining rafts for the rest of the journey; have some of the party hike out and meet us at the Chulishman; or hitchhike onto another group. Or, of course, we could rely on the Latvians' sense of improvisation to figure out something else—like building a completely new raft from scratch.

Luckily, by nightfall all boats and bodies make it across unscathed. But there is no happy ending; that evening is our most miserable yet as we try to glean a campsite out of a landslide. It starts with dinner. By the time everyone ropes over to our side of the river, it's dark. If earlier we were at Camp Glum, tonight it's Camp Ankle Break. The cooking area is littered with shin-high potholes that bruise everyone. A lightning storm and cold rain crowd us together under one tarp with just enough wiggle room between rocks to lie prone. The roar of the river is deafening and further amplified by its echoes rebounding off the canyon walls. Thunder rages in the distance, adding to the roar. Still, both sounds are a far better rumbling to hear than rockfall. The night's sleep is fitful.

A lot of that might have to do with our dreams. With the past day's six memorials still fresh on our minds, and August 10 greeting us as soon as we wake, Van, Ben, and I all dream about someone dying. I dream that Edge drowned while kayaking a creek near Boulder. Ben dreams of a drowning and we're called upon to help find the body. Van dreams that I am lost underwater before finally being found. We share our subconscious nightmares over quiet cups of coffee.

After breakfast, we help the Latvians take down the Tyrolean traverse. The rope is stuck, and Sergei the Small's block-and-tackle system isn't helping. Five of them are pulling on the rope, to no avail. Van tries to explain how a Z-drag system of pulleys will provide a mechanical advantage. He draws a picture on his hand and shows it to Boris. An argument ensues among the Latvians. Sergei is embarrassed and asks Van not to tell Ramitch. Then Ben steps in and sets up the proper rigging. The system works, the rope is pulled free, and Team Cowboyshka earns some renewed respect.

So does *ploht* captain Vladimir Vinogradov, who runs everything we portage. Like Jib's group in 1988, however, they miss the eddy on the right where they'd carried their gear. Stuck on the left, he, too, has to set up a Tyrolean traverse to get back across. We paddle past, knowing they're in for another Russian novel's worth of frustrating rope rigging. Hopefully, it will go better than ours.

Soon, we round a corner to, again, another sharp horizon line. After what we've been through, we deal with it methodically. We eddy out, give it a scout, set up safety, talk (but less now), play the fingers game, and push on. We're not as scared anymore. Rather, we're efficient and businesslike, going about our decisions and tasks just as we would while shopping the grocery aisles back home.

As with navigating any Class V river, the Bashkaus has instilled in us a fresh perspective of fear. Those we face here are different from the more mundane fears we encounter in ordinary life back home. They're not the helplessness you feel from airplane turbulence or riding in a friend's car in a snowstorm. Those are fears from being powerless over your own fate. All you can do is change your state of mind by accepting what you cannot change. You adjust your attitude and rely on destiny to carry you through.

Here, we're not passive. We're acute agents of our fate

and our attitudes toward our fears. Like a snowbound moun-
taineer, we might not have absolute control all the time, but
we can control how and when we act. If our raft gets caught
in a hydraulic, we keep our wits together and wait until an
opportunity arises to act. When it comes—a chance to dig in a
paddle stroke to launch us free—we respond instantly, alleviat-
ing our fears through action. If that doesn't work and we swim,
the cycle starts all over. Ride out the wave train until you can
take a breath, swim to shore, or grab a throw-rope.

In the intensity of those moments, there's no time to be
scared. Adrenaline actually clears our judgment and energizes
our ability to act, to dig ourselves out of a hole, so to speak. In
an odd way, it's analogous to our food situation. When things
are out of our control, we wait, staving off hunger and subsist-
ing on rations until the situation changes. As soon as it does,
whether from a mushroom goldmine near camp or a vodka trade
for part of a sheep, we react instantly to improve the situation.

We accept risks, but not foolish ones, and have learned
to tell the difference. We evaluate a rapid, decide how to best
manage its risk, and then do our best to get through it or
labor around it. If we're too scared to run it, we don't. If we do
run it, we do so knowing that we're the ones at the helm and
have an active hand in its execution. It's only the unforeseen
circumstances—the unpredictable surge that catches you off
guard—that makes things go awry. And you mitigate and
accept those in the scouting process. We'd all be far more
scared if we were simply sitting in someone else's oar raft with
our fate out of our hands.

The river, any river, is not evil, or even deadly, on its own.
Barring a freak flood, like a mountain, it just is. Only when
interacting with it is its potential for harm unleashed. Perhaps
no one knows this better than Vladimir Vinogradov, who is
attempting to run every rapid on the Bashkaus for the first time
ever. For him, the river's potential for harm has increased pro-
portionally. In trying to meet everything the Bashkaus throws
at him, he has ceded some control over his life to it. He's now

playing Russian roulette with the river. But he's not leaving his fate to an unknown and random chamber in a pistol barrel. He's accepting the river on its own terms, but tackling it on his. And he has an active role in the outcome. If he makes it, he won't conquer the river. He will have lived on it successfully.

Despite Ramitch's declaration of wanting "to run our strongest rapid ever," we have no such preconceived notions ourselves. All we want to do is get down alive. As one saying goes, good judgment comes from experience and experience comes from bad judgment. Since bad judgment here could be fatal, we want to rely on our existing experience to get us through, not the experience gained from a poor decision earlier on the Bashkaus. This is not the place to be learning from bad judgment.

We do, however, learn from the river. Each day, we get a better feel for its nuances and moods. We learn how pushy it is, how fast it moves, how sticky its holes are, and how squirrelly a boiling eddy might be. We learn how hard you have to paddle and at what angle to successfully ferry across its currents. And we learn from our mistakes and misjudgments, hopefully minor, and apply that gained knowledge as we progress. We tackle more difficult situations without taking greater risk.

Just as in the fingers game when I don't throw three again if it made us run first the time before, if an eddy accidentally grabs our pontoon, we give the next one a wider berth. But we don't seek hard lessons. What we've learned about the Bashkaus each day, combined with our past experience, has gotten us this far. We're counting on both to carry us the rest of the way.

In one of Ben's early letters, he wrote as his sign-off line, quoting Franklin Delano Roosevelt, "There is nothing to fear but fear itself." We are learning this truth for ourselves on the Bashkaus. The cross-cultural human truism goes far beyond Ben's tongue-in-cheek rhetoric.

I've been scared on a river before. The first time I camped above Crystal Rapid on the Grand Canyon, my butterflies fluttered louder than the river. Putting in for my first Class V kayak run on Alaska's Six Mile Creek brought the butterflies

up to my throat. Dropping into Rapid Number Nine slightly
off line on Africa's Zambezi had me thinking "Oh, shit."
These epiphanies have also surfaced while rock climbing and
skiing couloirs in the backcountry. But they can be managed
and need not arouse panic, or paralysis, or cloud judgment.
All these experiences help to better deal with fear whenever it
next arises. And between Van, Ben, Edge, and I, we've made
it through enough of these types of situations that we're confident in our abilities and craft.

Yet, today is August 10, the Bashkaus Memorial Day.
We're on the edge of our cataraft seats the whole time. Thankfully, we make it through without perishing. The Latvians
historically lay over on the thirteenth, maintaining it's their
bad-luck day. But for us it's neither the tenth nor the thirteenth
that is troublesome. Our bad luck comes on the twelfth.

After breaking camp that morning, we're left with no
choice but to run a rapid called Kamikaze that disappears
around a blind corner. We're nervous about it because we
can't see what's downstream nor can we set up safety. A cliff
blocks us from scouting. It's a river runner's worst fear. There's
nowhere to portage, no way to scout, and no way to set safety.
We're trapped.

We don't play the fingers game. Ramitch, who has been
here before and apparently knows that the rapid doesn't lead
into a deadly sieve, goes first. He ferries hard over to a slot on
the far left. But his relative familiarity with the river doesn't
help him. He makes the slot okay, but the drop is bigger than
he (or we) thought. Just before he slips out of view, his cataraft
rises up toward the canyon walls and spills over backward.
It's the first flip of the trip, with all five occupants—including
Olga, who was riding on top of the gear—now swimming in
unseen waters.

Immediately, we hop in our raft and peel out for the
same slot to give chase. We think we can hit the line better
and punch harder through the hydraulic at the fall's bottom by
keeping the boat straight. Wrong. We, too, are mistaken.

There are guides who have flipped and those who will. I leave the latter and join the former for the first time in my rafting career, here on a homemade cataraft in the middle of Siberia. After hitting the slot, our boat, too, rises up and topples over backward just like Ramitch's, spilling all of us into the Bashkaus's well. With two out of our three boats upside down, nine of our party of fourteen is now swimming in the lower canyon.

Our fears of getting caught in the homemade thigh straps are erased as we're instantly thrown clear of the raft. I manage a quick breath midair before hitting and being pulled under. I pop up a few seconds later, crashing down a wave train with crests as high as the train cars we rode from Moscow. A couple of holes bury me, leaving me gasping for air. Finally, I swim for an eddy behind a row of rocks on the left. On shore stands Sergei the Tall from Ramitch's raft, as well as Van, who washed up fifty yards below.

"You okay?" I ask Van, before he can ask me. We are cold, wet, and shaken. We can't see what happened to Ben and Edge, or any of the other swimmers.

"Yeah," he says, rubbing his knee. "I hit a couple of rocks, but I'll be all right."

We're the only three people on the left bank. We can't communicate with Sergei, but drowned rats don't have to. We're all dumped from the same proverbial boat and stuck on the bank together. He pulls a pack of matches and cigarettes out of the canister stashed in his survival pocket. He offers Van and I each one and we accept. We've got other things to worry about than lung cancer. Soon we have a roaring fire and start to warm up.

"Nice little amenities, those survival canisters," Van says, taking a drag. "I might just have to get one of my own."

While Van and I were thrown clear, Edge, who was on the bow left, came up inside the upside-down frame. Ben, on stern left, emerged next to the raft. Had Yevgheny been manning the Little Ship, theoretically, they could have climbed back aboard the upside-down raft, pulled the pole from its perch along the bottom, reached for the Little Ship's line, clipped it with the pole's carabiners, and then pendulumed to shore. Instead, when they finally reached calmer waters, they climbed back on top and paddled it upside down into an eddy farther down on the right where the rest of Ramitch's crew had ended up.

To get over there, we'll have to swim the river again. Like the cilia on the pork fat rinds, the hair of the dog is hard to swallow. It's psychologically difficult to leave the moment's safety, relative comfort, and warmth of our fire to jump back into the Bashkaus. But it's our only choice. We all smoke, procrastinate, warm up, wait some more, and then slowly put out the fire. We boulder-hop down the bank as far as we can, until another cliff blocks our way. Then we cannonball in. The water is cold, but the current has slackened. I kick my legs and freestyle across the river. Soon, we're all together again on the right bank, where everything else from both boats—food, clothes, sleeping bags, and people—is laid out to dry. Our gear fared better than the Latvians', whose germ-warfare bags were no match for the Bashkaus.

Sergei the Small's team is still upriver. They do not know our fates, and have yet to run. After seeing our flips, Sergei, the captain, is short on confidence, the worst of all situations. But there's no other way for his raft to go. Ferrying across the river, the raft lines up above the slot and shoots in. When they hit the hole, the raft also juts skyward, but then falls forward right side up. By better chance, they've made it, and a few minutes later, join us downstream.

We make camp for the day where we are, having been on the river for about three minutes total. We're behind our two-kilometer-a-day average. Worse, some of our foodstuffs are now ruined.

Though it is completely soaked, the tooth-breaking dry bread is still hard. Boris tries to squish some of it into a mashed potato–like pulp by putting it in a pot and pounding it with a log. It works, but doesn't make the end result any more palatable.

"Not so good still," he says, dipping his finger into the soggy dry-bread pudding.

The sweet bread doesn't fare even that well. Our entire stock has been reduced to bags of goopy glop, the Bashkaus easily penetrating the plastic bags. If there's a bright side, it's that tonight we'll have plenty of food—if you can call it that. There's nothing left to do with it all except eat it. The downside is that there's now even less food for the rest of the way. And dinner is simply soggy sweet-bread soup, the only salvation for the mush. Olga tries to spice it up with moist sugar cubes and formerly dehydrated fruit that has now rehydrated in the bag. But the plan backfires. It somehow tastes worse. No one can finish his bowl, not even the insatiable Boris. Worse still, the provisions Olga sacrifices to try and make it more edible are wasted. I feel bad throwing my bowl away after being so ravenous yesterday, but everyone else does the same. Olga Soup is one more punishment for flipping.

"Makes you want to treat all that hot fish water with a little more respect, doesn't it?" I say.

"I'd give my right eye for an eyeball right now," Ben answers.

In an odd turn of events, Edge even tries the old "Look, is that another group?" trick to get Boris to look away while he puts some of his mush *into* Boris's bowl (usually we're employing the opposite tactic). But Boris catches him.

"Hah!" he says. "Nice trick. You have to eat."

Before giving up completely, we try a few other tricks. Sergei the Small tries to fry his soup, but it just turns into bubbling mush. Van adds some flour and tries to make soggy sweet-bread pancakes.

When he tries to turn it over, it stays on the spatula and, unlike our raft, resists the flip. Fancy name or not, it still tastes like waterlogged bread. The glop coats our teeth and makes us smack our lips. With the reminders of less-than-rigorous oral hygiene everywhere, from gold caps to missing rows, tonight, we're extra diligent scouring off the fried pancake soup sticking like plaque to our teeth.

The next days are filled with more rapids and more varia-
tions of soggy sweet bread. It's our staple meal for two and a
half wet, cold, adrenaline-addled days straight.

The first of these mornings, I play the numbers game
with Ramitch and Sergei. The result: the exact same order as
yesterday's flip fiasco in Kamikaze. We look at each other, all
realizing its implications. Luckily, this time we have plenty of
carbs to power us through the hydraulics: soggy sweet bread in
two thinly veiled disguises—porridge and leftover pancakes.
We start to make the classic big IHOP special, but Sergei the
Small sets us straight: five cakes per pan rather than one big
one. Even the soggy sweet bread is allocated.

With dough lumps knotting in our stomachs, we push
off. We're glad for the calories when our raft gets caught in a
hole after an hour on the river. It's an innocuous-looking reversal, but we clip it with our right tube just enough for it to suck
us back in. The result is another near flip and an uncontrollable
surf that repeatedly spins our boat around. For the rotating
two on the upstream side of each spin, not much can be done
except to hold on and yell for the people on the downstream
side to dig in with their blades. Then the positions rotate, and
the opposite two yell and the former yellers dig deep. We spin
again. And again. Seven times.

When spun to your turn on the downstream side, the
deeper you can plant the blade, the more green water you
can grab to hopefully pull the craft out. But just as the blade
digs in, the boat spins again, yanking those two back on the
upstream side, with water careening over their thighs. It's like
riding a Brahma bull in a rodeo, never knowing which way
you'll get tossed, spun or twisted. And everything happens
so fast, there's no time to devise an escape plan. You can only
react, synchronized, all together.

In conventional rafts, a key to surviving such a ride
is to highside by moving to the higher, downstream side of
the raft—the side climbing the downstream portion of the

hole. This prevents the upstream current from grabbing the upstream tube and flipping the boat. But therein lies an inherent pitfall of Russian catarafts: you can't highside. If we're on the lower, upstream side, to help the other two highside we'd have to jump across the frame spanning the water we're trying to avoid. And even if we wanted to, we couldn't, as our thigh straps hold us down firmly in place.

"Dig! Dig! Dig!" I yell from the upstream side with Van.

Before I finish the third syllable, the boat abruptly spins 180 degrees and Van and I are now downstream in an adrenaline-filled game of topsy-turvy. We stab our paddle blades deep into the river with all our might, hoping to grab the faster current below the foam, while the same yells come from Ben and Edge, who are now on the upstream side. Then we spin again, and again, each time alternating between yelling and paddling.

We could easily flip during any one of the rotations. Eventually, the Bashkaus shows mercy and releases us, exhausted and spent. To swim then, thoroughly tired at the top of a long Class IV, might not have been lethal, but it would have been exhausting, as well as an unnecessary expenditure of calories. We regroup with Ramitch and Sergei at the bottom of the rapid. Finally, we catch our breath.

At the next rapid, I realize the jury is still out on Yevgheny's Little Ship. Though it saved Sergei earlier, this time it nearly clotheslines me off of the raft as we paddle toward shore. It's a great idea, but like the country's new market economy, it still has a ways to go.

Boris explains another Russian safety device that night at camp. As with the pocket, rock, and parachute combination in some of the life jackets, some boats also have their own special built-in pouch holding a rock and a parachute. When the boat flips, the rock falls out and unleashes a nylon awning that fills with water and theoretically pulls the raft out of the hole to safety.

"It worked once," he says, remembering a friend getting

pulled out by the contraption. "But sometimes, it no work so good."

He tells us that on Ramitch's last trip here, he saw a cataraft break in half in the same hole that surfed us. All this on an *unnamed* rapid.

Named or not, a lot that has happened to us has happened to the boat in front of us. After Ramitch flipped, we flipped in the exact same spot. Before we got surfed in the hole that merry-go-rounded us, Sergei's boat took a similar ride.

"We just don't seem to learn," Van says.

"*Nyet,*" Edge replies, on cue.

Though we've all had a few rough days, spirits are remarkably high at camp. Adrenaline leaves a residue of joy at simply being painless, safe, and warm. Ramitch hoists the drinking flag to celebrate Valeri's birthday, and the joking escalates. Since we lost three paddles in yesterday's flips, and the spare blades are now fastened to new shafts to replace them, Ramitch uses the bottom of his guitar as the new, improvised serving tray. After the first round, he stands and makes a toast.

"We will name the American's new boat *Draigan*," he says through Boris, of the cataraft we're piloting. "It's named after a famous philosopher, because, like him, it's always getting stuck in holes." The group laughs at our expense. Still, we're glad we managed to influence such a ceremonious rite.

As usual when drinking, the next ceremonial rite follows shortly when the guitar is turned back over. Once again, Yevgheny is quick to ask us to play "American Pie." I'm not sure what their infatuation with it is, but the request is made every night of merrymaking. I know Van, Ben, and Edge are sick of it.

Thankfully, dessert quickly takes their minds off of my umpteenth rendition of the song. This time, using a broken oar blade he found near camp as a Dutch oven lid, Ben has baked—guess what?—a soggy sweet-bread cake for Valeri's birthday. When he pulls it from the coals, Yevgheny makes a joke.

"There is American pie," he says.

More laughter. But then Ramitch makes the moment even sappier by requesting "The Sound of Silence," getting Boris to translate the words onto paper. I see Van, Ben, and Edge's silent groan; they'd rather have my sounds remain silent. Luckily, things get more lively—and more what you'd expect from a night of vodka drinking—when the Latvians pass the guitar on around.

Between songs, Yevgheny, a child of the Cold War, turns serious and tells Van, "As a child in school, they told us that every day when an American wakes up, he says to himself, 'Today, I must kill Russians.' Is that true?"

"Hell, no," Van replies, laughing.

"Besides," adds Edge, "We can always leave that to your rivers."

Everyone laughs, but Yevgheny's statement underscores the wide gap our countries have nourished between us. Still, like the narrowing river, the gap is shrinking the deeper we head into the canyon and the more we continually rely upon each other for survival. Although our home lives are separated by two continents and an ocean of politics, propaganda, fear, and distrust, we are slowly bonding as brothers on the Bashkaus.

CHAPTER SIXTEEN

The Rapids Continue

Yet another ankle-breaking portage in the lower canyon (note the use of a derriere-covering *sidushka* by Yevgheny in the rear).

It's a good thing we're bonding. The next morning, we face four consecutive Class V rapids as soon as we put on.

"If that's the case," Van says, pouring coffee into the pot as nonchalantly as John Wayne gearing up for another shoot-out, "then we'd better make a pot of some good ol' American joe. Olga be damned."

He's only half joking. In analyzing our previous flip (and buying into superstition), a couple of things went wrong beforehand: I accidentally left my cotton underwear on beneath my pile suit and rain gear (it was my turn to forego the wet-suit); Van only left *one* cigarette behind at one of the memorials; and perhaps most importantly, he didn't have any coffee before we shoved off.

"I'm telling you, that's what did it," Van says. "Never underestimate the power of coffee."

"Strong coffee, strong country," Edge chimes in, on cue.

"And strong cataraft," Ben adds hopefully.

189

During a rare flat section leading up to the day's first rapid, Edge repeats what has become his calling card: "Are you aboard? Are you a team player?" Then he launches into a soliloquy about the difference in team concepts between us and the Latvians.

"Think about it," he says. "Where we brought four cameras, they brought one. Where we brought four journals, they brought one. Where we brought four books each, they brought one that they pass around page by page."

"At least they don't share their underwear," Ben says.

"At least not that we know about," Van adds.

We hit all the rapids and then camp, after a rock-strewn portage, at the only available site, a sandy alcove at the bottom of a rapid called Obstinate. It figures we'd have one of our hardest portages the day after hoisting the Russian drinking flag for a birthday party. Everyone was sluggish in today's rapids, not only because of last night's celebration, but because rations continue to be curtailed. Tired, famished, hungover, and dehydrated is no way to run a Class V.

I try to make up for the lack of food at tonight's dinner. It's more fish-eyeball soup, and I calculatingly plan my pick. By now, everyone has gotten pretty good at sizing up portions. If you get to the lineup early, you have a few extra seconds to pick your bowl before the hordes move in. While deciding, I see Boris go for one bowl and then put it back in favor of another. That's all the data I need. Since he at least touched it, I figure it has to be a good choice. The same tactic holds true when picking out pieces of dry bread. Does the wider girth make up for the broken-off corner? Watch Boris.

We also get good at holding on to the piping-hot aluminum soup bowls, even if they sear our hands. More than one of us has yelped from being too quick on the draw. But once grabbed, like a raccoon with his paw caught in a trap, we don't dare let go. We just don't make those clumsy knock-a-glass-of-milk-off-the-countertop moves as we would in our land of plenty. The stakes (my diary says *steaks*) are too high.

After the eyeballs come the cigarettes. The only night I've seen them smoke this many was the night before running and portaging the Key. Tonight's nervousness stems from debating whether or not to run Obstinate tomorrow and, if so, what line to take. The sand is a welcome mattress compared to the rocks of the past few nights. I fall asleep to the overbearing thunder of tomorrow's rapid.

Their lung impairment turns out to be for naught. After scouting thoroughly the next morning, we all get through Obstinate, wet but fine. A hole buries and drenches us, but only momentarily. We keep the craft straight and emerge well positioned for the rest of the rapid.

Our first portage of the day takes us across bedrock, a welcome change from incessant boulder-hopping. Another welcome change is that I'm starting to develop a rapport with Sergei the Small. Since we're often scouting the easier rapids together and then reporting the lines back to our raft mates, we're starting to catch each other's eye a bit, before and after our respective runs. Despite the language barrier, he is even making a more concerted effort to communicate at camp.

Later, we come upon a rapid called Stubborn. The main rapid is meaty enough that even Edge says it might be worth lining our raft down it. But Ramitch and Sergei each have good runs, so Van, Edge, and I, with Boris subbing in for Ben, who chose to walk around and meet us below, give it a go. We clip an eddy and spin but make it past the crux.

Just after the rapid, leading the pack around a tight corner, Sergei the Small's raft hits an undercut on the right and promptly flips when the river grabs hold of its bottom tube. There's not much you can do when this happens. The high tube climbs the wall and upends before there's any chance of reacting. The scarier part here is that the wall is undercut and it could easily trap a body. Thankfully, everyone remains in the main current. We help gather them up and usher the overturned boat to shore, pushing it with our bow. This rapid isn't named either, but it broke their raft's frame—an indication of what we face every time we confront a rapid *with* a name.

Although in the United States a broken raft frame might pose a problem, here, we hop out, hike into the woods, and chop down a tree for spare parts. Soon, the broken pole is replaced with a fresh one from the forest and we are on our way again.

"Nice parts store," Van says once we're back underway. "Everything you need to fix something grows right on the spot."

"Except it doesn't have any candy bars at the front counter," Ben says.

Soon, the canyon narrows and tightens even more. A series of waterfalls cascades down from dizzying heights on the left. Yesterday, the Ogozo River careened over a hundred-foot cliff into the river. Today, we pass another called Kyzyltak, this one falling in even longer curtains.

We feel as if we're at the bottom of a giant funnel, its tight spout surrounding us down at the river with a broader, expansive rim surrounding us above. At a rapid aptly named Cramped, the entire river pinches into a channel barely wider than our catarafts. We get out and walk around. I glance upward and actually see the upper level of the canyon broadening out, letting in more of the Siberian sky. It's a welcome change from the claustrophobic, vertical confines of the past weeks. Today, we also have our first relatively mellow water in nine days: a Class II to III section without horizon lines that we can just read and run as we go. Paddling is actually fun again. We feel like we've made it and left the worst behind. But it's just a feeling, a momentary high, not grounded in knowledge.

By now, the meager rations have everyone lethargic around camp. Still, Yevgheny pawns off scraps to those who happen to be in the right place at the right time. Usually, it's Boris and Sergei waiting like dogs. Though we miss out on this round of Yevgheny's handouts, we make up for it with dessert. Tonight, it's a surprise. Valeri has found some *oblebiha* berries near camp. You can rub them on your hands to combat dry skin and then eat them. They're sour and different. And most importantly, they're nutrients and calories.

"Kind of like edible Vaseline," Ben remarks.

Valeri also pulls a coup for breakfast: fresh mushrooms with boiled beans. I can tell it's going to be a good day when Yevgheny sits next to me and dishes off his dry bread and left-over beans—like getting through a rapid when the same drop flips someone else, it's a simple case of luck of the draw. I get the handout despite the fact that Edge strategically cleared a seat on the log next to him for Yevgheny.

"You bastard," he says when he sees me with the spoils.

The progressive lack of food relative to the physical hardships we're enduring weighs on everyone. Even Yevgheny's handouts are smaller and fewer. Today's portage is epic, not so much for its difficulty, but for all the little aggravating things that go wrong. Bow and stern lines become unraveled and catch in crevasses. We carry the boats over slippery, wobbly rocks that zero-in on shins. Crossing moss-covered logs makes us wish for ice skates. Edge and even mild-mannered Ben lose it at times with sudden outbursts. Edge slips and hits his knee, has to untangle a rope, and then slips and hits the same knee again. It becomes overwhelming. When the Latvians start conversing away in Russian at the end of the portage, it triggers a psychological breakdown.

"Ooga, ooga, booga, ooga!" Edge shouts back at them in a tantrum.

He's reached his breaking point. We can't blame him. If the conditions are tough, the language barrier is even harder. A few *ooga boogas* is all their words mean to us. Russian is not a romance language where you can second-guess meanings. Ninety-nine percent of the time we simply have no idea what they're saying. The times when they're laughing are worse—we never know if it's at our expense. We're constantly left out of conversations and the whole communication loop. When Boris and Olga aren't around, we end up simply figuring things out for ourselves. Rather than brothers on the Bashkaus, at times, it feels like we're simply ignorable little brothers, at best.

Language barriers have surfaced on other trips I've been on, but never to this degree—and never day in, day out in the stress of life-or-death situations. When the Tambopata flooded in Peru, my Spanish was good enough to listen and understand, and try to communicate. Other times, I've been just as much in the dark, but for shorter time spans and with less severe consequences. While in Prague to watch a World Cup slalom kayak race, my cousin Homer and I paddled the course naked (we didn't have any shorts) at night with Czech security guards yelling from the banks. We couldn't understand a word they were saying, but we got the gist. Another time, at the end of a four-day canoe trip down Japan's Omono River, I almost paddled out into the strong currents of the Sea of Japan because I didn't understand directions to get out at a fish camp on the left. I've paddled in Spain, Africa, Fiji, Bali, and, perhaps most linguistically challenging of all, Australia ("Fancy a coupla' tinnies of the amber fluid there, mate?"), all of which required reading inflections in pitch and voice as much as reading the water. But it was nothing like this, where decisions are crucial and, absent context, you have no idea what's being said. Edge's *ooga-booga* breakdown said it well for all of us.

Sign language, at least, is universal. When Ramitch, Sergei, and I play the fingers game to run the next Class V, we all three throw fists, which count for zero. Though we're fully prepared to run the rapid, Ramitch sees it as an omen. He looks at Sergei and I and wiggles two fingers upside down in the air. We'll walk. It's another portage. This simple twist of fate, all of us throwing zeros, could have saved our lives. Not really wanting to run the rapid anyway, we carry the boats and gear around. The almighty fingers have spoken.

Ramitch's physical communication tonight at camp is just as easy to understand: he raises the drinking flag for a toast.

"Even though we have only one more day in the lower canyon," Olga translates, "we are not out. We still have to be careful. Sergei's flip yesterday could have been far worse than just a broken frame. We have been lucky."

As if on cue, Sergei the Tall breaks out a ziplock bag of sugar cubes and passes them out to help everyone be more alert tomorrow.

The toasts then turn to being "real men" on the river. As with Boris's earlier comment about wanting to "prove" himself by running strong water, they seem to have a thing about it, a desire to show that they can survive in the outdoors.

"We are real men on the Bashkaus," Ramitch continues through Olga.

It sounds funny coming from Olga, but he means what he says. For them, running difficult whitewater is a way of proving themselves. Back home, they have little else in life to stimulate them. We, meanwhile, are constantly overstimulated. In a socialist society, if you work hard and do a good job at something, there is little reward. In a capitalist society, if we do a good job, we'll likely see a reward. On the river, however, they can do a good job and get rewarded instantly.

When we ask Olga about Ramitch's "real men" comment, she tries her best to explain.

"Our boys are not satisfied," she says. "They need strong water to be men."

The Bashkaus certainly is a good testing ground. When something goes wrong, like Sergei's flip, the cigarettes go in, the axes come out, the trees go down, and the situation gets remedied. Most men in the United States would simply get up from the couch, call a repairman, and go back to the ball game.

"Still, I don't know too many real men who suck sugar cubes," Ben says under his breath.

The ramblings aren't all talk. With their cigarettes and chiseled features, any one of them could easily star in a Marlboro commercial. While we feel soft, they're hard—from home lives as well as their lives in the canyon. To them, real men survive at all costs. Thankfully, they've proven remarkably good at it here on the Bashkaus. Like our namesake cowboyshkas, they also seem impervious to discomfort. Not that we can understand them, but they rarely complain or whine. Apart from Valeri and Sergei pounding rocks with sticks during the Tyrolean headache, there have been no tantrums, sulking, or other signs of discontent.

Their quest to become "real men" seems not to be based on machismo, but on a recognition of the fact that on a river such as this, we all share a common ancestral denominator: we're all simply trying to survive, learning that we can, and getting better at it daily. Our time on the raft reaffirms our very existence as humans. We're fully aware that we have the capacity to control our destiny. Every paddle stroke that steers us from danger strengthens this recognition. We're not drift-wood, but active in our fate. If we're heading toward a rock, we paddle to change our course. We're using equipment of our own making to tackle life's challenges.

True freedom is being aware of this ability to act. I think of "Me and Bobby McGee," a song I belted out for them around the fire. Nothing left to lose also means everything to gain. We all have our lives to lose, but the Latvians perhaps have a greater need to be here than we do. With less freedom over their own fate, they have less to lose. Conversely, we have less to gain from being here. Unlike Olga's comment about her "boys," we *are* satisfied with our normal existence. We don't feel we "need strong water to be men." While this trip has made us appreciate our own freedom, we don't need to prove anything here to anyone, not even ourselves.

Only, we do want to prove our worth to the Latvians, to show that we have the mental and physical fortitude to belong side by side with them in the canyon. And we're fast learning that this is far easier to achieve when you work as a team.

Like Indian tribes coordinating a buffalo jump, to survive here, we have to place trust in both ourselves and our compan-ions. While we arrived as individualized Americans, we've now become a communal family whose bond is based on respect, dignity, and reliability. The trust we now place in each other has been earned every stroke of the way.

Working together toward a common goal is imperative to the survival of most species. For us, this goal is getting down the river safely. Our rafts help us with this. The beauty of paddle rafting is that the whole is greater than the sum of the parts, and everyone has a say in their craft's fate. Emerging safely after a rapid is far more important than any personal accomplishment en route. One hero can't always raise the performance level of the entire raft. A brilliant, course-saving rudder stroke does little good if the next wave knocks us over.

Just as each raft comprises a team, all three rafts work together to make up an even bigger team. We share a mutual responsibility for safety, share opinions about routes, and share camp chores for the common good. We all contribute equally to the expedition's success.

Because of their upbringing in a system that better develops a sense of sharing and group-centeredness, the Latvians seem more socialized to this sense of community. We noticed it first when they loaded the train back in Moscow, and we see it each day on the river. They know how to work together without individualized competition, which is a harder concept for us to grasp. We're more individualized, self-centered, and competitive. It might not be coincidence that four-person catarafts were invented in Communist Russia and one-person oar rigs in the United States.

Here, deep in the canyon, we're relearning something we've intrinsically known all along but have somehow forgotten. Synergies arise in working together. Like throwing a draw stroke right when it's needed or hitting a swimmer with a throw-rope, the team experience is natural and reflexive for the Latvians. And it's become so for us.

CHAPTER SEVENTEEN

Perestroika

Sergei the Small (right) and Andrew threading an unnamed slot toward the end of the lower canyon (note the paddle shaft's Ensolite foam for flotation).

Due to rain or a landslide upstream, the next morning the river has turned a deep brown from the previous day's green. Because of our position at the bottom of a scree field, I'd like to think it's from rain. But the skies are Siberian blue. Time for some coffee and Class V.

If the previous portages were real-man material, today's is Herculean. After an hour on the water, the river calms abruptly. It becomes a lake. Still in the heart of the canyon, the tranquility feels eerily out of place. So do the dead trees sticking out of the water with ghostlike driftwood caught in their branches. Rounding a corner, we see why. A giant landslide has careened down a side canyon on the right, completely blocking the river. The scale is stupefying, like a wheelbarrow full of gravel poured in front of a garden hose.

We have to crane our necks skyward to see where it came from. After the landslide, a wall of boulders backed up the river for miles. The water has now gnawed a new way through on the left. The result is Perestroika, the worst rapid we've seen yet. So seemingly near to being out of the canyon, we are still so very far. Maybe farther than ever.

The landslide and its political namesake occurred at about the same time. Perestroika is the Russian word for the economic reforms introduced by Mikhail Gorbachev in 1987. Its literal meaning, "restructuring," is as apt for the abrupt change in the river caused by the landslide as it is for the restructuring of the Soviet economy.

Unlike the water, which eventually found its way through, the political perestroika hasn't been as successful; the country's economy has yet to resume its course. One reform enabled state enterprises to determine output levels based on demand (like Yevgheny's food handouts, they could dispose of oversupply however they wanted). Others allowed private ownership of businesses, permitted the government to trade, and even let foreigners invest in the Soviet Union. Though the walls of Communism were slowly crumbling, however, the basic tenets of Stalinism still remained, including price controls, money inconvertibility, and a government monopoly on production. By 1990, the economic chaos was as unmanageable as the maelstrom below our current horizon line, and there was no Yevgheny manning the Little Ship for rescue. It's no wonder Konkas relished the chance to escape into the wilderness. The unknowns of Mother Nature were far preferable to the whims of the mother country. At least here, the only inflation to worry about is that of the rafts.

Still, if their lives are out of their control from Gorbachev's economic reforms, they'll be even more so if we decide to run the namesake rapid. Some blame Gorbachev for being out of touch with the people when instigating his reforms. We're all perfectly in touch with our decision now: our hardest portage yet.

"I think perestroika is the real revolution, only without fire," Yevgheny says as we paddle toward shore. "We're happy we've finished the period of Communism, but now, our life is very hard, like this rapid. There are no jobs and no money. I don't understand it. Our land is very rich. But foreign people in other places live better than we do. Why do they live better when our land is very rich?"

The rapid and new economy are about the same age. The landslide occurred just eight years earlier, a sign of the canyon's geologic youth. Ramitch's near miss with the rockfall earlier is another reminder. But unlike the new economy, the river is already flowing strong again.

Four previous rapids were drowned by the backed-up lake. The good news, if there is any, is that after the river finally carved its way through, there's now only one rapid instead of four. The bad news is that it's the longest and worst yet. All we can see is mist rising from below a stomach-churning horizon line.

There is no question about portaging. Unfortunately, this requires several mile-long round-trips over steep, unstable rockfall. The loads are heavy, the sun hot, and the footing precarious. Like walking across a hill of jacks, it takes every bit of effort not to stumble and bring down a pile of rocks with you.

We're now more accustomed to walking on the uneven terrain. Where earlier we were timid about trusting rocks with all our weight, now we just step on them, prepared to go with the fall should a rock give way. We've also grown adept at finding our route back and forth, recognizing certain footstep progressions across the scree. Your body memorizes them while carrying loaded backpacks so it's easier when you return carrying the raft, with leg-level tubes that often block your view.

Sergei the Small runs ahead and rigs a hand-rope to help with the traverse. Sagging uselessly whenever weighted, it's more of a placebo than anything else. I doubt it would do much good if anyone really slipped and fell. The hardest part is always carrying the frame, which must be carried horizontally while walking at the angle of the steep slope. It's a constant struggle to keep its uphill end off the ground. Two people tackle it, one in front and one behind, with relief carriers always close at hand—like an outrigger canoe race where paddlers switch off with other team members treading water. Manning the unenviable front position results in getting pushed onto a minefield of greased bowling balls. Taking the rear spot means getting pulled blindly along.

No one complains. It beats the alternative. The main drop is a fifteen-foot-high river-wide pourover. It has been run only once, by a group in a *bublik*, the donut-shaped raft that stands on end. One man was killed and his memorial is tacked to a tree at the end of the portage.

The rapid killed one of the few people who've run it. The portage nearly does the same to us. Yevgheny, who has been complaining of chest pains ever since the flip on the undercut, looks more fatigued than usual. If it's a heart attack, heaven forbid, he'd have to lay off the salt, pork fat, sugar cubes, vodka, and cigarettes. More likely, it's a cracked rib from the flip, exacerbated here by the hard breathing and heavy loads. He's obviously in great pain. Ben, using his wilderness first-aid training, looks him over.

"I think it's just his rib," he says after finishing his examination. "Besides, if he survived that portage, his heart's fine."

We see the tree with the memorial. It's dated 1991. Boris translates the writing.

"It was put here by the brother, Vladimir Chenebanov, of the man who died," he says. "He calls the rapid Heart of Vladimir, because of his sadness."

It's another Vladimir who now has his heart set on the rapid. Vladimir Vinogradov, the resolute *ploht* river runner we passed earlier, has portaged this monstrosity with his own monstrosity all three times he's been down the canyon. While he's still upstream of us, I can only wonder how he'll keep his vow once he sees the rapid at this flow.

It takes us most of the day to finish the portage. When we finally shuttle everything down below the rapid to the tree with the memorial, we're absolutely exhausted. But we can't stay. We must reassemble the boats and rerig the gear. Dead on our feet, and now dead on our knees, we nonetheless have to put back in on the rapid's tail waters. It's still formidable water, so bad that Ramitch flips again after broaching on a mid-current rock. And it was he who toasted everyone to stay attentive. We give chase and help corral the overturned raft to shore. Yet we can't linger here, either. Once more, we all put back on the river, and keep our eyes peeled downstream—especially Sergei, who gives subsequent corners a wide berth to avoid his earlier misfortune.

By now, it's late afternoon and the canyon's shadows reach high up the surrounding cliffs. By 5:00 P.M. Ramitch Time, we pass the Chebdar River tumbling out of a canyon on the left. The tributary's clear waters are instantly absorbed by the ever-growing Bashkaus. As the river grows, so does the breadth of the landscape. The canyon is opening up now for the first time in more than two weeks. We can finally see the sky. We're exhausted and famished. Yevgheny is affected the most by the day's hardships. He doesn't give away his customary food handouts at camp. "That portage was harder than anything else on this trip," he whispers while getting a back rub from Valeri. Edge asks Boris what he thought of the day's portage. The answer shouldn't have been surprising.

"Porridge?" he asks. "What porridge? Where?"

CHAPTER EIGHTEEN

Heading Home

(Left to right) Van, Andrew, Sergei the Tall, and Ramitch ending the suffer-fest with a smoke on Lake Teletskoe.

Two more days of this and at last we're delivered out of the canyon. After nearly a month, we join the Chulishman, floating into a broad, glaciated valley that offers the most expansive view we've seen in more than three weeks. Save for Yevgheny's ribs, no body part is more thankful than our knees, which have been bent like wishbones daily. When we pull over at a small village, Edge hops off the raft into knee-deep water but sinks in up to his shoulders. He doesn't realize that both legs have kneeled themselves to sleep and can't support his weight.

Though there are no roads to the village, two men race around the dirt streets on motorcycles with sidecars. Another whips by in a three-wheeled ATV. The vehicles were likely airlifted in during the Soviet days.

We send our best beggars, Sergei the Small and his main food rival, Boris, into the village for food while we pile onto two rafts and paddle down to set up camp at the confluence. They don't disappoint. A few hours later, they paddle down with ten loaves of bread and two goat quarters, which the villagers butchered while they waited. It cost us a half liter of booze and a throw-rope. Only here, I think, would you trade rope for a goat. So far, we've bartered away five of our twelve liters of booze for meat, and one for the last shuttle ride to the put-in. The rest has gone the way of the drinking flag.

It continues that way tonight. Safely out of the lower canyon and camping in a broad, flat meadow, the flattest sleeping area we've seen in weeks, Ramitch's first toast is to "surviving the Bashkaus." It draws a round of loud cheers. Looking back upstream, the accomplishment begins to sink in. The entire valley is flat with grassy fields, pierced only by a dark cleft in the mountains housing the Bashkaus. With its remoteness and rapids, it's not a river for play or conquest. It's a river you simply try to survive.

"It's amazing how you get spit out of the canyon," Ben says, sitting next to me by the fire. "Last night's camp was on a tight, boulder-choked hillside next to a roaring Class V rapid, and now we're here." He waves his hand across a wide open, serene, almost exotic-looking landscape.

Our reverie is interrupted by a toast from Yevgheny, this one to Sergei the Small because it's the first time he's done a trip with Team Konkas. Yevgheny was on Sergei's boat the entire time—except, of course, when it flipped. The toast is impassioned. He ends it by walking over and kissing Sergei on the lips. Not exactly real-man material, but it touches all of us.

Sergei follows with a toast to Ben for being such a good cook. Ben beams. Indeed, Ben stole the culinary show throughout the trip by baking birthday cakes, Dutch oven cinnamon rolls, and other fare the Latvians had never experienced before on a river trip. Sergei gives him his homemade paddle as thanks. Ben counters with a toast to Sergei and gives him his wet-suit. Ramitch then gives a toast to me as a third guide, having always to scout with him and lose so often at the fingers game. He then presents his own cherished homemade paddle, a personalized Team Konkas emblem inlayed with his name.

The toasts continue. We find it was a hard trip for them, too.

"You Americans are just like our boys," Olga compliments. She explains that when a German group joined them for part of the Kitoy last year, they didn't eat their pork fat. But the trip was so short, they probably didn't have to.

"You eat too much!" Sergei chimes in, drawing more laughter.

Everyone eats too much that night at the party. It's a true feast. We put down in one night what we'd normally eat in three days. It starts with coffee, full strength, and, yes, even hot chocolate; then bread, compliments of Sergei and Boris, with salami; then vegetables, beans, and rice (a whole bowl!); a scrumptious two-layer chocolate cake baked by Ben; glazed goat ribs cooked Argentine-style by Van over the fire (which cause Yevgheny to groan in pleasure); chocolate; pork fat and bread; and coffee again, followed by tea. And all of this is capped with two sugar cubes. Combined with Ramitch's continual pouring of shots, the feast and merriment lasts until the wee hours.

I find out from the trip meteorologist the next morning that we didn't go to sleep until 4:30 A.M. It had been a very long day.

"And that's Ramitch Time," Ben adds.

It feels like it. Luckily, Van returns an earlier favor by bringing a cup of coffee to my tent before I crawl out and face the day. It's 9:00 A.M. and we have more calories to burn.

We're not quite finished. We lay over for two more nights at this confluence camp. While Van opts to stay and fish, Edge, Ben, and I get conned into joining Ramitch and some of the other Latvians on a two-day Siberian march to a "must-see" waterfall on the Chulcha River, which dumps into the Chulishman upstream. The section below the falls is also one of the Altai Bars, all of it Class V to VI.

The hike is thirty-six miles round-trip over rough terrain, a gruel considering we've been kneeling in a freezer for more than three weeks. During the sales pitch—"It is very beautiful, you come with us"—we are told we will have two days and nights for the journey. So we pack and carry accordingly. But shortly into what we coin the Gulag March, Ramitch changes his mind and says we have to be back tomorrow to float to Lake Teletskoe to reach the steamship in time. Calorically deprived already—one night's feast does not make up for a three-week deficit—we now have to hike thirty-six miles in less than twenty-four hours, straight off the cataraft couch.

"Look on the bright side," Ben says once the news is broken. "At least we can eat two days' worth of food in one day."

"Two days' worth of pork fat," I answer.

"And get two days' worth of blisters," Edge adds.

The food is the only consolation I can find as I force my withered legs to take step after step through the broad valley. What real man would turn back in less than eighteen miles?

At least we have it better than those forced to march to the real Gulag. *Gulag* is an acronym that, translated, means "main camp administration." While our bodies feel as if we've been doing heavy labor for the past three weeks, especially now that we're on Ramitch's forced march, the real Gulag had far worse implications for banished Soviet citizens. Stalin's slave labor system was in place for a generation, from 1930 to 1960. With camps for everyone from criminals and politicians to women and even children, people were forcibly relocated to Siberia to work in mining and logging operations. The Soviets suppressed political opposition and reaped production rewards at the same time. By 1960, nearly 2 million people had died in Gulag camps from hunger, brutality, and harsh living and working conditions. At one time, there were rumored to be more people in Siberian prison camps than all European countries combined. And there was no Olga running around with iodine drops, no equitable portions of food, and no Yevgheny giving handouts or measuring your waist for *sidushkas*. Unlike the team we had become part of, corrupt officials stole everything from rations to the camps' output, forcing inmates to work even harder to make their quotas.

Even the pre-Stalin Siberian camps were so severe that after being imprisoned in 1849 for being a "utopian socialist," Russian author Fyodor Dostoevsky penned three books about his experience there, all of whose titles—*The House of the Dead, The Insulted and Injured*, and *Notes from the Underground*— hint of the camps' conditions. His follow-up work, *Crime and Punishment*, also bore scars from the Gulag.

Thinking about the long Gulag history helps me ignore the blister sizzling against my heel. I put it out of my mind and continue on, placing one leaden foot after another. During the drudgery, I think back to all the wars and suffering the Russians have endured. Two of the biggest came at the hands of empire builders, who quickly learned that the country doesn't give up easily. Napoleon attacked Czar Alexander's empire in 1812 with a 500,000-strong army, the largest of its time ever assembled. Russia retreated, but fought all the while until its army eventually sent Napoleon home with only 10,000 of his original troops. Fresh from victory over France, Hitler's Blitzkrieg invasion in 1941—employing a technique much like charging into a rapid blind—resulted in Bashkaus-type memorials for more than 25 million Soviets. But the Soviets persevered with the fighting retreat, and the tide shifted for good in a battle in Belorussia in the summer of 1944.

My time-killing historical reverie is interrupted shortly when we pass a rough-looking horseman riding toward a field of haystacks. He looks us over, and our Pavlovian response of trying to look Russian instinctively kicks in. Luckily, despite our relatively expensive sunglasses, it's easier now than it was on the train; the shared last three weeks here has done wonders for our ability to blend in with the Latvians. Our hair is long, matted, and mangy; we're emaciated; and we have stubby, patchwork beards and dark circles under our eyes. Our clothes hang loose and look as if we've literally been through the wringer. Only our mouths haven't changed, and we keep them closed.

Our surroundings are much more appealing. The valley is broad and green, with towering mountains rising on both sides. Golden hay fields are worked by kerchiefed women swinging scythes, the workers behind the country's hammer and sickle emblem. Like their annual cutting of the grass, there is a ritual to the hike: walk for twenty-five minutes, rest for five—all on Ramitch Time. We cover the entire thirty-six miles this way. The rest breaks occur not upon need or demand, but only by this schedule, even if no one's tired. One of them comes right when we're crossing a streambed.

"What does he want us to do?" Edge asks. "Sit down right in the creek?"

"Maybe next time it will be in a patch of nettles," Ben says.

If we're starting to get surly, noble Valeri keeps us in check. He hikes in the same black leather boots he's worn for the past twenty-four days. They've induced a severe case of trench foot, but he still doesn't complain. When we stop to attend to it, Ben pokes his finger into Valeri's swollen, blue ankle. Instead of springing back, the divot remains in his skin long after the finger is gone.

"Not good," Ben says.

"Almost like a piece of pork fat," I add.

Valeri just puts his boot on and keeps walking.

The next thing we know, we're walking through a Cheech and Chong movie. Fields of towering *cannabis* plants line the trail in full bloom, swaying in the Siberian breeze. At one point, Edge and I stop to chew their leaves to take the sting out of the trudge. It's a placebo more than anything else, but the prescription is especially appealing to Edge, whose knees are sore from the hike after contorting into pretzels on the cataraft.

It's ironic that though the Latvians seem to know every plant around, capably identifying mushrooms, berries, onions, and even grasses to make tonic for the vodka, they don't seem to know much about these. Neither, seemingly, do the peasants swinging their scythes in the field, chopping hay next to them.

Other plants are in full bloom also, trying to launch their seed into the breeze before winter. It's late August and we're in the middle of a Siberian pollen factory. The fresh, heavy smell of plants rising from the valley floor presents a stark contrast to the rocky confines of the gorge. Unfortunately, with the foliage comes pollen; our shoes are covered with yellow dust and I count my sneezes by tens.

Despite the hike's hardships, we feel pampered compared to the Latvians. While we're wearing sunscreen, baseball hats, sunglasses, and insect repellent, they're making do without anything but their grit. While we put iodine tablets in our water, they drink straight from the creeks. Where we have lightweight, Gore-Tex hiking boots, Valeri has calf-high leather boots. They also have no sense of hydration. We chug relentlessly during our five-minute breaks, while they sit and smoke cigarettes, the smoke dehydrating them even more. There's definitely something to be said for our indulgences—Olga's face is as red as a lobster, Sergei's foot has a blister the size of the lower canyon, and I wouldn't wish Valeri's trench foot on anyone.

Soon we pass a steep canyon emptying into a small village across the river. This is the canyon Igor stumbled out of after his four-day hike out of the lower canyon. I try to see where it goes, but it simply disappears into the mountains. Canyons like this are everywhere here. Where the five rivers of Altai Bar fame converge, the sport has evolved all on its own, giving rise to a rich river-running heritage with legends like Vladimir, Misha, Igor, and even Ramitch. But throughout the repeated river explorations in the area, the region's domestic culture has remained largely unchanged. Perhaps conquerors like Ghengis Khan failed to subdue the region simply due to natural barriers like the Bashkaus and Chulishman. As well as fostering a new culture of river running, these canyons might also have been responsible for preserving the area's indigenous ways. When outsiders did enter, cultures blended, just like the Bashkaus and Chulishman do at the confluence, creating a new bloodline that carries parts of each ancestor. The marriage of Russian and Mongolian cultures is evident in the yurts, horsemen, and women tending the fields.

The hours pass, and my mind still wanders. Hike for

twenty-five minutes, rest for five. Hike for twenty-five minutes, rest for five. Eventually, we reach the Chulcha, whose confluence was where Boris's group camped when he beat away the drunken horsemen with his paddle. Once we reach the cascading waterway, we head upstream toward the waterfall, beginning a more difficult ascent. The trail fizzles out and we end up in Siberian death bush. Waist-high nettles and thorn bushes scratch at our bare legs, and new scratches scratch our old scratches. No wonder Khan retreated.

Sergei The Small—Plain and Tall had the sense to stay behind—is the first to defy Ramitch and pick his own route. Ben and I follow, hopping boulders along the shore instead of staying high. Then I lose Ben and end up solo back in the death bushes. Despite the concept of team, it's every real man for himself. Eventually, we all regroup at Uchar Falls, appropriately meaning "unapproachable" in Russian.

"Now we find out what it means," Ben says.

Again showing the young, volatile nature of the mountains we're in, a huge landslide careened down the surrounding mountains about 150 years ago, but it didn't stop the Chulcha for long. As the Bashkaus did at Perestroika, the river eventually found a way back down to the Chulishman. Today, the falls, which were only discovered about twenty years earlier, compose a towering cascade that would likely be protected as a national park in the United States. Here, it's one of many such breathtaking views, protected only by the terrain. As well as with the view, we're rewarded with fresh pine nuts, which we eagerly devour.

Still, it's not worth the caloric expenditure of the hike. Van might have made the better call, staying behind with most of the Latvians.

We make it about halfway back to base camp before calling it a night. The Siberian stars are out in full force, but we're too tired to pay much notice. We're up at 6:00 A.M. Ramitch Time with a breakfast of beans for the final ten-mile push home. When we arrive in camp around noon, fresh sheep ribs are roasting Argentine-style over the fire. The group that stayed behind bartered more rope and a few dry flies for more meat. But the local interaction had its downside. Word got out, it seems, that there were Americans around. Yesterday, two horse-men rode into camp. They were cordial enough at first, and even let Sergei the Tall ride one of their horses. Someone else showed up with the sheep to trade. Later, near dark, two more horsemen showed up, this time obviously drunk. While one was apparently friendly, the other was loud and obnoxious. Whether it was a setup or not, that morning Van noticed his fishing vest and headlamp were gone. Others found gear missing, too.

Boris wasn't there to beat them off with a paddle. He had hitched a ride with another raft group coming down the Chu-lishman to a village downstream to inquire about the ship that would carry us across the fifty-mile-long lake. We'll pick him up at the village tomorrow on our way down to Lake Teletskoe.

Tomorrow is our last day on the river. We might be on the lake for a few more days, but as far as paddling on current, we have one last fifteen-mile stretch of the Chulishman before its name, too, vanishes into the depths of Lake Teletskoe. As soon as the gradient disappears, so do their names, absorbed like their water by the lake. By the time their waters reach the far end of the lake the Bashkaus and Chulishman will be fully absorbed, becoming the Biya and eventually the Ob. It's a fit-ting end. The two rivers' waters are at peace now, merged and moving slowly as one body. Unlike an athlete playing beyond his or her prime, there's nothing to dilute their legacies, no extended flats softening the memory of their canyons.

Everyone retired early to sleep. Soon, only Edge and I remain by the fire. Earlier, against our American comrades' advice, we had picked the stalks of a few *cannabis* plants grow-ing near camp. Edge retrieves them and tosses them onto the fire, and we watch the smoke rise up out of the valley. Then we, too, retire to ready for the next day.

After a quick swim the next morning and a refreshing mutton breakfast, we load our gear and head downstream. It takes about four hours to reach Lake Teletskoe, where Father

Altai threw his gold. We pick up Boris, waving on shore, along the way. The ferry, he says, left the day before and won't be coming back for a week. The prospect of paddling fifty miles across the lake against the wind with depleted rations begins to sink in, as does the fact that we missed it because we joined Ramitch on his waterfall tour.

The Altai name for the lake is Altyn-Kyol, which means "Golden Lake" in Russian. It's considered a smaller replica of Baikal, the world's deepest fresh-water lake nearly 700 miles east. Rumors have it that the lake might well have more than just gold buried beneath its surface. Stories say it is polluted with the remains of Soviet spaceships that were launched in the 1980s from nearby Kazakhstan.

By this point, however, it's hard to find fault with any aspect of civilization. Though rested, we're tired. Though feasted and fed, we're still hungry—scratch that, starving. We're ready for the trip to end. Inching our way closer, we're still not out of the proverbial woods. The nearest town with electricity and running water is still fifty miles away, further perspective on the remoteness of the villages we passed earlier.

When the current slackens, we see the group that gave Boris a ride. They look hardened, as if they've been through a war. It turns out they have. They flipped and lost a boat in the last major rapid on the Chulishman and now have everything, seven people and all their gear, crammed onto one lone cataraft. They've rigged a makeshift sail and plan to sail across the lake. Down to our last bag of rations, we hope to get out sooner. How they made room for Boris, I'll never know. But as it is in the States, river running is a fraternity here. People routinely sacrifice to help each other all the time.

If earlier we faced Camps Glum and Broken Ankle, tonight's is Camp Calamity. It starts with a rainstorm of Siberian proportions. Rain slaps us horizontally in sheets, ripping tarps and blowing away tents. Immediately, everything is soaked. Then the realization hits again that the weekly ferry left yesterday. The boat used to run more often, Olga says, back when the lake was a popular tourist destination. But because of the poor economy, tourism has dried up. No one travels here anymore. Our dilemma is a lose-lose proposition: wait a week for the next ferry or paddle heavy catarafts for days without any food against rainy headwinds. While we mull our fate, the crossbeam over the fire breaks, spilling our last pot of kasha onto the ground. Then the tarp line falls, letting the torrential rain pound us from all sides. It's our most miserable night yet. Finally out of the canyon, we're as far as ever from comfort or even return.

As he has shown a propensity for averting crisis, Ramitch pulls another coup the next day. After paddling with Plain Sergei, Valeri, and Andrew over to a closed-down lodge across the lake, he stumbles upon a fellow Latvian working on a twenty-eight-foot sailboat. He strikes a deal and persuades the captain to give us a ride. The cost is thirty dollars, or about two dollars per person. When Ramitch returns with the good news, we cut up the last remaining sheep meat, which has been simmering all night over the meager coals of the rain-drenched fire. We have a late breakfast of spaghetti. Sergei the Small has to chop the noodles with an axe because they're saturated together. Then we deflate the rafts, bidding official farewell to the river portion of our journey. After spending such a long time on them, and relying on them to carry us through the lower canyon, it's a bittersweet moment. We're glad to be going home, but it's like leaving your dog behind on a vacation. We unfasten the webbing from the frames, stow it in plastic bags, and leave the logs on shore. Then we roll up the pontoons and stuff them back inside the backpacks we unfurled them from so long ago.

The boat comes to our shore in the early afternoon. It has a light blue stripe running above the waterline, and a yellow windsock flapping at the top of the mast. Below the windsock is the Team Konkas flag Ramitch gave the captain. Below that is another for the Washington Huskies. Why the captain has it, we're not sure. Not that we're Huskies fans, but it's a nice reminder of home.

With seventeen people—the fourteen of us, and the captain and his two crewmen—and all our gear crammed onto its twenty-eight-foot length, we limp out onto Lake Teletskoe. The sailboat's stern is awash in water, our perpetual wheelie causing surges of Lake Teletskoe to flood the back deck. It's another improvised Russian mode of tranportation. Only now it's a sailboat instead of a bus, train, car or cataraft. It's also too many people jammed aboard too small and decrepit a vehicle. Most of us are outside on deck, holding onto shrouds extending down from the boat's mast. Our life jackets are draped over the boom. We bum cigarettes from Valeri because it seems like the thing to do. We look and feel as if we could get train tickets at the Russian rate anywhere.

When it begins to rain again, everyone crams down into the claustrophobic cabin. The wet, cramped quarters don't dampen anyone's joy at heading home. On cue, Ramitch breaks out the vodka and everyone joins Boris's singing with the guitar. When he's through, the captain takes a turn and belts out a fast-paced song in a surprisingly high falsetto voice. The smoke is stifling. Feeling seasick, I head back outside for some fresh air in the rain.

Eventually, we make it across the lake and camp near the village of Artibash. In the morning, the final piece of the puzzle falls into place: still drunk from a night on the town, our bus driver, Yuri, backfires up to camp in his dashboard-steaming, *Playboy*-pictured jalopy. I never thought I'd be so happy to see it or him. The same pinup girl smiles from above the radiator-erupting dashboard when I climb on board. She seems a lot better looking this time around.

Though it's only early afternoon, it doesn't take long for the vodka to be broken out yet again. The driver, as expected, willingly joins in. Then it's on to the town of Bisk, an eight-hour ride. Our first stop to fill the radiator comes outside a little store where we pick up another bottle of vodka, a jar of jam, and a bucket of crab apples. We siphon fuel from the gas tank to prime the carburetor and get the bus started again.

Realizing we are now close to civilization, I finally sacrifice a piece of pork fat at lunch to a readily waiting Boris. Shortly, our bus is stopped by a soldier brandishing an AK-47, looking for a prisoner who escaped nearby. Though we look the part, he peeks inside, talks to Ramitch, and lets us pass. Our final fingers game comes at dinner to see who has to cook the last meal. Edge throws a peace sign, relegating the task to Sergei the Small.

"And no skimping on portions," Van says.

Despite the communal drinking and merry-making with Yuri, the bus ride ends prematurely. Facing a broken tire he can't fix, Yuri says he can't take us all the way to Bisk as promised, and drops us off in Gorno-Altaisk still expecting full pay. It's like negotiating with the gunmen all over again, only this time it's for our shuttle rather than sheep. When Yevgheny argues with him, Yuri goes into a fit and starts driving away with most of our gear still on the bus. He tries to run over the gear we have already unloaded, but Boris jumps on board to stop him. Eventually, we settle things, unload the rest of our gear and make a deal with another bus driver to take us into Barnaul. "The whole country is like that bus and driver," repeats a disgusted Yevgheny.

Before departing Gorno-Altaisk, we return to the bus station to retrieve the equipment we had left there four weeks earlier. Though the woman we made the deal with is nowhere to be found, our mound is still there, in a room behind the main office. Boris tells the clerk that it is ours and Valeri and Sergei the Small help us carry it to the bus. Although we're glad to see it, we're not so glad to have to lug it all over the place again.

The new bus takes us to the train station in Barnaul, where the Latvians will spend three days camping on the floor waiting for the next departure. While there, we bump into Vladimir Vinogradov's group from the Bashkaus. They made substantially better time than we did in the lower canyon and did not lay over at the confluence of the Chulishman. We learn through Boris that he did, in fact, run Perestroika, fulfilling his vow to run every rapid on the Bashkaus. His giant *ploht* disappeared in the gigantic hole completely, resurfacing with its middle pontoon completely blown-out. But he did it, becoming the first person ever to raft every rapid on the river. We all feel a fellowship with him, proud to have been on the water with him at the same place and time of his amazing determination, bravado, and accomplishment.

We're still traveling Latvian-style, but after sleeping on the hard, cold, marble-tiled floor of the train station that night, we're ready to revert to Western visitor. Rather than wait for three days, we decide to fly back to Moscow, bringing Olga along as an interpreter. She'll hook back up with "her boys" in Moscow. Before we leave, we try both calling and faxing Andre in Moscow to let him know we have finished our trip and are in Barnaul. Then we try in vain to find a ride to the airport. We can't catch a bus, can't stop a cab, can't place a call, and can't send a fax. We are back in civilization.

It's a long round of heartfelt good-byes, 10:00 A.M. vodka shots, and last meal of fourteen equitable portions as we bid farewell at the train station. We exchange more gifts, the Latvians making out with wetsuits, dry bags, watertight Pelican boxes, river knives, and other gear more readily available to us in the States than to them in Latvia. In return, they present us with a homemade, two-man cataraft that they stashed in the train station before heading to the river. It will add to our load flying home, but we are extremely grateful for the Siberian specimen. But we're even more grateful for the gracious and generous gesture.

Edge gets everyone to sign his guitar, the one we had left at the bus station in Gorno-Altaisk and picked up when we retrieved our gear. Grabbing it by the neck, Ramitch turns it over and scribbles something on the front of it.

"What's it say?" Edge asks Boris.

Boris reads it and laughs. "It says, 'May your life not be like Kamikaze Rapid.'"

It's one of the most cherished souvenirs we have.

Finally, bribing a private driver, Ramitch and Olga accompany us to the airport. The plane is overbooked, of course, just like the boat. But again showing his bartering prowess, Ramitch once more improvises a solution. He tells the reservationist we are writing a Russian travel novel. We also play our Western ace-in-the-hole, a gold-seal-stamped letter that Van procured from the mayor of Jackson Hole, Wyoming, saying we are his personal emissaries. The ticket clerk examines the letter upside down. These two lies and a ten-dollar bribe get us boarding passes.

We're the last people to board the flight, and end up loading our gear ourselves into the belly of the plane. Luckily, we've been loading and unloading gear for the past month and we quickly form a chain gang to get everything in the hold. Our bribes also get us seats, which is better than a lot of the other passengers. Two people sit on their luggage on top of the toilet seats in the bathroom. Another couple kneels in the aisle. We wonder about the plane's weight limit.

"Thank God Van brought that letter from the mayor," Ben says. "At least we're not on the toilet seats."

Until 1991, most foreigners had to use a travel organization called Intourist when traveling in Russia. Even now, the majority still use it for their travel and accommodations, though it means expensive taxi rides and hotels. With Olga, we are still traveling Latvian-style.

We're made fully aware of this when, still blessed by good fortune, we arrive safely hours later in Moscow. We land at a domestic airport, but there are no baggage attendants to help with our gear. Stuck on the tarmac, we find and wheel a ladder up to the cargo hold, unlatch the door, and climb deep inside the belly of the airplane. Then we shuttle it all out like we have so many times already in other circumstances. Van and I wait with our pile on the runway for two hours while Edge and Ben go inside with Olga. Ben has our passports, and we wonder what might happen to us should we be found without any documents while standing on the runway with a pile of unknown gear.

Igor was supposed to meet us, but Olga says he has been drinking all day and isn't coming. After four hours of travel-weary logistics inside the airport, we store some of our gear—the clerk wants thirty dollars, but Olga gives him three—and make our way to a hotel a quarter mile away. It takes four hours of dodging hundred-dollar taxis to figure out that a bed, our first in a month, is just a rapid's length away. On the way, Olga points out some grass under three replica airplane sculptures. "After last trip our boys sleep here," she says. We want nothing to do with it and insist on a hotel.

We forget to be careful what we wish for. A broken elevator sits discarded in a wreck outside the hotel's front door.

"We might want to take the stairs?" Ben suggests.

Olga argues again when we try to book a room. Eventually, we secure one and drag ourselves upstairs. We are dead tired. As we insert the key, the door opens and four Russians file out, a bottle of vodka still wobbling on the coffee table and three cigarettes still burning in the ashtray. They were poaching the room but we don't even care. The five of us fall asleep before our heads hit the pillows, or appreciate that they're even there.

We head to a fancier hotel the next night, dropping, by Latvian pocketbook, two months' salary for two rooms. I look out the window into dismal gray and see a large hammer and sickle sign atop a nearby building. Below it, the Moscow River flows aimlessly, civilized by concrete. I think of the free-flowing Bashkaus, a river even a massive landslide couldn't contain. Edge snaps me out of my reverie with his typical dry wit.

"It's so hard leaving when it's like this," he says of the gray sleet. We are all longing to return home.

In the afternoon, we meet Sasha Tokarev, one of our Russian contacts we lined up in the United States. He tells us over beers on a park bench how he, Andre, and others got delayed by a storm on the Black Sea on their return from the Project RAFT championships in Turkey. He adds that Andre wondered what happened to the Americans he was supposed to meet, and that it was good we didn't go on the Kalar.

"Very boring and bugs," he says. "You end up doing good trip." This Andre remains a phantom, however, whom we never meet.

Later, we take a cab over to visit the river runner's library where Ramitch secured his maps of the Bashkaus. After an hour drive we arrive at a tiny brick building sandwiched between larger apartment buildings. It's nondescript. We're here on a Wednesday, the only day of the week it's supposedly open, but it's closed due to a power failure.

"Very Russian," Sasha says, obviously frustrated. "Everything here is like this. That's why it's nice to go to rivers. Everything there is more predictable."

Rather than take a cab back, we work our way across Moscow Sasha-style—hiking between occasional subway rides. He tries to get us into a private club but he gets kicked out for wearing river sandals. We all feel more at home on a river.

On our final homestretch to Sasha's apartment we pass a line of women selling bread for 200 rubles that they bought earlier for 50 rubles. A new open and public market is slowly taking hold.

That night we drop another two months' Latvian salary at a restaurant, where Igor and Sasha join us and listen to our tales from the Bashkaus. Halfway through a story, Edge feels something odd in his shirt pocket and pulls it out. It's a piece of dry bread.

"Ahh, *zanachka!*" Igor says, well familiar with the art of squirreling food away. Though it's a waste from two weeks ago, we don't need it anymore. Our plates are full for the second time in a month.

We absorb the details Igor relates in his stories of the deaths he witnessed on his Bashkaus trip three years ago. The stories sink in now that we've been there and know it first hand. We relate our series of near misses. During the telling, I think back to the countless nights around the fire, the guitar playing, the rapids, and the "fairy landscapes" and "high psychological tenseness of the long staying alone in the canyon."

My recollections are interrupted by Olga, who now, after spending two days with us in the city, realizes how far apart we are again now that we are no longer on the river. There, dependent on each other and lives in each other's hands, we truly became brothers. Now, with the river removed as a common denominator, our differences surface like Vladimir's *ploht* in Perestroika. We're like Huck Finn and Jim, returning to their lives of separation off the river.

"You men are like spacemen to us," Olga says, holding back the tears.

The next morning we pack our bags and fly away.

Epilogue

The team at the train station in Barnaul, where the Latvians will wait another three days for the four-day train ride home. (Clockwise from top left) Sergei the Medium, Ramitch, Sergei the Tall, Sergei the Small, Plain Sergei, Andrew, Edge, Boris, Olga, Van, Yevgheny, Eugene, Ben, and Valeri.

A year later, a package arrives in the mail. It's from Boris, address Riga, Latvia. Inside is a letter written in broken English, as well as a cassette tape. I walk over to our living room stereo and plug it in. It cackles at first, and then Boris's hearty voice fills the room in a thick Latvian accent. A flood of memories instantly pours out of the speakers. I am no longer in my home, but back on the Bashkaus.

We had all looked at photos and given slide shows of the trip, but visual reminders can only do so much. It's the other senses that bring memories back to life. My throat tightens upon hearing the all-too-familiar strum of Boris playing his broken version of "Rocky Raccoon," with accents and words in all the wrong places.

"Somewhere in black mine Dakota, there live boy named Rocky Raccoon ... Hah!"

Then he stops strumming and starts talking. "Hi Euge, Hi Bruce, Hi Ben, Hi Van, it's me, Boris. I'm sitting in front of, uh, Olga and Ramitch's tape recorder and we are all ready to sing the songs of our journey for you and we feel it is pleasure that you remember us and send letters to us and maybe sometimes we will see each other and I hope we make another trip as well … "

The archaic ring of a rotary phone drowns him out in the background, forcing him to stop. Then the whole group breaks straight into "Gogia," their fast-paced song about Georgians in the "key of H," which we heard countless times around the campfire. A hearty chorus is punctuated by heartier yells and laughs. I'm on the river all over again. I even feel hungry.

Then comes Olga's voice, still, as ever, the matriarch.

"And now we want to record another Russian song by a group. We enjoy it very much, but Ramitch can't play it yet." At the end of that selection, they play a fusion-jazz pop song straight from the floor of the B2 dance club in Moscow. Olga's voice fills the cackling tape again. "And now, our best songs about whitewater athletes. Please listen and enjoy it."

Ramitch's voice comes on as crisp and clear as his commands on the river. It's a song they played often, with rhymes in all the right places and a simple, repeating melody that lifted our spirits countless times on the Bashkaus. It does so again now, although we are thousands of miles away.

When the tape is over, a hollow feeling settles in my stomach. We have talked about trying to get Team Konkas over for an American-style trip on a run such as the Grand Canyon. Their eyes would pop at such luxuries as lawn chairs, coolers, solar-powered blenders, and more weight in beer than they bring in food. But we also know that it would be far easier to just get one of them over. Boris seems the likely candidate.

That summer, I bring the tape up to Jackson for Ben's wedding. Van and Edge also make it to the ceremony. It has been a while since we have all gotten together, and we listen to it in one of the wedding cabins.

ॐॐॐ

When we parted ways back at Kennedy airport—Van off to the U.S. Open with a friend, Edge, Ben, and I on separate flights back west—we split off before having much time to digest what we had been through and shared together. Like the slabs of pork fat, for each of us, the trip needed its own time to be digested and settle in. We all went our separate ways.

Out of work after quitting his environmental remediation job to go on the expedition, Edge went straight to a three-week trip on the Grand Canyon with friends from Boulder. (The Latvians would have enjoyed their dry-iced ice cream on day fourteen.) Ben went back to Lander and his position at NOLS. Wanting nothing more than to watch the opening Broncos game with five everything-on-them pizzas, I was immediately whisked away from the Denver airport to my wife's grandparent's fiftieth wedding anniversary in Lead, South Dakota. The cultural shock was as profound as it was in Igor's apartment, on the train, and during our days at the put-in. It was as opposite a lifestyle imaginable.

The table of octogenarians, instant mashed potatoes, white bread, frozen peas, and processed turkey was a far cry from our log bench service on the Bashkaus. It made me long for hot fish water, dry bread, and soggy sweet-bread soup. During speeches, I craved Ramitch's toasts. I thought back to the freshly butchered sheep roasting over the fire on Argentine spits, and my comrades' guitar playing. Attempts to make small talk with my table neighbors distracted me from daydreaming, which seemed so much more real. It was hard to bring my mind back.

"So, Denise says you just returned from Russia," the questions came. "Did you see any polar bears? Do they still have those prison camps over there?"

They were truly interested and more than polite, but I could not respond adequately. How could I let them see Omsk, the horsemen, the memorials? How could I explain the exhilaration of plunging through Siberian Class V water, with no way out but down?

I tried to answer as best I could, and then found solace in the food. Lean to start with, I had lost more than twenty pounds on the trip, according to the South Dakota scales—and that was after a week of solid, off-river eating. My only lingering ailment was a swollen right foot, infected from a sandal strap that had rubbed the top of it raw. It hurt the last few days on the river and made me limp while following Sasha across Moscow, but now it was worse. Even a slight brush from a pant leg forced a grimace of pain. When I returned to Steamboat Springs, I went to a physician friend and asked her to look at it. Her finger depression lingered long after she removed it—just like Valeri's did on our march to the waterfall. While Olga dosed his with iodine, only antibiotics stopped me from getting blood poisoning.

When we finish listening to the tape in Ben's wedding cabin, talk turns to trying to get Boris over to the United States. We agree to pursue the plan.

In the fall, Ben and his bride, Lisa, travel to Scandinavia for their honeymoon. There they hop a flight to Riga to visit Team Konkas. Ben has been in contact with Boris for a few months about a possible job at NOLS and now has the chance to score him a J-1 student visa allowing him to work here legally. As well as making a social call and seeing the others, he plans to hand deliver Boris's visa and some cash for a ticket.

Yevgheny meets them at the airport and drives them through pouring rain to a local river camp to meet the rest of Team Konkas. On the way, his car fishtails on the muddy, steep road and crashes into a tree, buckling the front hood. They are forced to walk in the rain the rest of the way.

"He was laughing like a maniac the whole time," Ben remembers. "I think he was just excited to see us."

At the camp, they see all but a few of our comrades from the river trip, along with their wives, girlfriends, and children.

Mushrooms stew over a huge, smoky fire and the guitar and vodka get passed around equally.

"It was like we were right back on the Bashkaus," Ben remembers, adding that he had to sneakily dump his toasts onto the grass to survive the reunion.

Six months later, Boris arrives in Jackson for a job at the NOLS Teton Valley branch in Driggs, Idaho. Van and I meet him at the airport. He's still wearing a beard and ponytail. I wish I had taped a sign to a paddle to welcome him. It's March, so we rent him telemark equipment and take him to Snow King, the local ski area downtown. He's never been on skis before, or a poma lift, which shows when the contraption whisks him uphill, legs and arms flailing. We barely get our pole straps on before he barrels down ahead of us, more out of control than he ever was on the Bashkaus. He looks like a Russian bear on skis.

"Watch out!" Van yells, more to innocent bystanders than to Boris.

As always, Boris survives both the slopes and the partying that night when we take him to the Million Dollar Cowboy Bar. We toast to his arrival and promise to stay in touch.

It's easier said than done. His job starts the next day, and once I head back to Steamboat, I don't hear from him for months.

He proves very helpful at work, taking care of all the outdoor equipment and helping with the cooking and cleaning. Everyone loves his quick wit, laughter, and enthusiasm, and he quickly makes friends, as well as an indelible impression on the students. His room and board is covered, and he has a minimum-wage job—about ten times what he was earning in Latvia. He quickly applies his work ethic and avoids the temptations of a free-market economy by saving all his money. A month later, he confides to Ben his grand scheme. His life, it seems, has taken the plot of a Russian novel. He's in love with a married woman named Rita, and plans to return with his savings to Latvia and buy an apartment for her husband to move into. Then

Boris will move in with Rita and her children.

Shortly thereafter, he wins a scholarship for a NOLS River Instructor's Course. He takes it very seriously and trains relentlessly, every spring morning skating around a makeshift track in heavy mountaineering boots and telemark skis. To further prepare, he takes ice-cold baths and holds his breath for minutes at a time in case he ever needs to maintain his composure underwater. Later that spring, I get a letter from him describing another unorthodox training approach. He sticks his head upside down in a sink filled with ice water and holds his breath.

"I am up to two minutes," he writes.

When his work tasks slow down in Idaho, he gets repositioned to the NOLS headquarters in Lander, Wyoming, to continue fixing equipment and tidy up the bulk-food warehouse. It's a kid-in-a-candy-store job placement for him, akin to unleashing mice in a cheese factory. None of us would have ever trusted Boris to manage a bulk-food warehouse.

Still living out a Dostoyevsky novel–like life, Boris is more focused on saving money than ever. He lives rent-free in a tent in the town park and eats "refugee food," the camping rations leftover from students' trips. It's not far from life on the banks of the Bashkaus. He saves, makes more friends, and improves his English.

His river course is a multiday trip down Colorado's Yampa River. Though he would have been the first to swing a paddle if armed horsemen rode through camp, the NOLS way proves markedly different than what he was used to with Ramitch and Team Konkas. There's no chopping down trees for benches and cooking structures, all waste is carried out, and there are rarely even any fires. When they do have one, it's dutifully contained in a fire pan and all ashes are carried out. There's friction between him and the trip leader, and in the end, both part ways, realizing there are different ways to accomplish things.

"I had a different paddling style," Boris tells me later.

"But NOLS kept to their policy, which is how it should be."

He heads home to Latvia that fall with more than $5,000 rolled up in his socks. Rita's husband moves into the new apartment without a whimper. Boris later confides to me that the only reason it worked out was because of us, and that he cherishes our help greatly.

Save for a few e-mails, I don't hear from him again for several years. He now works in sales for a bar code–scanner company ("It's not fun like river running," he says, "but it's a job that pays"), and still runs rivers whenever he can.

His trip to the United States, he says, was as foreign as ours was to Siberia.

"At first, people seemed to behave like caricatures," he writes, his English now much improved from what it was on the Bashkaus. "Everybody seemed to overdo everything all the time—like laughing too loud at jokes, dressing out of style, or even burping without blushing. They matched the stereotype I had of them. But everyone also was very helpful, hardworking, friendly, and caring. They seemed to enjoy their hobbies and life in general. I felt like I was part of big family."

Boris also better appreciates NOLS' dedication to the environment. "I learned it for life and now try to teach it to my paddling buddies here," he says.

He also appreciates our country's work ethic, noticing that everyone chipped in when they needed to. "Nobody did unnecessary work or wasted time," he says. "And it wasn't below my boss's status to help load a truck with gear. In Latvia, bosses are too proud and lazy to help their subordinates.

"It's weird," he adds, "but I felt that the U.S. was a very young country. Everything felt possible and easy to achieve, and people seemed very open-minded and free."

In a way, Boris's time with Team Konkas proved a natural fit for NOLS. The school's founder, Paul Petzoldt, believes expeditions fail when their members fail to act as a team. To Boris and Team Konkas, that's second nature.

"On a difficult river," Boris says, "everyone must think of

the team's needs before their own and work toward a common goal."

Over there, at first we joked among ourselves about their emphasis on the team, from gathering berries in wetsuits to passing the pages of a novel back and forth.

"This vill be good for zee team," we'd jest. "This vill make our country strong." But after a while, we, too, came to fully appreciate and apply the practice.

In 1998, NOLS used our trip as a newsletter case study on what makes expeditions fail or succeed. The concept of *team* quickly rose to the surface.

"It's a different culture over there," Edge sums up in the essay. "They've grown up to think like groups, not as individuals."

Adds Ben: "It would've been a disaster had we splintered off as our own group. It was way more successful for us to go along with a different way of doing things."

Says Van: "No one person, nor one boat, had all the tools to get down that river. Both as boatmates and teammates, we all benefited from everyone's different strengths."

Having us along, Boris says, added a calming nature to the trip. "It's like a big family where everyone gets tired of the same faces," he says. "Suddenly, you have four guests who live with you for a month and the atmosphere gets healthier. Everyone is better."

In our grant application, we mentioned that "expeditions, like organisms, take on a character and life all their own once the wheels have been set in motion." An organism is a team, all working toward a mutually beneficial outcome. It's not a bunch of contracted individuals. Diversity matters within such a team, as well as openness to qualified newcomers. But every team also needs a leader, and chains of command based on experience and knowledge. For this, we were lucky to have Ramitch, whose leadership style is a wise blend of knowledge, experience, authority, responsibility, and equality. He treated all members with dignity, which held us together under extreme conditions while bringing out our best. His is leadership with respect and celebration.

The Latvians' team practice is still alive today. Though Ramitch's new tarp business kept the team from running rivers for awhile, several of the original Team Konkas members ran the Chulishman in 1995, returned to the Bashkaus in 1998, and then rafted the Argut in 1999. It was on that trip that they experienced their first rafting death of a fellow expedition member. Halfway through their trip, Voronko Slavjan, who joined them on their 1998 Bashkaus trip, met up with another group attempting the Class V to VI Karagem Gorge, which Konkas was portaging. Short one person to help paddle their two, two-man *bubliks* on the descent, the group asked Voronko to join them. Against Ramitch's wishes, fatefully, he did, drowning during the attempt despite Ramitch's cataraft positioned downstream as safety.

"For Ramitch and all of us it was very difficult," says Olga. "We had run rapids for fifteen years and never had such an accident. And Ramitch, as our leader, had the last decision in difficult decisions."

The death deeply affected them. They took the next year off before putting it behind them, as Voronko would have wished, and then kept at it, notching the Uda in Sayan in 2001, Ukuchikta near Lake Baikal in 2002, and the Kitoy in 2003. There, under Ramitch's guidance, they wisely backed down after the first section due to the river's rapid rise. Others weren't as fortunate.

"That one was most difficult," Olga says, giving me chills of déjà vu from when Ramitch drew a skull and crossbones on his map on the train ten years earlier. "It was the Black August. It rained very hard and the water was very high. We had to carry and hike a lot, because it was dangerous to paddle. Some groups were not as clever as Ramitch. Fifteen people died on that river and others in the region that August. We know of seven who died on the Kitoy alone that year."

Since then, they've toned down their whitewater wanderings

a notch, sticking to easier runs closer to home. "After that trip, we realized that it's difficult at our age to carry on the shoulders all the equipment needed to run Class V to VI," says Olga. "Maybe in the future we will have water trips only on Class IV rivers that don't require any hiking."

The same year Konkas was on the Kitoy, a different group returned to the Bashkaus for the twenty-fifth anniversary of Sergey Papush's historic descent in 1978. With modern-day kayaks and catamarans, they blitzed the lower gorge in five days. A year later, a group of American kayakers ran the lower canyon in three days, calling it some of the toughest whitewater they had ever faced. They saw our journal entry in the logbook and were incredulous that we paddled it in homemade catarafts.

Ramitch, Olga, Yevgheny, and Sergei (I'm not sure which one) still work for Ramitch's truck tarp company, which is now called Roskon and is based in St. Petersburg. Ramitch and Olga have become Russian citizens, and Boris doesn't see them much now that they have moved away.

The move to a better location went smoothly thanks to easier travel restrictions. Restrictions have also eased with regard to Latvia's naturalization of minorities, in particular its Russians. Latvia's bid to join the European Union sped this process up. New rules allow non-Latvians to gain citizenship by taking a language and history exam. Boris took the test recently and finally secured the same rights as other Latvian citizens.

"It is good for travel and paddling," he says.

The same year travel restrictions were eased, however, Andrew died while driving from St. Petersburg to Riga. As much as Andrew's death rocked Team Konkas, a more recent death shook up Russia's rafting world. Rafting pioneer Misha Kolchevnikov, who first opened Russia's rafting doors to Westerners, passed away August 10, 2005, at age fifty-seven, while rafting Siberia's Katun River. He was on a high-water descent of the upper section when his raft flipped in a rapid named Ak-Kem. The coincidences are startling—it's the same day of the August 10 Bashkaus memorials, and the same river that gave Project RAFT founders their first glimpse of Soviet river running.

Misha's legacy lives on. "The events served their purpose," he once said about the cultural mixing of his international raft rallies. "They were a meeting of everybody who loves water, the outdoors, peace, and, of course, a little competition."

Two months after his death, as if cementing their role in using rafting to foster international camaraderie, Team Russia won the World Rafting Championships for the first time in the country's history, besting eighteen other nations, including the United States. And in August 2006, an international rafting competition was hosted on the Katun for the first time since 1989.

"Misha was a true citizen diplomat," eulogizes Project RAFT's Jib Ellison. "He understood that the human bond forged on a river expedition could make a positive difference, and that river running is a great metaphor for life. It doesn't matter if you speak the same language, believe in the same god, or even like each other; we all must learn to paddle together through the rapids of our time."

We lived this with the Latvians on the Bashkaus. It's not that they taught us so much, but more the river, just like Misha's rafting festivals did for their participants.

This theory is strengthened in July 2006 when Boris, on a company trip to New Jersey, detours with his wife, Rita, to pay us a visit in Colorado. Edge picks him up at Denver International Airport and shuttles him and Rita up to Dillon, where I meet them after driving south from Steamboat.

"Hah, twenty-one minutes late," Boris admonishes when I show up to meet them at the Blue Moon coffee shop. "That means twenty-one push-ups for you."

He's sitting in a booth eating an egg-bagel sandwich with Rita and Edge. He looks pretty much the same, save for the absence of his beard and shorter hair, which is now salt-and-peppered with gray. He's also the same underneath, as affable and happy-go-lucky as ever.

After a couple of jokes about food, we head to the Pine Creek and Numbers sections of the Arkansas River. Instead of taking catarafts, we will all be kayaking. On the drive, we share stories about the trip and our lives. Boris says he still sees "Sergei the Hungry" occasionally, referring to Sergei the Small, as well as certain other members of Team Konkas. He is happy with Rita and her two full-grown sons from her earlier marriage.

At the river, I escort Rita downstream and show her where to drive the car to meet us at the take-out. We snap a few pictures and put on, the first time we three have been on a river together in thirteen years. The run, straightforward Class III to IV at this low-water level, goes smoothly. Boris has become a proficient kayaker, his "breath-holding-in-the-sink" antics apparently paying off.

We're surprised Rita isn't waiting for us at the take-out. Turning our heads toward the highway intersecting the dirt road, we see why. The spiraling luminescence of siren lights tells us something has gone wrong. When she was turning left onto the dirt road, two teenagers tried to pass her, clipping the car. Edge's car, a new Honda SUV, is wrecked, the front driver's side corner mashed into the wheel and exposing the radiator. A tow truck is already on the way.

"Now it's just like our bus on the Bashkaus," says a surprisingly unrattled Edge.

"Maybe we should run the radiator hose up to the windshield," I add.

Rita is in no mood for joking. She's distraught, even though the accident wasn't her fault.

We get towed back to Dillon, where I load everyone into my car and we drive to Boulder for a barbecue at Edge's house. We invite some of our friends to meet Boris, and the night ends with him playing the guitar to a captive audience on the porch. The first song is "Gogia," which instantly transports Edge and me back to the Bashkaus. Like clockwork, he then passes the guitar our way and requests "Rocky Raccoon." I take the guitar and strum.

"Somewhere in the black mine hill of South Dakota ... "
I sing, mimicking Boris's translation and wrongly placed
accents.

That we haven't seen each other for more than ten years is
inconsequential. It's as if the river trip was only yesterday. The
river bonded all of us, and it will take more than time or distance to sever our connection.

On the Bashkaus, each stroke took us deeper into self-
reliance and self-discipline. But it also took us deeper into
trust of one another, trust of people who started as strangers
and emerged, one by one, as lifelong friends. By trip's end, we
were one cohesive group—not the two that started on the river.
It's our cultures that are different, not our desires to challenge
ourselves and help and learn from each other. Real men, we
learned, are not cowards in life, or fools. They earn and share
the dignity, respect, and trust of their comrades.

Our differences surfaced quickly back in civilization; at
dinner in Moscow, Olga seemed to recognize it instantly. On
the river, however, they dissolved like so much sediment being
carried toward the Arctic Ocean. Swiss philosopher Jean-
Jacques Rousseau argued that civilization has destroyed man's
natural goodness. For us, things simply became more real on
the river. Social constructions and cultural assumptions disappeared. We weren't dependent on the rules of society any more
than we were the river's currents. Freed from these constraints,
we discovered that integrity grows easily across social and cultural boundaries.

This is what river running does. It evaporates socially con-
structed attitudes into a far more pertinent bonding process of
trust and reliance. It deconstructs social conditioning, creating
a Land of Oz where bonds between strangers form naturally
and transcend all barriers. Perhaps this is what the Latvians
were seeking in their quest to become real men on the river.
And perhaps life on the river, then, represents the real world
after all.

Selected Bibliography

Trading armed horsemen vodka for freshly butchered sheep, which we'd subsist on three meals a day until it was gone.

Early Bashkaus River Descent History (1969–1981)
Source: www.whitewater.ru

1969—V. Dvoryashin; *ploht*; upper section.

1971—Alexey Fomin (Tomsk); *ploht*; upper/middle section.

1972—Nikolay Telegin; *ploht*; upper/middle section.

1972—Vladimir Povitsky; LAS; upper/middle section, portion of lower gorge.

1972—Nikolay Ryazansky (Moscow); *ploht*; upper/middle section.

1973—S. Gulidov (Leningrad); *ploht*; unknown parts.

1974—Vladimir Krasnikov (Moscow); *ploht*/LAS/modified *baidarka*; upper section.

1974—G. Geyn (Tula); modified Salut *baidarka*s; upper/middle section.

1974—A. Sumbaev; *ploht*; unknown parts.

1974—O. Varivoda; *ploht*; unknown parts.

1974—Mikhail Kolchevnikov (Barnaul); *ploht*; upper/middle section, portion of lower gorge.

1976—G. Geyn (Tula); modified RZ *baidarka*s; up to Saratansky Canyon.

1977—Sergey Chesnokov (Tomsk); *ploht*/LAS; unknown parts.
1978—Sergey Papush (Moscow); catamarans/*baidarkas*; upper/middle sections (without portages), lower gorge.
1978—Polyansky; LAS/catamarans; all parts.
1980—A. Sazhnev (Novosibirsk); *ploht*/catamaran; "up to mouth."
1981—Vladimir Semenov (Leningrad); catamarans/kayaks; upper/middle section (without portages), lower gorge.

Additional Sources

Books

Draper, Hal. *The Adventures of the Communist Manifesto*. Berkeley, CA: Centre for Socialist History, 1994.

Newby, Eric. *The Big Red Train Ride*. New York: St. Martin's Press, 1978.

Gonzales, Laurence. *Deep Survival: Who Lives, Who Dies, and Why*. New York: W. W. Norton and Co., 2003.

Ratchnevsky, Paul. *Genghis Khan: His Life and Legacy*. Translated by Thomas Haining. Oxford: Blackwell, 1991.

Siebert, Al. *The Survivor Personality: Why Some People Are Stronger, Smarter, and More Skillful at Handling Life's Difficulties ... and How You Can Be, Too*. New York: Perigee Trade, 1996.

Web Sites

Internet Modern History Sources: www.fordham.edu/halsall/mod/modsbook.html
Rousseau Association: www.rousseauassociation.org

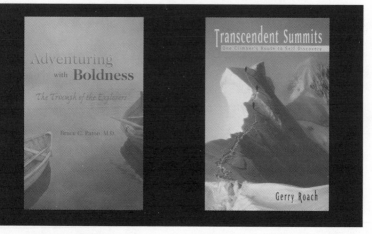